PHYSICAL
EDUCATION
AND
SPORT
PHILOSOPHY

THE PRENTICE-HALL FOUNDATIONS OF PHYSICAL EDUCATION AND SPORT SERIES

JOHN E. NIXON
Series Editor
Stanford University

Earle F. Zeigler
The University of Western Ontario

PHYSICAL EDUCATION AND SPORT PHILOSOPHY

PRENTICE-HALL, INC., ENGLEWOOD CLIFFS, N.J.

Library of Congress Cataloging in Publication Data

ZEIGLER, EARLE F
    Physical education and sport philosophy.

    (The Prentice-Hall foundations of physical
education and sport series)
    Published in 1968 under title: Problems in the
history and philosophy of physical education and
sport.
    Bibliography: p.
    Includes index.
    1. Physical education and training—Philosophy.
2. Professionalism in sports. I. Title.
GV342.Z43 1977   613.7   76-12549
ISBN 0-13-668731-8

© 1977 by Prentice-Hall, Inc., Englewood Cliffs, New Jersey

Printed in the United States of America

10 9 8 7 6 5 4 3 2 1

PRENTCE-HALL INTERNATIONAL, INC., *London*
PRENTICE-HALL OF AUSTRALIA PTY. LIMITED, *Sydney*
PRENTICE-HALL OF CANADA, LTD., *Toronto*
PRENTICE-HALL OF INDIA PRIVATE LIMITED, *New Delhi*
PRENTICE-HALL OF JAPAN, INC., *Tokyo*
PRENTICE-HALL OF SOUTHEAST ASIA PTE. LTD., *Singapore*

280390

Contents

III PROFESSIONAL CONCERNS 109

Series Preface

It is a professional privilege and pleasure to introduce The Prentice-Hall Foundations of Physical Education and Sport Series of textbooks. This revised series has been expanded to include more comprehensive books written by well-known authorities in various foundational areas of physical education and sport.

As knowledge and experience expands in the various foundational areas of physical education and sport, young scholars are electing to specialize in detailed study and research, not only in the traditional fields, but also in the newer foundational areas. This series is well represented with books written by selected authors who bring scholarly expertise and proven literary skills to their assignments in both the traditional and emerging areas.

Because of the recent rapid expansion of specializations within the general field of physical education, and also because the term "sport" is gaining broad recognition and use as an area of intensified study, research, and practice, the scope of the revised series has been extended. There are differences in definitions of these terms among physical educators, sport leaders, and scholars around the world. Some authorities now conceive of the term "sport" as being separate, or different, from the term "physical education." Others still retain the traditional definition that sport constitutes one of several domains of human activity typically included within the overall definition of physical education, along with such terms as "dance," "aquatics," "gymnastics" and "designed exercise."

Each volume has been expanded, enabling authors to provide suitable conceptual depth concerning the specialized subject matter. One of the major contributions of the books in the revised series is their completeness and careful coverage of the latest theories, facts, and concepts which make up the body of knowledge of the area under discussion. Each book is now a complete text in its own right. No longer should the books in this series be regarded as supplementary to other textbooks.

The central purpose of the revised Foundations of Physical Education and Sport Series has not changed. These textbooks present warranted generalizations from related fields of knowledge which contribute to a sophisticated understanding of physical education and sport.

These generalizations form a basis for educational decision making and policy formulation by teachers, coaches, and administrators in educational institutions as well as in other public and private agencies which organize and conduct physical education and sport programs.

Physical education currently is defined as the art and science of voluntary, purposeful human movement. Its central concern is the individual engaging in selected motor performances and the significance of these experiences. Thus, physical education and sport are broad interdisciplinary subjects. Scholars and practitioners of these areas need to be familiar with the most contemporary hypotheses being generated in the closely related disciplines which explain phenomena associated with human movement. Disciplines which provide the most relevant foundational knowledge in physical education and sport include anatomy, anthropology, aesthetics, biology, history, kinesiology and biomechanics, neurology, physiology, psychology, and sociology.

With rare exceptions, scholars of other academic disciplines have not devoted their major attention to investigations which concern important phenomena in physical education and sport. The historian has virtually neglected the history of sport in general history books. Few sociologists have elected to conduct careful research in selected aspects of sport or physical education as a major scholarly commitment.

Nonetheless, a vast accumulation of knowledge in the foundational fields is rapidly appearing in many countries around the world in the form of research reports, scholarly articles, books, pamphlets, and other literary formats. Most of this knowledge has not been accumulated systematically nor reported and interpreted accurately on a broad scale to members of the physical education and sport disciplines. This difficult task of selecting and reporting relevant generalizations from any one academic discipline and commenting on their meanings requires a physical education scholar who also has a background of graduate study and research in the related disciplinary field.

The authors of books in this revised series are recognized, distinguished physical education and sport researchers and scholars and are acknowledged specialists in the foundational fields covered in their respective books. Each volume reports and synthesizes recent knowledge into understandable and usable form for students, teachers, coaches, and administrators. The reader is instructed in the vital process of developing his or her own *principles* of physical education and sport as knowledge and understanding accumulate from these foundational fields. Comprehensive bibliographies list basic references and source materials for further study and research.

Most, if not all, of the authors have had extensive intercultural experiences in other countries and thus are highly qualified to bring to the series the perspective of varied societal norms and cultural values as well as to expose the student to a greater range of relevant academic and professional literature than typically has been the case in past American textbooks in this field.

This series is appropriate for courses in the Foundations or Principles of Physical Education at both the undergraduate and graduate levels. Individual volumes are written to serve as definitive texts for relevant subject matter courses or seminars. These books are also valuable for collateral reading and provide excellent resource materials for students working on special assignments, individual study projects and related research compilations and reviews.

Overall, this series provides an important source of scholarly literature which contains the latest scientific, behavioral and humanistic insights about the subject matter of physical education and sport. It also provides the foundational knowledge necessary to guide the selection of teaching and coaching practices which will be of most educational benefit to participants in programs of physical education and sport.

JOHN E. NIXON

Preface

There are at present a number of books and texts relating to what might be called physical education and sport philosophy in English and other languages. Usually these volumes have the words "philosophy" or "principles" in their titles. As with the first edition of this book, the question may now be asked again: is another such book needed? (It should be pointed out that the first edition, which appeared in 1968, included the word "history" in the title as well. Subsequently, the decision was made to separate history and philosophy as subdisciplinary areas. An additional volume covering physical education and sport history will appear in The Prentice-Hall Foundations of Physical Education and Sport Series within a few months of the publication of this revised and enlarged volume.)

Something new usually appears either because new sources demand that earlier books be updated, or because changing times and new purposes demand that we look at our past and present differently because of altered systems or sets of values. This present volume fulfills both these purposes to some degree. It is designed primarily to offer a persistent or recurring problems approach to the philosophy of physical education and sport.* Following each chapter or section, each persistent problem is analyzed in terms of the leading philosophical tendencies in the Western world.

I would like to say that the idea for this new approach came to me in a brilliant flash of insight while atop a high mountain, but, alas, the occurrence was much more prosaic. Although many of the specific ideas originated with me and some of my colleagues and graduate students, the

---

* No apology is being offered at this moment for calling the field "physical education and sport." This term seems to be gaining credence around the world. However, if we were to grant the unity of the human organism, it follows that there is no such thing as *physical* education. Many other names have been offered, but this is a good "holding pattern" term for now.

credit for this unique approach must go to John S. Brubacher, professor of the history and philosophy of education at Yale (and of higher education at Michigan), who was selected as one of the outstanding men of professional education of the century. Thus, it is the adaptation of this approach, the selection of certain persistent problems of both types (social forces and professional concerns), and the delineation of the implications for this field that may possibly be considered new contributions. Of course, Professor Brubacher should not be held accountable for any changes and/or possible deficiencies brought about by the transferral.

Some concepts and statements in this book remind us that the second half of this century may come to be known as the time when scholars and research-minded leaders in the field became truly concerned with the need to develop bodies of knowledge from related areas of study (so-called subdisciplinary areas). The accumulation of this knowledge may well enable the profession, within a reasonable period, to assume what many of us already believe is our rightful role in education and society at large. As the late Dean Arthur S. Daniels remarked at a unique conference of the Big Ten Physical Education Directors at the University of Illinois (Urbana-Champaign) in December, 1964:

> If we are to gain greater recognition in the academic world, we must follow pathways similar to those traversed by other disciplines. This means a greatly expanded program of scholarly research and development in which the body of knowledge in physical education is defined as nearly as possible in terms of its fundamental nature, and in its relationships with other disciplines.

Philosophy is one of these related disciplines to which we must turn for guidance, as well as to one of its corresponding subdivisions—the philosophy of education. The profession of physical education and sport must be aware of where it has been, how it developed, what its persistent problems are, and what it should do about them. Sound historical and philosophical research, plus investigation of a descriptive nature related to administration (management) as a developing social science—not to mention the social, psychological and sociological research endeavor—are the types of endeavor to which our best minds should be devoted in increasing numbers. Scientific research is vitally important, of course, but we *cannot* afford to slight the humanities and social science aspects of physical education and sport research. We do so at the very great risk of elimination through subversion to established or emerging disciplines. A greater amount of scientific truth will create more tenable theory, but we *act* according to our own systems of ethical and/or religious values within the boundaries outlined by the society's values and norms.

For these reasons, curriculum planners in professional preparation for physical education and sport should include in a body-of-knowledge core an articulated series of course experiences in the areas of professional orientation, history, sociology, social psychology, philosophy, and administration—quite probably in roughly that order—in every curriculum related to teaching, coaching, and administration. Such course experiences, each offered on the basis of prerequisites, are just as important in the development of a professional physical educator/coach as anatomy, physiology, biomechanics, motor learning, growth and development, and the health aspects of sport and exercise (as a natural science sequence). Coupled with beginning, intermediate, and advanced professional courses should be basic arts, social science, and natural science courses (and courses in general professional education if the student wishes to qualify eventually for state or provincial certification).

This volume in The Prentice-Hall Foundations of Physical Education and Sport Series is based on my own philosophical inquiry—and directly and indirectly on the endeavor of many colleagues within and outside this specialized field. The contents are introductory in nature and should be regarded as such. Some of the other volumes in the series will be based on more scientific generalizations available through the efforts of researchers in physical education and related disciplines. Such an approach was not possible, of course, in a subdisciplinary area such as philosophy. The philosophical analysis of persistent problems, as identified, is not usual either.

If the professional student is able to obtain an early understanding of the *nature* of the persistent historical problem and how they might possibly be *resolved* according to what seem to be the leading philosophical positions (or stances) in the Western world, this volume may stimulate the person to greater depth of thought. One last word—do not automatically accept what this book and your teachers tell you. This field desperately needs intelligent, inquiring, and dedicated scholars and researchers, teachers of teachers, and professional practitioners. Our future depends on you.

I am very pleased to recognize the very happy relationship I have had with Prentice-Hall over a period of twenty years. To Walter Welch, assistant vice-president; John Nixon, the series editor; Barbara Kanski, production editor; and to Howard Petlack, designer, may I say simply: Thank you very much.

E.F.Z.

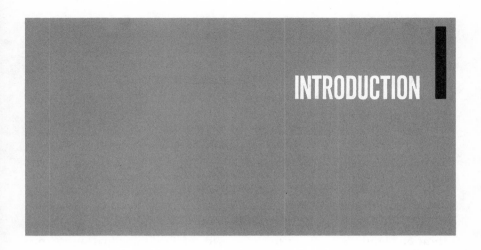

This book will identify and describe some of the major persistent problems in physical education and sport philosophy. The various terms now in use to describe what only a few decades ago was accepted universally as the field of physical education would fill this entire page. Although some readers may take exception, here we will use the term "physical education and sport."

DEFINITION OF PHYSICAL EDUCATION

Physical education could be exemplified by a child bouncing a ball on a school playground, an overweight man doing a situp, or a woman taking part in modern dance.[1] From another standpoint, physical education could be explained by a halfback scampering for the goal line in the Rose Bowl, boys and girls playing volleyball in a church recreation room, or a high school boy pinning his opponent in an interscholastic wrestling match. A Ph.D. candidate might be analyzing the contents of a Douglas gas bag full of a runner's expired air in a physical education exercise science laboratory, or a person might be trying out rhythmic exercises at home. Any of these activities could well be designated as aspects of physical education.

Until recently "physical education" has generally been employed as a broad, inclusive term comprising the fields of physical education, health education, safety education, athletics, recreation, dance education, kinesiology, and so on. Now many of these earlier subdivisions of the field have

[1] Some of this material was originally prepared for inclusion in the *Encyclopedia of Physical Education* to be published through the efforts of Professor T. K. Cureton and the Research Council of the American Alliance for Health, Physical Education, and Recreation.

become professions in their own right. Quite often now one sees the terms "physical education and sport" (as used in this book), or "sport and physical education" (for example, the National Association for Sport and Physical Education of the American Alliance for Health, Physical Education, and Recreation).

After an extensive study of physical education literature, Cobb (1943, p. 6) stated that there were four basic beliefs about the place of physical education in education: (1) There is no place for physical education in education; (2) physical education is for the maintenance of health in order that students may carry on their intellectual work with less strain; (3) physical education should develop students physically, mentally, and morally (mind-body dichotomy implied); and (4) physical education should contribute to the growth of the individual as an integrated personality by discovering the health, recreation, and personality needs of individual students and helping them to meet those needs through the program.

Beliefs three and four imply a "total fitness" concept. It is true that people now are much more successful than their predecessors in making an adjustment to the environment. They have had the experience of their forebears upon which to base the judgments that underlie actions. Their "adjustment" is dependent, however, upon complicated procedures. Their teeth depend upon the services of competent dentists. Their eyes very often must be aided to see well by highly trained ophthalmologists, optometrists, and opticians. Medical doctors and surgeons preserve the health of their hearts, lungs, and other vital organs (even with transplants when necessary). Protruding neck, round shoulders, sagging abdomen, pronated ankles, and weak feet are the results of modern society with its advanced technology. Muscles become weak, and the constant force of gravity upon the vertical body exacts a toll. A sedentary person's heart pounds wildly when he or she runs fifty yards after a departing bus, or to catch a subway train, or climbs a flight of stairs fairly rapidly.

Still further, most people often have difficulty adjusting their elemental emotions to the habit pattern of "do's and don'ts" that represent today's civilization. When this occurs, and it seems to be happening with increased regularity, the person cracks under the strain and is referred to a physician, and perhaps a hospital, another victim of what has been designated as psychosomatic difficulty. The field of physical education, and those subfields related to it within the educational pattern, has an important role to fulfill. It can provide the health knowledge, the physical activity, and the recreational outlets whereby boys and girls, and young men and women, will learn how to take care of their bodies, how to use them effectively, and how to provide themselves with healthful recreational activities.

The ambiguity of the term physical education may be clarified by approaching it from another direction. An extension of Frankena's categorization (1965, p. 6) transposed from an analysis of the meanings of education indicates that physical education may mean at least any one of five things:

1. The *activity of physically educating* carried on by teachers, schools, and parents (or by oneself)
2. The *process of being physically educated* (or learning) that goes on in the pupil or child (or person of any age)
3. The *result*, actual or intended, of (1) and (2)
4. The *discipline* or field of inquiry that studies or reflects on (1), (2), and (3) and is taught in departments, schools, and colleges as the theory of physical education
5. The *profession* whose members practice (1) above, try to observe (2) taking place, attempt to measure and/or evaluate whether (3) has occurred, and base their professional practice on the body of knowledge developed by those undertaking scholarly effort in the discipline (Zeigler and Vander-Zwaag, 1968, p. 8)

A PLETHORA OF OBJECTIVES

However the field is designated or defined, there can be no argument with the statement that its leaders have made a great many—and often unverifiable—educational claims for it over the years. Notable among those who have defined a variety of objectives, dating from the 1920s to the 1950s and thereafter, have been Hetherington (1922), Bowen and Mitchell (1923), Wood and Cassidy (1927), Williams (1927, 1930, etc.), Hughes (1930), Nash (1931, etc.), Sharman (1937), Wayman (1938), Esslinger (1938), Staley (1939), McCloy (1940), Clark (1943), Cobb (1943), Lynn (1944), Brownell and Hagman (1951), Scott (1951), Bucher (1952, etc.), and Oberteuffer and Ulrich (1951, etc.).

Hess (1959) assessed the objectives of American physical education from 1900 to 1957 in the light of certain historical events. These were (1) the hygiene or health objectives (1900–1919); (2) the socioeducational objectives (1920–1928); (3) the sociorecreative objectives, including the worthy use of leisure (1929–1938); (4) the physical fitness and health objective, including the broader objectives of international understanding (1946–1957).

It appears that the profession should take positive steps to plan for the possible achievement of a significant amount of consensus among the various philosophies of physical education extant in the Western world. This seems especially important because the field is increasing its efforts to relate to other countries in *all* parts of the world. Some possible common denominators are as follows:

1. That regular physical education periods should be required for all schoolchildren through sixteen years of age (approximately).
2. That children should develop certain positive attitudes toward their own health in particular and toward community hygiene in general. Basic health knowledge should be taught in the school curriculum.
3. That physical education and interscholastic athletics can make a contribution to the worthy use of leisure.
4. That physical vigor is important for people of all ages.
5. That boys and girls at some stage of their development should have experience in competitive athletics.
6. That therapeutic exercise should be employed to correct remediable physical defects.
7. That character and/or personality development may be fostered through physical education and athletics. (Zeigler, 1967)

SPORT HAS BECOME A POTENT SOCIAL FORCE

There are those both in North America and elsewhere who are arguing strongly that the field should adopt the name "sport" and that the area of study should be known as "sport studies." It is quite true that the social phenomenon known as sport, whether it be highly organized, reasonably well organized, or disorganized, has become a potent social force within the past century.[2] It can now be characterized as a vast enterprise that quite obviously demands wise and skillful management. Such a statement is presumably as true on the North American continent as anywhere else in the world. In Canada, for example, increased interest and emphasis on sport at both the provincial and national levels is certainly a most interesting and important development of the 1970s. While this was occurring, it became increasingly evident that qualified coaches for all levels of competition in all sports were not readily available. Provincial and federal officials have been forced in many instances to seek the services of qualified personnel from other countries. To what extent the established field of physical education (and/or kinesiology) will be able to provide the necessary highly qualified people for the rapidly developing profession of sport coaching remains to be seen. The opportunity for the profession of physical education and its related disciplines to be

[2] Adapted from a paper prepared for presentation at a CAHPER Preconvention (Learned Society) Program sponsored by the Philosophy of Sport and Physical Activity Committee, Saskatoon, Saskatchewan, June 25, 1975.

of direct and immediate service is now most certainly apparent. Whether the colleges and universities will rise to this challenge—and do it rapidly—depends on a great many factors, some of which will be discussed in this presentation.

Sensing the urgent need for much more careful study of the social impact of sport on culture, I have made an analysis of the situation in an effort to develop a model that would be both logical and consistent—a model of the social force known as sport. Subproblems of this analysis revolved around discovering preliminary answers to the following questions: (1) What have been some of the persistent historical problems of sport? (2) What diagrammatic pattern composed of what "ingredients" which best serve as a model for any field, profession, or even for an aspect of a society or culture (including sport)? (3) How might a disciplinary approach to sport (perhaps designated as "sport studies") be conceived in regard to its recommended composition? (4) What types of questions seem to arise as a result of such an analysis and proposal? (5) What reasonable conclusions can be drawn at this time?

Before attempting to answer these questions, a few definitions will be offered so that the reader will understand precisely how these terms are being used (these definitions are quite ordinary and can be found in just about any reliable dictionary).

Model

A diagrammatic structure indicating postulated relationships among the designated components of said structure (or pattern), some or all of which may be axiomatic in nature

Social force

A power that influences human relations in a society or culture to a greater or lesser, or good or evil, extent and/or direction

Sport

An outdoor pastime, as hunting or fishing done for recreation, or an outdoor athletic game, as baseball or lawn tennis, extended to cover such indoor games as bowling and rackets, and more recently, a variety of team activities typically identified as athletics, games, or contests

Culture

The characteristic attainments of a people or social order

Discipline

The subject matter of instruction; a course of study; a branch of knowledge

Profession

That of which one professes knowledge; vocation, if not purely commercial, mechanical, agricultural, or the like; calling, as of the profession of arms

SPORT'S PERSISTENT
HISTORICAL PROBLEMS

Over a period of years, I have been concerned with the careful delineation and description of what have seemed to be the persistent historical problems of physical education and sport. My efforts have been an adaptation of the unique approach developed by John S. Brubacher, retired professor in the history and philosophy of education (Yale and Michigan). Thus, what appears here is a further adaptation of this approach as related specifically to the social force known as sport. (Later in this introductory chapter, the persistent problems of physical education will be stressed.)

It should be pointed out immediately, however, that this approach does not really represent a radically different approach to history. The processes of investigation employed in traditional historical concerns are the same for those related to sport history. This approach does differ markedly, however, when the organization of the collected data is considered: It is based completely on the problem areas of the present, with a concurrent effort to illuminate them for those with an interest in sport history. There is a conscious effort to keep the reader from thinking that the subject is of antiquarian interest only. The reader moves back and forth from early times to the present as different aspects of the various social forces or professional concerns are considered. This might be called a longitudinal or vertical approach as opposed to the horizontal, chronological view typically employed. These persistent problems, then, recur again and again down through the ages, and they will in all probability continue to occur in the future. A problem used in this sense (based on its Greek derivation) would be "something thrown forward" for us to understand and/or resolve.

As indicated above, these problems have been divided into two categories: (1) social forces, of a pivotal or lesser nature; and (2) so-called professional and general educational concerns for the person involved professionally with sport or the individual concerned from the standpoint of general education and/or interest. The *social forces* identified are as follows (adapted from Zeigler, 1968):

1. Values (aims and objectives)
2. The influence of politics (or type of political state)
3. The influence of nationalism
4. The influence of economics
5. The influence of religion
6. Ecological concerns

The *professional* and/or *general educational concerns* are undoubtedly numerous, but the following are some that have been identified:

7. Relationship to the use of leisure
8. Relationship to the concept of the healthy body
9. Classification of amateurism, semiprofessionalism, and professionalism
10. The relationship of women to sport
11. Management theory and practice applied to sport
12. Curriculum for professional preparation and for general education
13. Teaching and/or coaching methodology
14. The ethics of coaching
15. The concept of progress in sport

A Model for the Optimum Development of Sport

Throughout the world the social force known as sport has been gathering momentum steadily and increasingly during the twentieth century. In the field of physical education—after an initial period of disenchantment with sport's many excesses—some practitioners have begun a disciplinary type of scholarly endeavor and research, but there are still many who are attempting to move in the opposite direction for fear that they may become further tainted and disenfranchised unless they establish a separate identity. This development is particularly true in the United States, but there is some evidence of similar feelings in Canada as well. The organizational structure of sport within the many other countries of the world, with the possible exception of Japan and a few others, is such that the concept of sport in education as a highly competitive, interinstitutional matter has not demanded investigation.

In an effort to clarify for myself, and perhaps for others, what has most certainly been a muddled matter for the past fifteen years, I have developed a model for the optimum development of a social force known as sport (see Figure 1). It is a model that can undoubtedly be adapted to other social forces or to the professions as well. The model includes the following five subdivisions: (1) professional, semiprofessional, and amateur involvement in theory and practice; (2) professional preparation and general education; (3) disciplinary research; (4) a developing theory embodying assumptions and testable hypotheses; and (5) an operational philosophy.

Professional, semiprofessional, and amateur involvement in theory and practice can be categorized further as (1) public, (2) semipublic, and (3) private. Professional preparation and general education involve the education of (1) the performer, (2) the teacher/coach, (3) the teacher of teachers/coaches, (4) the scholar and researcher, and (5) all people in the

FIGURE 1. A Model for Optimum Development of a Social Force Known As Sport

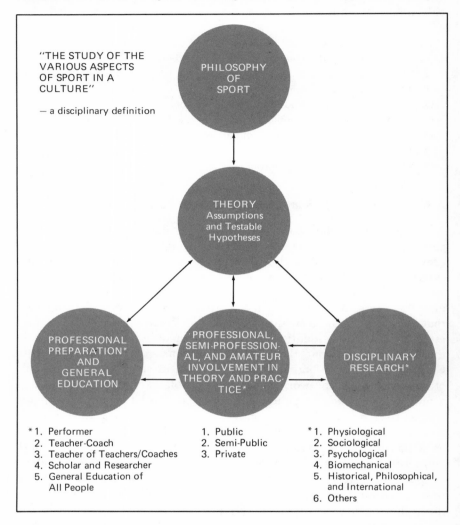

"THE STUDY OF THE VARIOUS ASPECTS OF SPORT IN A CULTURE"

— a disciplinary definition

PHILOSOPHY OF SPORT

THEORY
Assumptions and Testable Hypotheses

PROFESSIONAL PREPARATION* AND GENERAL EDUCATION

PROFESSIONAL, SEMI-PROFESSIONAL, AND AMATEUR INVOLVEMENT IN THEORY AND PRACTICE*

DISCIPLINARY RESEARCH*

* 1. Performer
2. Teacher-Coach
3. Teacher of Teachers/Coaches
4. Scholar and Researcher
5. General Education of All People

1. Public
2. Semi-Public
3. Private

* 1. Physiological
2. Sociological
3. Psychological
4. Biomechanical
5. Historical, Philosophical, and International
6. Others

theory and practice of sport generally. Disciplinary research includes (1) the physiological, (2) the sociological, (3) the psychological, (4) the biomechanical, (5) the historical, philosophical, and international aspects of sport, and (6) other subdisciplinary areas as yet unexplored (for example, anthropology).

The assumptions and testable hypotheses of a steadily evolving theory should comprise a "coherent group of general propositions used as principles of explanation for the phenomena" (*Random House Dictionary*, 1967) exhibited in human movement or motor performance in sport. Finally, inclusion of the philosophy of sport as an overarching entity in the model is based on the belief that the value system of a society will in the final analysis be realized, albeit gradually and unevenly, within the culture. This means that decisions regarding the development of the profession by its professional practitioners, or regarding the control or influence of sport as a social phenomenon, are usually based on the prevailing social values. Stresses and/or strains may bring about pressure to change these values or their hierarchical arrangement. This might occur as the result of new scientific evidence or other factors that could well lead to social unrest and upheaval.

A Disciplinary Approach to Sport

The recommended composition of sport studies as a developing discipline can be perceived reasonably well at this point, but it will undoubtedly evolve and expand in the years immediately ahead. I have devised a tentative disciplinary definition of a sport studies area—"the study of the various aspects of sport. in a culture." For purposes of curriculum development and discussion, the discipline is viewed as containing an arts and social science division and a natural science division (see Table 1.) The development of a subject matter or discipline to be

TABLE 1.   Sport Studies: A Discipline Definition Based on Descriptive Aspects of the Subareas of Study (with related discipline affiliation)

ARTS AND SOCIAL SCIENCE DIVISION		NATURAL SCIENCE DIVISION	
Description	Related Discipline	Description	Related Discipline
Meaning and significance	History, philosophy, international; etc.	Biochemical analysis	Physics; anatomy
Social and cultural aspects	Sociology; anthropology	Anthropometry	Anthropology; physical medicine
Esthetic aspects	Fine arts	Motor learning and development	Psychology; medicine
Behavioral aspects	Social psychology	Physiological aspects	Physiology; medicine
Administration and management Curriculum development and instruction	Administrative science (and related disciplines) Education	Health aspects (including injuries and rehabilitation through exercise)	Physiology; medicine (physical); psychology; public health
Measurement and evaluation	Mathematics	Measurement and evaluation	Mathematics

known as sport studies is, of course, in an early stage. This is true because the field of physical education has not been geared up for such investigation, and also because the more well-established disciplines have not been far-sighted enough to realize either the impact of culture on sport—or the impact of sport on culture. Such a seeming unwillingness to be concerned with sport is not unique to the area of sport studies. The field of sociology, for example, has been extremely slow to recognize the place of leisure in society either as an influence or as being influenced by society and its social forces (Zeigler, 1972).

There have been a number of articles during the past ten years analyzing the situation in physical education, kinesiology, and related disciplines insofar as disciplinary orientation is concerned. The late Arthur Daniels envisioned this approach in the 1960s, and he was followed by Loy and Kenyon (1969), Sheehan (1968), VanderZwaag (1972, 1973), Cosentino (1973), and others abroad (notably Hans Lenk in Germany). But it is misleading to list those to whom credit should be given without a careful investigation. Certainly Paul Weiss's effort in sport philosophy deserves mention (1969), as does Harold VanderZwaag's definitive *Toward a Philosophy of Sport* (1972). Obviously, all these scholars followed Seward Staley of Illinois, who was talking about "sport" and "sports education" more than forty years ago!

Despite these noteworthy efforts, it seems quite safe to state that sport or sport studies, from a disciplinary standpoint, is still multidisciplinary but on the way to becoming cross disciplinary (see Figure 2). Speaking about physical education as a discipline in the late 1960s, Cyril White, Irish sport sociologist, postulated that physical education had many multidisciplinary characteristics—and some cross disciplinary ones. His point was that physical education's "future development to interdisciplinary level will require a far greater degree of sophisticated research abilities and orientations than the field at present possesses" (White, 1968). Considering the paucity of intradisciplinary research efforts—where scholars from one subdiscipline within the subject matter area, conceived as sport studies, work together actively and cooperatively on joint scholarly endeavors—it still seems safe to state that sport studies is currently multidisciplinary on the way toward becoming cross disciplinary.

Some Questions That Arise

If it is indeed true sport has become an important—indeed, integral —aspect of culture, certain changes in the way sport questions are now analyzed will need to be made. In the first place, sport should be declared

FIGURE 2. Sport Studies: A Multidiscipline on the Way Toward Becoming a Crossdiscipline?

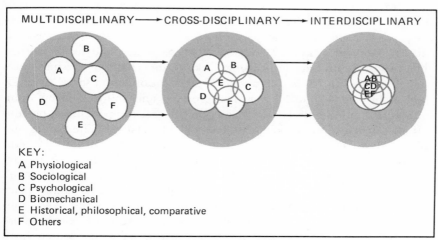

MULTIDISCIPLINARY ———► CROSS-DISCIPLINARY ———► INTERDISCIPLINARY

KEY:
A Physiological
B Sociological
C Psychological
D Biomechanical
E Historical, philosophical, comparative
F Others

Courtesy of Cyril M. White, Ph.D. (Adapted by Earle Zeigler)

officially an integral component of what has long been considered the physical education base of departmental, division, school, and faculty (college) titles. Names and titles should be changed to include the term "sport." (For example, I have for some time now been recommending that the term "physical education" be supplemented by the words "and sport." This would seem to be a desirable approach while the profession and the public make up their collective mind as to which term will ultimately be accepted.)

Further, it seems absolutely necessary that the research components of the various college and university units should be greatly improved. This is not to say that outstanding teachers of sport performance and teachers of coaches should not be available in each institution. It does mean, however, that the present quantity and quality of research leaves a great deal to be desired if sport studies is to come into its own. It would be a tragedy to lose our birthright by default—that is, to see other disciplines gradually assume the responsibility for various types of research related to sport. This may occur in any event, but the study of sport as an integral aspect of the culture is presently much more closely aligned with departments of physical education and athletics. Thus, it would seem highly desirable for the study of sport to be planned through these educational units, with joint appointments in related disciplines where it seems desirable and appropriate.

Conclusions

If it is indeed true that sport has become a potent social force within the past century and that almost all colleges and universities are poorly prepared to conduct scholarly inquiry and research about *all* aspects of this development, it seems reasonable to suggest that a body of knowledge about sport is indeed the missing link in the chain of circumstances whereby sport can be used as a valuable, educational and social force for the benefit of people of all ages, backgrounds, and abilities. In my opinion, sport should be declared officially an integral component of the educational structure of schools, colleges, and universities. The names and titles of departments and schools should be changed to include the term "sport." A case must be made for significant improvement of the research components of the various college and university units. Such improvement is urgently needed in the face of developments taking place in the various East European countries, where both "frontier" and "mission-oriented" research are proceeding apace. There must also be more reflective inquiry on the part of scholars associated with research institutes devoted to sport studies. Failure to meet this urgent need for scholarly endeavor and scientific investigation will result in (1) a steady —and continuing—decline in the status of physical education and/or kinesiology departments and/or schools; (2) a gradual, but belated, assumption of research responsibilities relative to sport by other disciplines (sociology, physiology); and (3) an inevitable assumption of leadership in all phases of sport by the Iron Curtain countries. It seems quite obvious that positive action in the direction indicated should be taken at the first possible moment.

THE GROWING INTEREST IN PHILOSOPHY

That there has been an upsurge of interest in philosophy is self-evident: Rapid progress in science and retrogression, or dubious progress, in the realm of social affairs have forced intelligent men and women everywhere to take stock. Unfortunately, it is next to impossible to gain historical perspective on the rapid change that is taking place, and a seemingly unprecedented burden has been imposed on our understanding of ourselves and our world. Everywhere we see a need for research, and then for more research. With all this endeavor, the rate of scientific and technological progress accelerates, and it becomes an exciting but vicious circle. One wonders whether the pace can continue, because research has a way of multiplying questions much faster than we can ever

hope to answer them. We may have already exceeded our ability to as-
similate the research findings that are being reported daily, but who can
answer this question? Certainly it is true that our knowledge of the
physical fields and the biological processes has vastly exceeded the development of fundamental knowledge about human behavior. Eventually
someone, or some group, is going to have to decide to what extent further
research in particular directions should be supported financially. Can we
manage this whole affair in such a way that wise and intelligent decisions
will be made in the light of the many scientific findings, and in such a
way that the good life, whatever that may be, will be available to everyone on earth? We must learn quickly to employ and direct science in
the best possible way to serve humanity. Thus we encounter the question
of the values by which we live, and we have come full circle to explain
the upsurge of interest in philosophy.

A study covering literature that has a relationship, no matter how
tenuous, to the philosophy of physical education and sport could conceivably run into hundreds of pages, and this would never do. On the
other hand, if a discussion were presented about only those studies that
employed the structural analysis technique of philosophical research, it
would be noticeably brief. Obviously, a compromise is necessary. This
discussion therefore limits itself to providing some of the answers to two
questions: (1) What is the philosophic task? (2) How may philosophical
investigation be related to physical education and sport activities? A third
question—What studies have been conducted in this field along philosophical lines during the past three decades?—will be left to the end of
each of the presentations of the various persistent problems (and all these
studies are included in the general bibliography at the end of the book).

The Philosophic Task

Probably there are as many definitions of the philosophic task as
there are philosophers; hence, no effort will be made to be all-inclusive.
Furthermore, any attempt to gain consensus on this point is automatically
doomed to failure. The safest approach for any quasi-philosopher is simply to state at the outset that his or her opinions about the philosophic
task have been developed from personal background reading and experience, and from association with others of like interest.

Proceeding from this premise, we see philosophers as scholars dedicated to, and perhaps ultimately responsible for, the outlook and values of
the various societies and cultures in which they live. Still further, philosophers attempt to evaluate what we know and believe about the universe
and our own sphere of human affairs. Subsequently they may evolve a systematic and coherent plan by which a human being may live. Following

this, they may attempt to justify their position in various ways against other competing philosophical approaches. In the process they may analyze these other positions carefully; they may make comparisons; and they may show what they believe to be their deficiencies. It is conceivable that they may gradually, or even suddenly, change their own position because of cumulative scientific evidence which appears to refute what was previously held to be true. Finally, they may even abandon the traditional or "scientific" approaches to philosophizing completely, if they become convinced that up to now it has not been possible "to be clear about exactly what we are saying or even exactly what the question is that we are asking" (Hospers, 1953, xii).

Up to this point, therefore, we have said that philosophers may approach their work *speculatively, normatively,* or *analytically.* They may speculate about what we know and believe about the universe and our own sphere of human affairs within this framework. They may approach these questions normatively and evolve a systematic and coherent plan whereby a human may live. They may seek to analyze other philosophical approaches critically and to make comparisons. In this latter approach they will probably attempt to clarify concepts and to present evidence that seems to bear out one position or the other. Finally, they may go so far with critical analysis that language analysis and semantics will come to seem their primary task.

The difference between the traditional philosophic method and the scientific method should be made clear. Rather than aiming at a solution of a limited number of the factors and variables through rigid experimental control, the philosophic method attempts instead to include every factor or variable that is either directly or remotely relevant to the problem. In this way an effort is made to arrive at "a synthesis which is not only consistent with the best current data but also with the best experience drawn from the past." As Brubacher makes clear (third edition, 1962, p. 6), ". . . philosophy itself uncovers no new facts. It processes the facts of other disciplines but owns none of its own."

The philosophy of physical education is a subdivision of the philosophy of education, itself a subdivision of the whole discipline of philosophy. Let us see what the philosopher Frankena, who himself has evidenced a deep interest in both the philosophy of education and in language analysis, has to say about the subject matter of education:

> We come, thus, to the subject of education. What is it? Actually, the term "education" is ambiguous and may mean any one of four things:
> 1. the *activity of educating* carried on by teachers, schools, and parents (or by oneself),
> 2. the *process of being educated* (or learning) which goes on in the pupil or child,

3. the *result,* actual or intended, of (1) and (2),
4. the *discipline* or field of enquiry that studies or reflects on (1), (2), and (3) and is taught in schools of education (Frankena, 1965, p. 6).

Writing in 1956, Frankena spoke about being able "to distinguish at least the outlines" of speculative, normative, and analytical philosophy of education. At that time he said, "Of these the first and second can now seem to belong to the philosophy of the process of education and the third to the philosophy of the discipline of education" (Frankena, 1956. p. 98). In his later writing, however, Frankena seems willing to include normative philosophy of education under the discipline of education when he states

> The philosophy of education is part of the discipline of education as defined earlier. It may either be *analytical* or *normative.* It is normative insofar as it is concerned to propose ends or values for education to promote, principles for it to follow, excellences for it to foster, or methods, contents, programs, etc., for it to adopt or employ, in general or specific situations. It is analytical insofar as it is concerned merely to analyze, clarify, or elucidate, or to criticize and evaluate, our thinking about education—the concepts or terms we employ, the arguments we use, the assumptions we make, the slogans we proclaim, the theories we formulate. (Frankena, 1965, p. 8)

This statement would seem to indicate that Frankena still feels there is really a legitimate place in schools of education for normative philosophers of education (and physical education!) who write texts in which the aims, principles, and means of a particular educational position are delineated for those involved in the "activity of educating."

To the reader it may now be obvious that true philosophizing is a highly complex discipline that may be practiced adequately only by a highly intelligent professional person. For this reason it seems logical that philosophizing of a speculative nature (if practiced at all!) should be left to true experts.[3] To what extent educational philosophers (and physical education philosophers) should involve themselves with speculative philosophy is debatable, although there is no doubt that some educational philosophers do qualify for this type of endeavor. We should keep in mind, of course, that many "pure" philosophers have given up this aspect of the work because of what they feel is its futility. Where physical education philosophers fit into this picture at present is self-evident.

Physical educators may well ask if they have a place at all. The answer again seems to be self-evident—yes! But it stands to reason that the assumption of such a role should not be taken lightly—certainly not as

---

[3] This is not to say that any person, and especially a teacher, does not have the right, or the responsibility, to develop his or her own philosophy of life, religion, education, and so on.

lightly as it seems to have been taken in the past. Unless physical educators have adequate backgrounds in the discipline of philosophy (and philosophy of education), they should not be encouraged or allowed to select thesis topics in these areas. To be sure, these related departments would undoubtedly view the selection of advanced fifth- and sixth-year courses in their subject matter most unfavorably, if they would even allow such selection. In summary, therefore, *adequately prepared* physical educators ought to be able to approach the philosophy of physical education and sport normatively and analytically and should do so increasingly in the future. The era in which the scholarly contributions to the philosophy of physical education were made by physical education leaders and administrators *with inadequate backgrounds in philosophy* is over. This is not to say that their statements will not be welcome, or that perhaps the rank and file of the profession will not pay greater heed to their words than those of the philosophy specialists, but well-informed professional physical educators will be forced to take into consideration the sources and the backgrounds from which these individuals speak. In any case, there is certainly a continuing need to train physical educators systematically and thoroughly so that they may undertake normative and analytical philosophical research of high quality.

Relating Philosophical Investigation to Physical Education

At the present moment in North America, the field of physical education and sport is being affected by certain social influences so strong that it is almost being swept along out of control by the fast-moving current. On the one hand, we are groping toward an understanding of the concept of internationalism in a shrinking world; in sharp contrast, there are also strong forces of a nationalistic nature at work driving our field into a position where it could conceivably be called "physical fitness" or even "sport" (in some people's eyes). The fact that acceptance of these terms as the primary function may relegate the field to secondary status in the educational system, and in the hierarchy of values in our society, does not seem to be bothering many physical educators. Of course, many feel that this is where the field belonged anyhow, and it is just now finding its rightful place. The typical physical fitness advocate believes that young people (and adults) are deficient in bodily musculature and endurance anyhow, and here is a way to start children early in life, exercise them vigorously, discipline them thoroughly, and thereby give them a sound physical base upon which intellectual competence can be superimposed.

There is one major difficulty with the approach of those who would raise physical fitness to such a paramount position in the program: Rightly or wrongly, a considerable percentage of the male physical educators and coaches, and a still larger percentage of the women in the field, are not ready to accept all that such a physical fitness emphasis implies. This latter group believes that physical education is really education *through* the medium of the physical, and that there is no such thing as education *of* the physical—that the mind-body dichotomy is something from the past, long ago disproved by psychologists and others. The term "total fitness" means something to these people; they see health education, safety education, physical education, sport and athletics, dance, and recreation education as integral phases of the curriculum. The term "social intelligence" as defined by Dewey, or perhaps even the term "social self-realization" as stressed by Brameld, involves knowledges, competencies, and skills related to citizenship, personality traits, and moral values in the broadest sense.

On the one hand, therefore, the pendulum seems to be swinging sharply to the right in the direction of an essentialistic educational philosophy. The result is that many physical educators are searching rather frantically for a discipline involving a body of scientific knowledge that will bring, they hope, a certain amount of academic respectability to the field. Progressivists, because of their allegiance to the scientific method, can work hand in hand with all other discipline seekers. The President's Council on Physical Fitness is striving for a much greater amount of vigorous physical training in our programs, and those who venture the belief that physical *education* has a greater role to play in the educational process are challenged to produce substantial proof. Admittedly, this is quite difficult to do. But despite the advent of the cold war and the space age, many educational leaders in our profession are standing by their belief that physical education does contribute to the educational process in many ways. It does seem to be true, however, that many important members of our lay public are siding, occasionally quite vociferously, with the rising tide of essentialism in education.

These current trends in the philosophy of physical education and sport, which undoubtedly are the result of conflicting philosophies of education in each of the fifty public educational systems in the United States, have perpetuated such a blurred image of the field that professional practitioners are typically quite confused. This confusion is often unconsciously transmitted to professional students, who find themselves at a loss when faced with a need to explain to parents and the general public what our field can and should do with the nation's children in the recommended daily program of physical education.

To understand how physical education and, for that matter, the entire educational structure got itself into this situation, we must look to our philosophical foundations. For the first time in the history of physical education, scholars have become truly aware of the need to turn to philosophy in an effort to delineate the implications for our subject of the leading philosophical tendencies of the Western world. (The fact that no consideration is being given here to philosophical movements in the Orient reaffirms pointedly the narrow provincialism of a world that is technologically shrinking day by day.) At least we have begun to apply philosophical concepts and methods of analysis directly to physical education and sport. This experiment, still in its infancy, is of mutual importance to both philosophy and physical education, for philosophy must "bake bread" if it is to survive in our rapidly changing world.

Of late many people in our field have been using the word "philosophy" with increasing frequency. Currently there seems to be a "philosophy" of almost everything; for instance, a recently published article bore the title, "A Philosophy of Base Running"! This development should not cause too much concern, since it points to a new awareness of the need for reassessment of our value system. Such awareness is heartening, but often quite superficial, because most individuals lack a philosophical background. Furthermore, one can undoubtedly learn more about a person's value system by observing conduct than by listening to him or her describe a philosophical position, no matter how eloquent he or she may be. For those involved in teacher education, the task is to help the prospective teacher of physical education and sport to understand his or her own philosophical position. Because backgrounds are so varied, very few, if any, can accept any one philosophical position in its entirety. Most people seem to develop a type of "patterned eclecticism" that works for them. The teacher of philosophy has the age-old, intangible task not of imparting knowledge about a specific "thing," but of educing self-examination. He or she can only hope that a reasonable amount of internal consistency will evolve in this "process of becoming."

HISTORICAL BACKGROUND
AND PERSPECTIVE

It may be possible to gain truer perspective on physical education by viewing the question historically. If one of the primary functions of philosophy is to help decide what a person is or should be, the fivefold classification provided by Morris (1956) should be helpful. Morris explains that throughout history human beings have been defined as follows:

1. Man is a rational animal.
2. Man is a spiritual being. St. Augustine in the fifth century set the stage for a man consisting of mind, body, and soul—a three-dimensional man. With this came a hierarchy of values with the "animal nature" assuming the lowest position. (Excesses in athletics were roundly condemned.)
3. Man is a receptacle of knowledge, a "knowing creature" who should absorb as much knowledge as possible.
4. Man has a mind that can be trained by exercise. It was decided that education should exercise both mind and body. After all, man is an organic unity.
5. Man is a problem-solving organism. Dewey redefined man as a problem-solving animal in the process of evolution on earth. All his capabilities had come from his developing capacity to solve the problems that confronted him. Thus, man tries to make sense out of his experience, and reconstructs it to improve future experience. Physical education's task within this pattern is to teach man to move efficiently and with meaning and purpose within the context of man's socialization in an evolving world.

Those who have written about history, including education, appear to have slighted "physical culture" through bias. Woody (1949) tells us that "lip-service has been paid increasingly to the dictum 'a sound mind in a sound body,' ever since western Europe began to revive the educational concepts of the Graeco-Roman world," but that "there is still a lack of balance between physical and mental culture."

It is true that physical activity has been part of the fundamental pattern of living for every creature that has ever lived on earth. For this reason, the condition of a person's body must have always been of concern. In primitive society there appears to have been very little organized, purposive instruction in physical education, although early people knew that a certain type of fitness was necessary for survival. The usual activities of labor, searching for food, dancing, and games were essential to the development of superior bodies. With physical efficiency as a basic survival need, muscles, including the heart, had to be strong; vision had to be keen; and the body had to be able to run fast and to lift heavy loads.

Even if it were an objective, it would not have been possible to separate completely the physical and mental education of primitive youth. The boy underwent an informal apprenticeship that prepared him for life's various physical duties. A great deal of learning occurred through trial and error and through imitation. Tradition and custom were highly regarded, and the importance of precept and proper example were important aspects of both physical and mental culture.

Testing in early societies was carried out through various initiatory ceremonies designed to give the young man (and occasionally the young woman) the opportunity to test himself or herself in the presence of peers and elders. Although most education was informal, the educational pattern followed the same traditions and customs from generation to generation. The practical aspects of life were learned by doing them repeatedly, and strict discipline was often employed if the child was lazy or recalcitrant.

There was, of course, a great deal of ignorance about sound health practices. Vigorous exercise undoubtedly did much to help early people remain healthy. Health care in infancy and in early youth was probably even more deficient than the health practices followed by adults in the society. In preliterate societies, there does not appear to have been as sharp a division between work and play (or labor and leisure) as is found later in civilized societies. Children had many play activities because they were not ready for the serious business of living. Their parents had very little leisure in a subsistence economy.

Persistent Social Forces or Influences

At least five pivotal social forces or influences have influenced society—and directly and indirectly what has been called physical education—during the various periods of history (Brubacher, 1966; Zeigler, 1968). To these I have added what might be considered by some to be a *false* problem—the influence of an ecological ethic.[4] Thus, these social forces are viewed as (1) the influence of values and norms, (2) the influence of politics, (3) the influence of nationalism, (4) the influence of economics, (5) the influence of religion, and (6) the influence of a so-called ecological ethic (see Figure 3).

To these six social forces (or influences) have been added some ten professional and/or general educational concerns, the last of which—the concept of progress—could be placed in either of the two major categories. These concerns are (1) curriculum, or what shall be taught; (2) methods of instruction, or how shall the curriculum be taught; (3) professional preparation or training; (4) the concept of what constitutes a healthy body; (5) the role of women in physical education and sport; (6) the role of dance in physical education and recreation; (7) the use of leisure; (8) amateurism, semiprofessionalism, and professionalism in sport; (9) the role of management (administration); and (10) the concept of what constitutes progress (viewed both as a social force and as a professional concern).

---

[4] A "persistent problem" recommended by a graduate student at Sacramento State College in the summer of 1970.

FIGURE 3. Selected Persistent Historical Problems of Physical Education and Sport

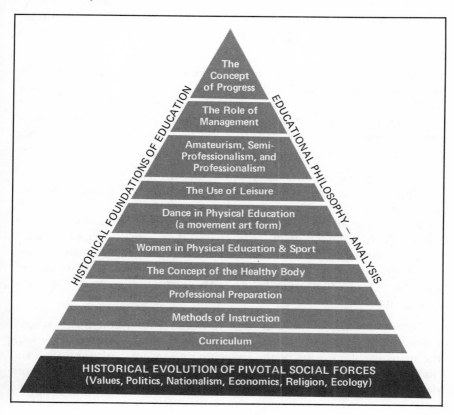

A BRIEF HISTORY OF THE MOTHER DISCIPLINE, PHILOSOPHY

Philosophy had its beginning in Greece over 2500 years ago, where the word originally meant knowledge or love of wisdom. The first method to be used by philosophers was speculation, a method many professional philosophers still employ today and which, interestingly enough, is an integral part of the scientific method first developed during the Renaissance. The ancients themselves in their search for a logical universe made a distinction between speculative knowledge and practical knowledge gained through experience and observation. In the course of this dialog on method, three leading philosophic tendencies emerged—idealism, realism, and pragmatism. Of course, they were not known under these titles until the late nineteenth and early twentieth centuries. The influence of these schools of thought is still very strong in the 1970s, despite the inroads that have recently been made by language analysis and existentialism.

Idealism, which can be traced through Plato, the Hebrew-Christian tradition in religion, Descartes, Spinoza, Leibniz, Berkeley, and Kant to Hegel, postulates that man is a real, existent being with a soul; that in each man is a spirit or mind which is basically real; that the essence of the entire universe is mind or spirit; and that man is a son of God, who created the universe.

Realism (or Nominalism), which got its start with Aristotle and developed through the philosophical thought of St. Thomas Aquinas, Descartes, Comenius, Spinoza, Locke, Kant, Herbart, James, and the various schools of the twentieth century, implies that man lives in a world which is undoubtedly real; that things actually happen exactly the way man experiences them; that man's experience does not change any knowledge that may enter into his consciousness; that things are just the same as they were before such experience occurred; and that reality "out there" is independent of man's mind.

Pragmatism may be said to have begun with Heraclitus; gathered momentum with Francis Bacon and John Locke; gained strength through the many early scientists of the sixteenth and seventeenth centuries; and blossomed into fruition with Comte, Peirce, James, and Dewey. Its position is that the world is *constantly* changing; that an idea is not true until it is tested through experience; that we can only learn what an idea really *means* by putting it into practice; and that we can't ever really discover the nature of the universe.

It is difficult to gain historical perspective on the philosophical trends and developments of the past century. It is apparent, however, that there have been strong attacks on many of the traditional approaches described above. Prior to World War I, idealism had lost some of the prestige it had enjoyed in the late 1800s. The defense of scientific investigation by Spencer and Darwin was a tremendously powerful influence. Pragmatism continued to be influential, especially in the United States. It gathered much strength from naturalism and from the rise of the spirit of scientific inquiry. Great emphasis was placed on the desirability of testing hypotheses through experience in order to gain "true" knowledge.

Philosophical Analysis, a development of the past forty years, attempts to provide an answer to the recurring question, "What is philosophical knowledge?" Developing the scientific method has forced many of today's philosophers to ask themselves, "In what kind of activity am I engaging? Does philosophical activity result in knowledge after all?" If true knowledge can come only from scientific experimentation, what is the justification for philosophy? A considerable group of influential people within the discipline of philosophy feel that, since knowledge must be communicable, philosophy's primary function is to use language terms clearly and correctly.

Existentialism is still another type of philosophizing that has emerged as a significant force during the past hundred years. This approach started as a revolt against Hegel's idealism, which held that ethical and spiritual realities were accessible to man through reason. One sector developed the position which affirmed that man's task was to create his own ideals and values. According to Nietzsche, science had shown that the transcendent ideals of the Church were nonsense—"God is dead." Thus man is on his own in a cold, cruel world. Man, spelled with a capital "M," is the only one who can give meaning and direction to a world lacking in these qualities. Can he so direct and guide his own existence that responsible social action will result? This is the fundamental question.

What *is* the answer to the many philosophical questions about the nature of the world, the problem of good and evil, the possibility of free will, the existence of God, the greater importance of some values as opposed to others, the possibility of man's really acquiring knowledge, and the nature of beauty—just to name a few of life's enigmas? It is safe to say that no one person or group has the answers organized in such form that anything close to universal acceptance would result.

Educational Philosophy, really a subdivision of philosophy, devotes itself to an analysis of the implications of the various philosophical positions for three major areas: (1) the relationships among society, school, and the individual; (2) educational aims and objectives; and (3) the process of education. More specifically, questions have been asked (and partially answered) about standardization of instruction, administrative control, teacher control, the psychology of learning, the definition of subject matter, the role of measurement and evaluation, the aims of the process of education, the importance of interest in learning, the need for indoctrination and discipline, and many others.

A DISCIPLINARY
STATUS FOR
PHYSICAL EDUCATION

Physical educators have realized the need for the development of a body of knowledge through a greatly expanded program of scholarly and research endeavor in a variety of subdisciplinary areas (Zeigler and McCristal, 1967). Some of the field's scientists had realized this earlier, especially in the physiological area and in certain aspects of psychology. Relationships are gradually being strengthened with such fields as anatomy, sociology, history, philosophy, comparative and international education, anthropology, and management theory within the behavioral sciences, business administration, and educational administration.

The effort to define the field as a discipline so as to provide a body of knowledge upon which the profession may practice may well assist us quite substantially to realize a wondrous future both on this planet and in space. The kinesiologists, exercise physiologists, psychologists, and sociologists within physical education should be able to discover how human beings move, what happens to them when they move in certain ways, and how this influences their social relations, but it will be the province largely of those interested in the historical, philosophical, and comparative aspects of physical education and athletics to assist the profession to contemplate the trajectory of this field in the space age.

As the body of knowledge within physical education increases and inventories of scientific findings from the various related disciplines improve in both quantity and quality, it will become increasingly possible to verify whether a planned program of physical education does actually result in the achievement of the many objectives that have been claimed over the years. Maybe then the field will be able to achieve consensus on certain common denominators in the "education of an amphibian" (Huxley, 1964) or a "naked ape" (Morris, 1967). What seems to be really important in the classification of a "relatively hairless ape," in addition to the obvious legacy from ancestors, is that the human being has now become almost non-apelike. And there remains ample opportunity for all sorts of differential development in the eons that lie ahead (Simpson, 1968). Physical education may eventually be called human movement, human motor performance, kinesiology, anthropokineticology, homokinetics, sport, or what have you. The important point is that the field has a significant role to play in human education and development.

For some time I have been recommending that philosophy, and specifically educational philosophy, has true meaning for us in physical, health, and recreation education, if we will only make the effort to comprehend our philosophical foundations (Zeigler, 1964, and other papers listed in the Bibliography). This approach will not give us the answers to all our problems overnight, but such analysis will place us in a much better position to meet our persistent, recurring historical problems intelligently *when we know where we stand;* and we can then discuss conflicting philosophies more logically and consistently than we have been able to do up to this time.

In relation to the philosophy of physical education and sport, the assumption has been made that physical educators with an adequate background in philosophy and philosophy of education ought to be able to philosophize normatively and analytically about their field in regard to its place in education and in society. An attempt is being made, therefore, to delineate the implications for our subject of the leading philosophical tendencies of the Western world. Thus, pragmatism, realism, idealism, philosophy of language, and existentialism have been related to corresponding tendencies in educational philosophy, such as experimentalism (pragmatic naturalism), reconstructionism, romantic naturalism, naturalistic realism, rational humanism, Catholic moderate realism, and idealism. Philosophy of language is being treated as philosophy "in a new key," and existentialism is conceived of as a "flavoring" influence.

The assumption has been made that philosophical analysis of the persistent historical problems will enable professional practitioners to realize the need for ordered, consistent, and logical personal philosophies. A consistent philosophy of administration, for example, will give direction to those administering programs in this field—direction that is sorely needed as we wait for the developing social science of administration to outline the most effective way to manage organizations. Here the objective has been to apply current administrative theory, based largely on the research conducted in public administration, business administration, educational administration, and the behavioral sciences. Our hope is that an analysis of the theoretical frameworks used in administrative research will enable us to develop our own unique theoretical framework for administration in the field of physical education and competitive athletics.

For all these reasons, the many graduate faculties in physical education are urged to develop a coordinated approach to scholarly and research endeavor in the history, philosophy, and administrative theory of physical education and sport. The greatest possible good would result if these areas, and others related to the humanities and social sciences, received an emphasis comparable to that of the natural sciences. Our overall goal is to discover what contributions physical, health, and recreation education can make to human development, to what extent society will accept this evidence, and how we may best administer programs of this type offered within the framework of general education.

CONCLUDING STATEMENT

In this chapter we have presented what is felt to be a primary need in our field now and in the future. It is a truism to state that we need a much stronger body of knowledge based on orderly and coordinated research so that we may eventually, and perhaps soon, call ourselves a fine profession. We have developed professional preparation that is intellectual in character; we are service-oriented; and we are not judged to be successful by the size of our bank accounts. Furthermore, we have a code of ethics (the enforcement of which, unfortunately, is rarely tested); we have certain public recognition (the level of which could undoubtedly be higher); we have professional leaders who are devoting their entire lives to the task; we are acquiring definite performance skills; and we have a fellowship with our associates through various meetings and published literature. Despite these dramatic advances, there still remains the basic need for an organized body of knowledge based on legitimate research—and this is certainly true in the areas of history and philosophy. Those of us involved in professional preparation can make decisions about who goes on this difficult road of scholarly and research endeavor. It is up to us to give bright young students the lead, to indicate to them where they should go, what they are after, how they may obtain it, and possibly what they can do with it. After that it is up to them. We can draw a rough blueprint for the cooperative research effort that will give us the body of knowledge that we need so desperately. "And so we had better strive to become clearly and fully conscious of who we are, where we are, how we got this way," and which path we should take (Muller, 1952, p. 33).

> Two roads diverged in a wood, and I—
> I took the one less traveled by —
> And that has made all the difference.   [Robert Frost]

REFERENCES

As we move forward to a consideration of some sixteen persistent problems selected for consideration in this volume, the reader is urged

to consider his or her own background in philosophy generally, and in
the philosophy of education specifically. This brief volume can stand
on its own, but despite its length it cannot cover such a vast area deeply.
The following list of references can be invaluable for supplementary
reading and browsing.

BOWEN, W. P., and E. D. MITCHELL, *The Theory of Organized Play*. New York:
A. S. Barnes, 1923.

BROWNELL, CLIFFORD L., and E. P. HAGMAN, *Physical Education—Foundations
and Principles*. New York: McGraw-Hill, 1951.

BRUBACHER, JOHN S., *A History of the Problems of Education* (2nd ed.). New
York: McGraw-Hill, 1966.

———, *Modern Philosophies of Education* (4th ed.). New York: McGraw-Hill,
1969. (The Third Edition was published in 1962.)

BUCHER, CHARLES A., *Foundations of Physical Education*. St. Louis: Mosby, 1952.
(There have been later editions of this standard work and certain others
listed in the bibliography at the end of the book.)

BUTLER, J. DONALD, *Four Philosophies* (rev. ed.). New York: Harper & Row,
1957.

CLARK, MARGARET C., "A Philosophical Interpretation of a Program of Physical
Education in a State Teachers College," Ph.D. dissertation, New York
University, 1943.

COBB, LOUISE S., "A Study of the Functions of Physical Education in Higher
Education." Ph.D. dissertation, Columbia Teachers College, 1943.

COSENTINO, FRANK, "A Case for Sport," *Journal of the Canadian Association for
Health, Physical Education, and Recreation*, 40, No. 2 (November–December 1973), 3–9.

DANIELS, A. S., "The Study of Sport as an Element of the Culture," in *Sport,
Culture, and Society*, ed. J. W. Loy and G. S. Kenyon. New York: Macmillan, 1969, pp. 13–22.

DAVIS, E. C., and D. M. MILLER, *The Philosophic Process in Physical Education*
(2nd ed.). Philadelphia: Lea & Febiger, 1967.

ESSLINGER, A. A. "A Philosophical Study of Principles for Selecting Activities in
Physical Education." Ph.D. dissertation, State University of Iowa, 1938.

FRANKENA, WILLIAM K., *Three Historical Philosophies of Education*. Chicago:
Scott, Foresman, 1965.

HESS, FORD A., "American Objectives of Physical Education from 1900–1957
Assessed in the Light of Certain Historical Events." Ed.D. dissertation,
New York University, 1959.

HETHERINGTON, CLARK, *School Program in Physical Education*. New York: Har-
court, Brace & World, 1922.

HUXLEY, ALDOUS, *Tomorrow and Tomorrow and Tomorrow*. New York: New
American Library, 1964.

KAPLAN, ABRAHAM, *The New World of Philosophy*. New York: Random House, 1961.

LOY, J. W., "The Nature of Sport: A Definitional Effort," *Quest*, No. 10 (May 1968), 1–15.

————, and G. S. KENYON, *Sport, Culture, and Society*. New York: Macmillan, 1969.

LYNN, MINNIE L., "Major Emphases of Physical Education in the United States." Ph.D. dissertation, University of Pittsburgh, 1944.

McCLOY, C. H., *Philosophical Bases for Physical Education*. New York: Appleton-Century-Crofts, 1940.

McNEILL, WILLIAM H., *The Rise of the West*. Chicago: The University of Chicago Press, 1961.

MEYERHOFF, H. (ed.), *The Philosophy of History in Our Time*. Garden City, N.Y.: Doubleday, 1959.

MORRIS, DESMOND, *The Naked Ape*. New York: McGraw-Hill, 1967.

MORRIS, VAN CLEVE, "Physical Education and the Philosophy of Education," *JOHPER*, 27, No. 3 (March 1956), 21–22, 30–31.

————, *Philosophy and the American School*. Boston: Houghton Mifflin, 1961.

————, *Existentialism in Education*. New York: Harper & Row, 1966.

MULLER, HERBERT J., *The Uses of the Past*. New York: New American Library, 1954.

NASH, JAY B. (ed.), *Mind-Body Relationships* (Vol. I). New York: A. S. Barnes, 1931.

OBERTEUFFER, DELBERT, *Physical Education*. New York: Harper & Row, 1951. (The second edition in 1962 was in collaboration with Celeste Ulrich.)

Random House Dictionary of the English Language. New York: Random House, 1967.

SCOTT, HARRY A., *Competitive Sports in Schools and Colleges*. New York: Harper & Row, 1951.

SHARMAN, JACKSON R., *Modern Principles of Physical Education*. New York: A. S. Barnes, 1937.

SHEEHAN, T. J., "Sport: The Focal Point of Physical Education," *Quest*, No. 10 (May 1968), 59–67.

SIMPSON, GEORGE GAYLORD, "What Is Man?" *The New York Times Book Review*, February 11, 1968.

STALEY, SEWARD C., "The Four Year Curriculum in Physical (Sports) Education," *Research Quarterly*, II, No. 1 (March 1931), 76–90.

————, *Sports Education*. New York: A. S. Barnes, 1939.

VANDERZWAAG, H. J., *Toward a Philosophy of Sport*. Reading, Mass.: Addison-Wesley, 1972.

————, "Sport Studies and Exercise Science: Philosophical Accommodation," *Quest*, No. 20 (June 1973), 73–78.

WAYMAN, AGNES R., *A Modern Philosophy of Physical Education*. Philadelphia: W. B. Saunders Co., 1938.

WEISS, PAUL, *Sport: A Philosophic Inquiry*. Carbondale: Southern Illinois University Press, 1969.

WHITE, CYRIL M., "Some Theoretical Considerations Regarding Disciplinary Development." Unpublished paper presented at a graduate seminar, University of Illinois, Urbana, 1968.

WILLIAMS, J. F., *The Principles of Physical Education*. Philadelphia: W. B. Saunders Co., 1964. (The first edition was published in 1927).

————, and W. L. HUGHES, *Athletics in Education*. Philadelphia: W. B. Saunders Co., 1930. (A second edition was published in 1937.)

WOOD, THOMAS D., and R. CASSIDY, *The New Physical Education*. New York: Macmillan, 1927.

WOODY, THOMAS, *Life and Education in Early Societies*. New York: Macmillan, 1949.

ZEIGLER, EARLE F., *Philosophical Foundations for Physical, Health, and Recreation Education*. Englewood Cliffs, N.J.: Prentice-Hall, 1964.

————, "The Need for Consensus and Research," *The Physical Educator*, 24, No. 3 (1967), 107–109.

————, *Problems in the History and Philosophy of Physical Education and Sport*. Englewood Cliffs, N.J.: Prentice-Hall, 1968.

————, "A Model for Optimum Professional Development in a Field Called 'X'" in *Proceedings of the First Canadian Symposium on the Philosophy of Sport and Physical Activity*, May 3–4, 1972, pp. 16–28. (Produced and distributed by Sport Canada Directorate, Department of Health and Welfare, Ottawa, Canada.)

————, and KING J. McCRISTAL, "A History of the Big Ten Body-of-Knowledge Project in Physical Education," *Quest*, No. 9 (December 1967), 79–84.

————, and H. J. VANDERZWAAG, *Physical Education: Progressivism or Essentialism?* (2nd ed.). Champaign, Ill.: Stipes, 1968.

SOCIAL FORCES

Values in Physical Education and Sport

Perhaps the most persistent problem that the physical education and sport teacher and coach faces is the determination of his or her educational values, and how the particular subject matter contributes to the achievement of these values in the lives of students. If certain values are available through instruction, then sincere teachers will obviously aim to bring about the realization of these values. Such values become the aims of education and, somewhat more narrowly, the aims of physical education and sport. The plan of this book is to help the teachers or coaches realize their underlying set of personal values so that they will pursue their profession with a reasonable degree of proficiency. Some very fundamental questions will be considered first so that we can discover what educational values may possibly derive from physical education and sport.

An examination of the diagram explaining philosophy and its branches (Figure 4) will indicate that axiology, the fourth subdivision, is the end result of philosophizing. The individual should develop a system of values consistent with his or her beliefs in the other three subdivisions. Some believe that values exist only because of the interest of the valuer (the interest theory). The existence theory, conversely, holds that values exist independently. According to this theory, a person's task is to discover the "real" values—to give existence to their ideal essence. The experimental theory explains value somewhat differently; values that yield results which have "cash value" bring about the possibility of greater happiness through more effective values in the future. One further theory, the part-whole theory, postulates that effective relating of parts to the whole brings about the highest values.

Axiology itself has various domains. First and foremost, we must consider ethics, which has to do with morality, conduct, good and evil, and ultimate objectives in life. There are several approaches to the prob-

FIGURE 4. Philosophy and Its Branches

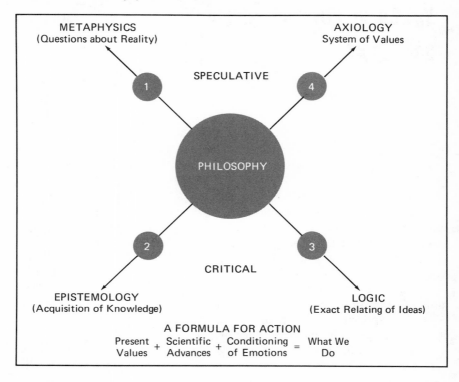

lem of whether life, as we know it, is worthwhile. A person who goes around all the time with a smile on his face looking hopefully toward the future is, of course, an optimist (*optimism*). Some people become easily discouraged and wonder if life is worth the struggle (*pessimism*). In between these two extremes we find the golden mean, *meliorism* (from the Latin, *better*), which implies that an individual constantly strives to improve his situation. This position assumes that the individual cannot make any final decisions about whether good or evil will prevail in the world.

Perhaps the key question to be considered in ethics is, "What is the purpose of *my* existence?" Under this heading we encounter the belief that pleasure is the highest good (*hedonism*). One approach that has developed in modern history from hedonistic doctrine is utilitarianism. Society, not the individual, is the focus, since the basic idea is to promote the greatest happiness for the greatest number of people in the community. Although the utilitarian recognizes the existence of various types of pleasure (ranging from intense, momentary emotional pleasure to the pleasure reflected in a placid life of contentment), he or she believes that seeking this type of pleasure will fulfill his or her own moral duty. Another important way of looking at the summum bonum (or highest good) in life is called perfectionism. Here the individual is aiming for complete self-realization and accordingly envisions a society of self-ful-filled individuals.

A logical outcome of an individual's decision about the greatest good in life is the standard of conduct he sets for himself. Certain interests are apt to guide our conduct in life. If we are too self-centered, people will say that we are egotistical (egoism). Some people go to the other extreme; they feel that a person best fulfills himself when he plays down the realization of his own interests in order to serve society or some social group therein (altruism). Once again, Aristotle's concept of the "golden mean" comes to the fore as a workable solution to this question.

One of the other areas of value under axiology deals with the "feeling" aspects of a person's conscious life (esthetics). Esthetics, the philosophy of taste, asks whether there are principles that govern the search for the beautiful in life. Because there has been a need to define still further values in human life, we now have specialized philosophies of education and religion. Further, we often refer to a person's social philosophy, which simply means that people make decisions about values intrinsic to various institutions; for example, the educational process.[1]

ARE VALUES OBJECTIVE OR SUBJECTIVE?

Now that we have a brief overview of the question of values, indi-viduals should ask themselves whether they believe values are objective or subjective; that is, do values exist whether a person is present to realize them or not? Or is it people who ascribe value to their various relationships with others and their physical environment? If a physical education program fulfills aims and objectives inherently valuable to youth, then it should be included in the curriculum whether students or parents recognize this value or not. If, on the other hand, it were proved that physical education has relatively little value, that the ma-jority of persons sees no need for it, then according to the subjective theory of value it should be eliminated.

Another facet of the question of values relates to their qualitative aspects. Some things in life are desired by the individual, whereas others may be desirable mainly because society has indicated its approval of

---

[1] For further reading on this subject, see J. Donald Butler, *Four Philosophies* (rev. ed.). (New York: Harper & Row, 1957), pp. 48–54.

them. A continuous appraisal of values occurs. If a value exists in and for itself, it is said to be an intrinsic value. One that serves as a means to an end, however, has become known as an instrumental value. When intense emotion and appreciation are involved, this gradation of value is called esthetic. Physical education and sport offer many opportunities to realize such esthetic values, although many well-educated people view the entire field far too narrowly and thereby confine esthetic values to experiences in the fine arts and literature.

A Hierarchy of Educational Values

Every culture seeks to develop its own hierarchy of educational values. In our own society, certain essentialistic philosophies of education, which hold that educational values are objective, encourage the gradation of these given values. Further, the disciplines at the top of their value hierarchy are those involving reason. If such values seem to coincide with eternal values inherent in the universe itself, they are considered still more valuable and are rated even more highly. So-called instrumental (pragmatic) values, conversely, are typically ranked much lower on the scale. Thus, physical education and sport might well be considered important by the idealist, but they would not take precedence over another subject that seemingly invokes rational powers to a greater extent, and that would thereby help a person achieve still "higher" goals in life.

To the experimentalist (as a progressivist), on the other hand, competence in, for example, self-defense or survival swimming might on a given occasion rate at the very top of the educational hierarchy—especially if such competence were necessary to save a life in an emergency. Thus, there is no question but that the role of physical education and sport in the educational pattern will vary depending on the final or ultimate aims of education to which the individual subscribes. Specific educational objectives in such situations would have to be chosen in the light of these educational goals.

A Self-evaluation Checklist [2]

With this introduction, readers may well be ready to involve themselves with a professional self-evaluation checklist that has been developed by the author over a period of years. By employing this instructional

[2] Earlier versions appear in Earle F. Zeigler, *Philosophical Foundations for Physical, Health, and Recreation Education* (Englewood Cliffs, N.J.: Prentice-Hall, 1964), as well as in the original version of this volume that appeared in 1968 in the Prentice-Hall Foundations of Physical Education Series.

device carefully and honestly, individuals will be able to determine quite accurately their philosophy of life, education, and physical education and sport. (Additional subsections cover health and safety education and recreation as well.) Keep in mind that the concept of "individual freedom" as proposed by Herbert J. Muller is basic to an understanding of the philosophy of education spectrum (Figure 5) located at the end of the checklist.

PROFESSIONAL SELF-EVALUATION CHECKLIST

Instructions: Read the statements below carefully, section by section, and indicate by an X the statement in each section that seems closest to your own personal belief. Check your answers only after all six sections have been completed. Then complete the summarizing tally on the answer page prior to checking your position on the philosophy of education spectrum at the very end.

I. The Nature of Reality (Metaphysics)

A. ☐   Experience and nature "constitute both the form and content of the entire universe" (multiverse?). There is no such thing as a preestablished order of things in the world. Reality is evolving, and humanity appears to be a most important manifestation of the natural process. The impact of cultural forces upon human beings is fundamental, and every effort must be made to understand them as we strive to build the best type of group-centered culture. In other words, "the structure of cultural reality" should be our foremost concern. Cultural determinants have shaped human history, which has now reached a crucial stage in the development of life on this planet. Our efforts should be focused on the building of a world culture.

B. ☐   Our world is a human one, and it is from the context of this human world that all the abstractions of science ultimately derive their meaning. There is, of course, the world of material objects extended in mathematical space with only quantitative and measurable properties, but we humans are first and foremost "concrete involvements" *within* the world. Existence precedes essence, and it is up to us to decide our own fate. This makes human beings different from all other creatures on earth. It appears true that a person can actually transform life's present condition, and thus the future may well stand open to this unusual being.

C. ☐   Nature is an emergent evolution, and the human frame of reality is limited to nature as it functions. The world is characterized by activity and change. The rational human being has developed through organic evolution, and the world is yet incomplete—a reality that is constantly undergoing change because of a theory of emergent novelty. We enjoy freedom of will; freedom is achieved through continuous and developmental learning from experience.

D. ☐   Mind as experienced by all persons is basic and real. The entire universe is mind essentially. We are more than just bodies; we possess a soul, and such possession makes us of a higher order than all other creatures on earth. "The order of the world is due to the manifestation in space and time of an eternal and spiritual reality." The individual is part of the whole, and it is our task to learn as much about the Absolute as possible. There is divided opinion within this position regarding the problem of monism or pluralism. We have freedom to determine which way we shall go in life; we can relate to the moral law in the universe, or we can turn against it.

E. ☐   "The world exists in itself, apart from our desires and knowledge." There is only one reality; that which we perceive is it. "The universe is made up of real substantial entities, existing in themselves and ordered to one another by extramental relations. . . ." Some feel that there is a basic unity present; others believe in a nonunified cosmos with two or more substances or processes at work. Things don't just happen; they happen because many interrelated forces make them occur in a particular way. We live within this world of cause and effect, and we simply cannot make things happen independent of it.

II. Educational Aims and Objectives

A. ☐   Socialization of the child has become equally as important as his or her intellectual development as a key educational aim in this century. There should be concern, however, because many educational philosophers seem to take the position that children are to be fashioned so they will conform to a prior notion of what they *should* be. Even the progressivists seem to have failed in their effort to help the learner "posture himself." And if it does become possible to get general agreement on a set of fundamental dispositions to be formed, should the criterion employed for such evaluation be a public one (rather than personal and private)? Education should seek to "awaken awareness" in learners—awareness of themselves as single subjectivities in the world. Increased emphasis is needed on the arts and social sciences, and students should "constantly, freely, baselessly, and creatively" choose their own patterns of education.

B. ☐   Social self-realization is the supreme value in education. The realization of this ideal is most important for the individual in the social setting—a world culture. Positive ideals should be molded toward the evolving democratic ideal by a general education that is group-centered and in which the majority determines the acceptable goals. Education by means of "hidden coercion" is to be scrupulously avoided. Learning is explained by the organismic principle of functional psychology. Acquired social intelligence teaches individuals to control and direct their urges as they concur with or attempt to modify cultural purposes.

C. ☐   The general aim of education is more education. "Education in the broadest sense can be nothing else than the changes made in human beings by their experience." Participation by students in the formation of aims and objectives is absolutely essential to generate the all-important desired interest. Social efficiency can well be considered the general aim of education. Pupil growth is a paramount goal, as the individual is placed at the center of the educational experience.

D. ☐   "A philosophy holding that the aim of education is the acquisition of verified knowledge of the environment recognizes the value of content as well as the activities involved in learning, and takes into account the external determinants of human behavior. . . . Education is the acquisition of the art of the utilization of knowledge." The primary task of education is to transmit knowledge, without which civilization cannot continue to flourish. Whatever men and women have discovered to be true because it conforms to reality must be handed down to future generations as the social or cultural tradition. Some holding this philosophy believe that the good life emanates from cooperation with God's grace and that development of the Christian virtues is obviously of greater worth than learning or anything else.

E. ☐   Through education the developing organism becomes what it latently is. All education may be said to have a religious significance, which means that there is a "moral imperative" on education. As the person's mind strives to realize itself, there is the possibility of realization of the Absolute within the individual mind. Education should aid the child to adjust to the basic realities (the spiritual ideals of truth, beauty, and goodness) that the history of the race has furnished us. The basic values of human living are health, character, social justice, skill, art, love, knowledge, philosophy, and religion.

III. The Educative Process (Epistemology)

A. ☐   Understanding the nature of knowledge will clarify the nature of reality. Nature is the medium by which the Absolute communicates to us. Basically, knowledge comes only from the mind—a mind that must offer and receive ideas. Mind and matter are qualitatively different. A finite mind emanates through heredity from another finite mind. Thought is the standard by which all else in the world is judged. An individual attains truth by examining the wisdom of the past through his or her own mind. Reality, viewed in this way, is a system of logic and order that has been established by the Universal Mind. Experimental testing helps to determine what the truth really is.

B. ☐   About the time of puberty, children experience an "existential moment" in their subjective lives—and are never the same thereafter. They become truly aware of their own existence, and of the fact that they have become responsible for their own conduct. After this point in life, education must be an "act of discovery" to be truly effective. Somehow the teacher should help young persons to become involved personally with their education and with the world situation in which such an education is taking place. Objective or subjective knowledge must be personally selected and "appropriated" by youth unto themselves, or else it will be relatively meaningless in those particular lives. Thus, it matters not whether logic, scientific evidence, sense perception, intuition, or revelation is claimed as the basis of knowldege acquisition; no learning will take place for that individual self until he or she decides that such learning is "true" for him or her in life. Therefore, he knows *when* he knows.

C. ☐   Knowledge is the result of a process of thought with a useful purpose. Truth is not only to be tested by its correspondence with reality, but also its practical results. Knowledge is earned through experience and is an instrument of verification. Mind has evolved in the natural order as a more flexible means whereby persons adapt themselves to their world. Learning takes place when interest and effort unite to produce the desired result. A psychological order (problem solving as explained through scientific method) is more useful than a logical arrangement (from the simple fact to the complex conclusion). There is always a social context to learning, and the curriculum must be adapted to the particular society for which it is intended.

D. ☐   An organismic approach to the learning process is basic. Thought cannot be independent of certain aspects of the organism; it (thought) is related integrally with emotional and muscular functions. The mind enables a person to cope with the problems of human life in a social environment. Social intelligence is closely related to scientific method. Certain operational concepts, inseparable from metaphysics and axiology (beliefs about reality and values), focus on the reflective thought, problem solving, and social consensus necessary for the transformation of the culture.

E. ☐   There are two major epistemological theories of knowledge in this position. One states that the aim of knowledge "is to bring into awareness the object as it really is." Th other emphasizes that objects are "represented" in man's consciousness not "presented." Students should develop habits and skills involved with acquiring knowledge, with using knowledge practically to meet life's problems, and with realizing the enjoyment that life offers. A second variation of epistemological belief indicates that the child develops his or her intellect by employing reason to learn a subject. The principal educational aims here must be the same for all people at all times in all places. Others carry this further and state that education is the process by which the person seeks to link herself or himself ultimately with the Creator.

IV. Values in Specialized Field (Physical Education)

A. ☐   I believe in the concept of "total fitness" implied in an educational design pointed toward the individual's self-realization as a social being. In our field there should be opportunity for selection of a wide variety of useful activities. Instruction in motor skills is necessary to provide a sufficient amount of "physical" fitness activity. The introduction of dance and art into physical education can contribute to creative expression. Intramural sports and voluntary recreational activities should be stressed. This applies especially to team competition, with particular stress on cooperation and promotion of friendly competition. Extramural sport competition can be introduced when there is a need; striving for excellence is important, but it is urgent that materialistic influences be kept out of educational programs. Relaxation techniques should have a place, as should the whole concept of education for leisure.

B. ☐   I believe that the field of physical education should strive to fulfill a role in the general educational pattern of arts and sciences. The goal is *total fitness*—not only physical fitness—with a balance between activities emphasizing competition and cooperation. The concept of "universal man" is paramount, but we must allow the individual to choose physical education and sport activities for himself based on knowledge of self—what knowledge and skills he would like to possess. We should help the child who is "authentically eccentric" feel at home in the physical education program, and also to find ways for youth to commit themselves to values and people. A person should be able to select a sport according to the values he or she wishes to derive from it. This is often difficult because of the extreme emphasis on winning in this culture. Creative physical activities such as modern dance should be stressed also.

C. ☐   I believe that education "of the physical" should have primary emphasis in our field. I am concerned with the development of physical vigor, and such development should have priority over the recreational aspects of physical education. Many people who believe in the same educational philosophy as I do recommend that all students in public schools should have a daily period designed to strengthen their muscles and develop their bodily coordination. Physical education must yield precedence, of course, to intellectual education. I give "qualified approval" to interscholastic athletics since they do help with the learning of sportsmanship and desirable social conduct if properly conducted. But all these things, with the possible exception of physical training, are definitely extracurricular and not part of the regular curriculum.

D. ☐   I am much more interested in promoting the concept of total fitness rather than physical fitness alone. I believe that physical education should be an integral subject in the curriculum. Students should have the opportunity to select a wide variety of useful activities, many of which should help to develop "social intelligence." The activities offered should bring natural impulses into play. To me, physical education classes and intramural sports are more important to the large majority of students than interscholastic or intercollegiate sports and deserve priority if conflict arises over budgetary allotment, available staff, and use of facilities. I can, however, give full support to team experiences in competitive sports, because they can be vital educational experiences if properly conducted.

E. ☐   I am extremely interested in individual personality development. I believe in education "of the physical," and yet I believe in education "through the physical" as well. Nevertheless, I see physical education as important, but also occupying a lower rung on the educational ladder. I believe that desirable objectives for physical education would include the development of responsible citizenship and group participation. In competitive sport, I believe that the transfer of training theory is in operation in connection with the development of desirable personality traits, but sports participation should always be a means, not an end.

V. Values in Specialized Field (School Health Education)

A. ☐   I believe that health is a basic value of human living and that the truly educated individual should be "physically fit," should live "near the maximum of his efficiency," and should have "a body which is the ready servant of his will." But even though I believe health is a basic value for all the others, I would have to place it at the bottom of the hierarchy of educational values. Worship must be placed at the top, because through it the person is brought "into conscious relation to the infinite spirit of the universe. . . ." Thus, it would not be included in a listing of the "essential studies" of the curriculum except where it would probably be included incidentally under biology. However, I am interested in "building wholeness of mind and body," "the development of strong, healthy bodies, good habits of mental and physical health," and "the right start in the teaching of health, safety, and physical education to children." There is no question in my mind but that educators should work for a larger measure of integration in the individual by promoting "more intensive study of the body, leading to scientific knowledge: anatomy, body chemistry, hygiene, physiology, etc.; and attention to sex characteristics and habits, leading to a greater understanding of the place of sex in human life, with implications for hygiene. . . ." But such knowledge is made available to boy and girls, and young men and women, as a "service" program in the schools—a service is provided to individuals, and through this contribution to their health they are enabled to pursue higher educational goals.

B. ☐ I believe strongly that the child must develop an awareness of the need for self-education about the various aspects of personal and community health. Such educational experiences will not take place, of course, unless the educational process itself is a natural one—a give and take situation in which the student is allowed to observe and inquire freely. Obviously, controversial issues should never be avoided with such an approach. Typically, the search for truth is an individual matter, but it is most important to test majority opinion when action is needed in a group situation. The debating of issues relating to health knowledge and practice will help students decide what is most important for them in this society at this time. In this way they will be able to commit themselves to personal and community health values.

C. ☐ I believe in the development of physical vigor and health. There is no question in my mind but that the school should provide "an atmosphere conducive to both emotional and physical health." Furthermore, "knowledge about the principles of physical and emotional health is a proper ingredient of the curriculum." I believe that the community does have a responsibility to provide clinical facilities for therapy, but this does not mean that they are part of the school program or curriculum any more than are boilers in heating systems. I assert that the home must have the complete responsibility for assisting youth to acquire desirable health habits—that is, unless we wish to establish some form of community youth organizations to accomplish this end. "The health of adolescents is for the most part too good and their sources of energy are too great to make health problems real to them." In a similar vein, sex education is certainly not a proper function of the school. It is logical that teaching of the means for securing health values would be incomplete anyhow until the perspective from which they are viewed is also taught; this perspective is found only in the humanities—in literature, art, religion, and philosophy. In summary, therefore, every person needs a basic core of knowledge in order to lead a human life, and this includes the learning of health knowledge. This is consistent with the central purpose of the school—the development of the individual's rational powers.

D. ☐ As I see it, there can be no such thing as a fixed or universal curriculum in physical, health, and recreation education. Men and women should be sturdy and possess vigorous health. Positive health should be a primary educational aim. Such a program would necessitate the cooperative involvement of many agencies. Health knowledge and attitudes should be realized through the provision of experiences involving problem solving. "Direct" health instruction should be offered, but such learning can take place indirectly in the science curriculum. Sex education and family relations instruction are very important. Instruction in mental hygiene needs serious attention in our highly complex society.

E. ☐   I believe that the human being should be a strong yet agile creature. Health, as I see it, is a primary objective of education, and the child needs health instruction. The success of the school health education program depends upon the degree of cooperation among home, school, and community agencies. An educated person must understand the difference between health and disease, and must know how to protect and improve his or her own health, that of dependents, and that of the community. As I see it, the program of school health, physical education, and recreation may be administered as a unified program within a school system. I believe that natural types of exercise promote sound mental health. All these aspects of the total program may be coordinated because they are related in many ways. Through unity these subdivisions, which are basically related, could probably serve the needs of schoolchildren and youth much more effectively than is the case so often at the present. To be truly effective, school health education must be concerned with helping the individual to lead a rich, full life. This means more than providing a health service so that students can maintain the minimum health needed to "pursue intellectual work with the least amount of strain." Health should be defined positively—as that quality which enables us "to live most and serve best."

VI. Values in Recreation (Education)

A. ☐   As I see it, work and play are typically sharply differentiated in life. Play serves a most useful purpose at recess or after school, but it should *not* be part of the regular curriculum. I believe that the use of leisure is significant to the development of our culture, but I realize today that "winning the cold war" is going to take a lot more hard work and somewhat less leisure. I see leisure pursuits or experiences as an opportunity to get relief from work while they serve a re-creative purpose in the lives of individuals. The surplus energy theory of play and recreation makes sense to me. So does the more recent biosocial theory of play—the idea that play helps the organism to achieve balance. I feel that the "play attitude" is missing almost completely in many organized sports. Play (and recreation) is, therefore, very important to me; I believe it should be "liberating" to the individual. People can develop their potential for wholesome hobbies through recreation. Furthermore, recreation can serve as a safety valve by the reduction of the psychic tensions that are evidently caused by so many of life's typical stresses. Even though play should not be considered a basic part of the curriculum, we should not forget that it provides an "indispensable seasoning" to the good life. Extracurricular play and recreational activities and a sound general education should suffice to equip the student for leisure activities in our society.

B. ☐   I believe that all types of recreational needs and interests should be met through recreation education. The individual should have an opportunity to choose from among social, esthetic and creative, communicative, learning, and physical recreational activities within the offerings of what might be called a "community school" in the broadest sense of the word. It is absolutely imperative, of course, that these choices be made according to the person's sense of personal values and in accord with his or her desire to relate to people. All are striving for self-realization, and the recreation education program can provide opportunities for both individual expression and for group recreational undertakings. Play seems necessary for people of all ages, and it assumes many different forms. We should not forget that one of its functions is simply personal liberation and release.

C. ☐   I believe it is difficult to separate the objectives of recreation education from physical education when physical activities are being considered. Within the schools I recommend a unified approach for physical, health, and recreation education. In this discussion I am only including those recreational activities that are "physical" in nature. All these leisure activities should be available to all on a year-round basis. I see recreation education as a legitimate phase of the core curriculum, but would include further recreational opportunities as well as opportunity for relaxation later in the day. My core curriculum is adapted from progressivism, and the extracurricular activities are quite as integral as "spoke and hub activities." In fact, the word "extra" is now most misleading.

D. ☐   I am inclined to favor the adoption of the name "recreation education" for the field. I see advantages in a unified approach whereby the three specialized areas of health, physical education, and recreation (in schools) would provide a variety of experiences that will enable the individual to live a richer, fuller life through superior adjustment to the environment. I believe that education for the worthy use of leisure is basic to the curriculum of the school—a curriculum in which pupil growth, as defined broadly, is all-important. Second, play shall be conducted in such a way that desirable moral growth will be fostered. Third, overorganized sport competition is not true recreation, since the welfare of the individual is often submerged in the extreme emphasis so frequently placed on winning. I believe it is a mistake to confuse the psychological distinction between work and play with the traditional economic distinction that is generally recognized. All citizens should have ample opportunity to use their free time in a creative and fruitful manner. I do not condemn a person who watches others perform with a high level of skill in any of our cultural recreational activities, including sport, so long as the individual keeps such viewing in a balanced role in his or her entire life.

E. ☐   I believe that the role of play and recreation in the development of personality and the "perfectly integrated individual" is looming larger with each passing year and that it has not been fully understood or appreciated in the past. For this reason it seems quite logical to me that education should reassess the contributions that recreation and play do make in the education of the person. That there is a need for educational research along these lines is self-evident. I believe further that we should examine very closely any theories of play and recreation that grant educational possibilities to these human activities. The self-expression theory of play suggests that one's chief need in life is to achieve the satisfaction and accomplishment of self-expression of one's personality. Here is an explanation that seems to consider quite fully the conception of the person as an organic unity—a total organism. I believe that a person is a purposive being who is striving to achieve those values embedded in reality itself. To the extent that we can realize the eternal values through the choice of the right kinds of play and recreation without flouting the moral order in the world, we should be progressive enough to disregard a dualistic theory of work and play. Another difficulty that confronts us is differentiating between physical education and recreation. Recreation has developed to the point where it is now clearly one of our major social institutions. I believe that recreation can make a contribution to the development of an "integrated individual in an integrated society growing in the image of the integrated universe." Mankind today is actually faced with a "recreational imperative."

> *Answers:* (Read only after all six questions are completed, and then complete the summarizing tally underneath.)

I. *The Nature of Reality (Metaphysics)*
   A. Reconstructionism
   B. Existentialism
   C. Experimentalism (pragmatic naturalism)
   D. Idealism
   E. Realism (basically essentialistic with elements of naturalistic realism, rational humanism, and positions within Catholic educational philosophy)

II. *Educational Aims and Objectives*
   A. Existentialism
   B. Reconstructionism
   C. Experimentalism
   D. Realism
   E. Idealism

III. *The Educative Process (Epistemology)*
   A. Idealism
   B. Existentialism
   C. Experimentalism
   D. Reconstructionism
   E. Realism

IV. *Physical Education*
   A. Reconstructionism
   B. Existentialism
   C. Realism
   D. Experimentalism
   E. Idealism

V. *School Health Education*
   A. Idealism
   B. Existentialism
   C. Realism
   D. Reconstructionism
   E. Experimentalism

VI. *Recreation (Education)*
   A. Realism
   B. Existentialism
   C. Reconstructionism
   D. Experimentalism
   E. Idealism

Summarizing Tally

	I	II	III	IV	V	VI	Totals
Experimentalism (Pragmatic Naturalism)							
Reconstructionism							
Existentialism (atheistic, agnostic and theistic)							
Idealism							
Realism (varying positions)							

Note: It should now be possible to determine your position based on the answers given in the various categories. At least you should be able to tell if you are largely progressivistic or essentialistic in your educational philosophy (see spectrum, Figure 5). If you discover considerable eclecticism in your overall posi-

FIGURE 5. Philosophy of Education Spectrum (Readers may wish to examine themselves—their personal philosophy of education—based on this spectrum analysis. Keep in mind that the *primary* criterion on which this is based is the concept of individual freedom.)

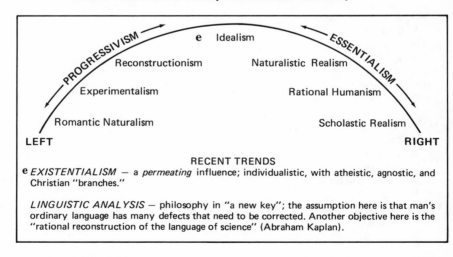

tion, closer analysis may be necessary to determine if your beliefs are philosophically defensible. Continued self-examination of aims and objectives should make you a better professional person.

46

Finally: After tallying the answer and keeping in mind the subjectivity of such a checklist as this, did the self-evaluation show you to be:

Strongly progressivistic	☐
Progressivistic	☐
Eclectic (checks in *3 or more* positions)	☐
Essentialistic	☐
Strongly essentialistic	☐
Existentialistic (and probably somewhat progressivistic)	☐

THREE MAJOR PHILOSOPHICAL STANCES

As a result of the foregoing self-examination, it is now possible to state that there appear to be three leading philosophical stances or positions regarding physical education and sport. There are, of course, those who say that the field has no place whatsoever in education, but they are extremists and decidedly in the minority—or perhaps they simply have not worked out their own educational positions consistently and logically.

Experimentalism

The first of these three philosophies is *experimentalism* (or *pragmatic naturalism*). Experimentalists are much more interested in promoting the concept of total fitness rather than physical fitness alone. They challenge the name "physical" education. They believe that what is presently called physical education can become an integral subject in the curriculum according to their definition of educational values. Students should have the opportunity to choose useful activities, and there should be a wide selection. Of these activities, many should be of the "socializing" type, since they help to develop what Dewey called "social intelligence." Furthermore, the activities offered should bring natural impulses into play.

Experimentalists believe that the term "evaluation" should be used rather than "tests and measurements," because the former implies concern with the individual and the individual's progress in relation to his or her environmental adjustment. They believe further that the concepts of grades and academic credit should be replaced by evaluation of student growth in keeping with the competencies and knowledges they have acquired. To experimentalists, physical education classes and intramural athletics are more important to the large majority of students than interscholastic or intercollegiate athletics and deserve priority if conflict arises over budgetary allotment, staff availability, and use of facilities. Experimentalists can give full support to team experiences in competitive sports because they can be vital educational experiences—especially if the elements of competition and cooperation are rather evenly balanced. Furthermore, athletic and recreational activities at a relatively high level of skill can be an esthetic experience of a fine type. The planned occurrence of educational situations within sports and athletics is also important to the experimentalist. If stress is placed on the continuous development of standards of conduct, such situations can contribute significantly to moral training. Rigorous physical activity for both sexes is desirable and necessary to produce strong, well-poised bodies. Last, experimentalists want to see the three branches of the field more closely coordinated so that experimental aims may be more fully realized.

School Health Education. In the area of health education, experimentalists view health instruction and first-class health services as vital to every school system. Since health is a primary objective of education for them, the concept of healthful school living should be made a reality at all levels of education. They believe further that natural types of exercise promote sound mental health. The school health education program depends upon the degree of cooperation among home, school, and community agencies. To be truly effective, school health education should be concerned with helping the individual to lead a rich, full life.

Recreation Education. Experimentalists believe that education for leisure is basic to the curriculum of the school. Overly organized sport competition is not true recreation; instead, play should be conducted in such a way that desirable moral growth occurs. If the proper foundation is laid in the educational system, individuals will have the opportunity to use their leisure creatively and fruitfully to ensure desirable individual growth.

Reconstructionist. Utopian experimentalists, the reconstructionists should be considered briefly at this point. Basically speaking, they would endorse much of what has been said under experimentalism, although they would advocate even more forcefully the individual's self-realization as a social being. The introduction of dance and art into physical education as stimulants of creative expression is one project of interest to them. Intramural sports and voluntary recreational activities should be accorded a high place; this would apply especially to team competition, with particular stress on cooperation as a strong element along with the promotion of friendly rivalry. Extramural sport competition could be introduced where the need arises—in other words, striving for excellence is important, but more important is keeping materialistic influence out of educational programs. In the area of health education, many experimentalist aims would be duplicated. Two important additions are courses in sex education and family relations, and in mental hygiene. For reconstructionists would provide a unified program, available on a year-round basis. Relaxation techniques should have a place, as should the whole concept of leisure education, because of the tensions of modern society. School facilities should be accessible for both curricular and extracurricular programs.

Realism

The second of the three major philosophical positions is realism (under which heading may be grouped *naturalistic realism, rational humanism,* and *scholastic, . or moderate, realism*). Broadly speaking, realists accept education "of the physical" as the primary goal. The name "physical education" by which the field is now generally known doesn't upset them at all. They are concerned with the "development of the maximum of physical vigor," even to the exclusion of the recreational aspects of physical education. Some educational realists recommend that all students in public schools should have a daily period designed to strengthen their muscles, develop their bodily coordination, and improve their cardiovascular endurance. According to the statement of the Educational Policies Commission in 1961, "an adequate physical basis for intellecutal life must be assured."

Realists believe that the intrinsic values are more important than the instrumental ones; hence, physical education, even though it is important, must "yield precedence to intellectual education" (some naturalistic realists, however, disagree). Most realists give at least qualified approval to interscholastic athletics, as they agree that the learning of sportsmanship and desirable social conduct is important. A leading scholastic realist stated that "sports is a school for loyalty, courage, endurance, determination, universal brotherhood. . . ." Another leading educational philosopher, who calls himself a classical realist, believes that, in the course of his schooling, every child should be required to learn one team game and two individual sports that can be played as an adult, but that such a requirement should be purely extracurricular.

School Health Education. For the realist, health education has an instrumental value; however, those inside the specialized area of physical, health, and recreation education seem to give health instruction and the development of health habits through the medium of the school a more important role. One realist believes that the home must have the complete responsibility for helping youth acquire desirable habits. He makes an interesting point that "the health of adolescents is for the most part too good and their sources of energy are too great to make health problems real to them." Although he states that sex education is certainly not a proper function of the school, he does advocate fostering the concept of healthful school living, and he suggests further that basic health knowledge does properly belong in the science curriculum. There appears to be general agreement that a program of physical education should be "based on authenticated health knowledge" and that physical fitness is an important key to a healthy body. The scholastic realist believes that health is decidedly important, but that "the primacy in the human composition does not belong to the body taken from the earth's slime, but to the spirit, to the spiritual soul."

Play and Recreation. There is a sharp contrast between the realist and the experimentalist when it comes to the question of the role of play and recreation. The realist typically believes that work and play cannot be identified under the same psychological rubric. As one leading educational philosopher explains it, "Play is all right on the playground at recess and after school, but it should not be imported into the regular curriculum." The belief seems to be that adults should think of play as "carefree activity performed for its own sake." With such an approach, the feeling is that recreation can contribute to self-integration through the reduction of psychic tension caused by so many of life's stresses. Some educational realists are concerned because the "play attitude" seems to be missing almost completely from organized athletics, and thus, unfortunately, what might be sport—or fun—is kept from being a truly recreational activity. Americans seem to have developed an ambivalent attitude toward play; in other words, if we can make our play serious business, then it cannot be implied or said that we are wasting our time in "sinful" or frivolous activities.

The realist would tend to argue that general education itself is education for leisure, and he would probably concur in the belief that people can develop a number of potentialities for wholesome hobbies through recreation. A leading realistic philosopher of the twentieth century distinguishes relaxation from recreation: "pure relaxation is a necessary condition of health . . . the normal recreation should be change of activity, satisfying the cravings of instincts." In summary, the more essentialistic one's educational philosophy is, the more one sees a sharp distinction between work and play. Although leisure activities of a purely individual benefit do have a place, winning the cold war is going to take a lot more hard work and somewhat less leisure.

Idealism

Although idealism is considered basically an essentialistic position because of its underlying value theory, its emphasis on the individual and his or her personality development impinges at certain points on the progressivist side of the educational philosophy spectrum. The idealist believes in education "of the physical," and yet believes in education "through the physical" as well. Like the realist, however, the idealist sees physical education as necessarily occupying a lower rung on the educational ladder.

Idealists strive to see the person as an organic entity, yet cannot avoid expounding upon the various aspects of human nature. A leading American physical educator wrote around the turn of the century that "man is capable of development physically, aesthetically, intellectually, socially, politically, religiously, and morally. A man who neglects one or more of these natures is one-sided." He went on to say that developing each of these "natures" to maximum potential was the way to approach life's main goal. A contemporary American physical education philosopher, while subscribing to the idealistic educational hierarchy of values, refuses to underestimate the task of physical education. He reminds us of the status accorded it in Greek idealism and of the new worth it assumes under the transfer of training theory. This psychological theory implies that attitudes of sportsmanship and fair play learned through desirable athletic competition can and do transfer to life situations.

In America, idealism is often associated with the Christian faith. The Young Men's Christian Association, a worldwide movement, has for many years applied Christian ideals to its work in physical education. In 1959, the YMCA listed its five objectives for physical education as follows: (1) Development of health and physical fitness; (2) education for leisure; (3) personality adjustment (learning to live with self and others); (4) development of responsible citizenship and group participation; and (5) development of a philosophy of life based on Christian ideals. The last of these objectives could have well been placed first, for as an outstanding YMCA international leader, Paul Limbert, has stated: "The central emphasis of Christian faith is not on development of the individual as such but on *equipment for service,* both to God and man."

Despite the support that idealism gives to physical education activities, some leaders are concerned about overemphasis, especially in the area of competitive athletics. Limbert warns that "focus on the development of physical strength or athletic prowess runs the risk of self-centeredness," and that sports participation may become an end rather than a means (1961, p. 9). It is feared by another leader that "growing specialization" in sport "tends to reduce the interest of people who are concerned for the whole personality of the participant." Recently established organizations like the Fellowship of Christian Athletes believe that a coach should hold high moral and ethical standards and should set a fine example for his athletes. They would agree with the 1951 position of the Educational Policies Commission that "the basic moral and spiritual value in American life is the supreme importance of the individual personality," and that "the teacher of sports is usually one of the most influential members of the school community in the shaping of moral and spiritual values" (p. 18). An educational survey conducted by Wilton (1956, p. 278) reported that a group of seventeen leading American physical educators ratified the idealistic thesis that "creative experience, noble achievement, true friendship, and spiritual satisfaction are encouraged by physical education." Character development is paramount; winning scores are incidental in the final analysis.

School Health Education.   In the area of health education, we find that the idealist recognizes the importance of sound health in the development of the individual personality, but that it remains at the bottom of the hierarchy even though it is "esteemed highly as a basic value for all the others, enhancing the richness of each and all of them" (Horne, 1942, p. 186). In an assessment of philosophical values, Clark (now Oestreicher) asserted that idealism stresses "building wholeness of mind and body, . . . the development of strong, healthy bodies, . . . good habits of mental and physical health, . . . and the right start in the teaching of health, safety, and physical education to children" (1943, pp. 310–311). Idealists are concerned as well with the teaching of health knowledge including "attention to sex characteristics and habits, leading to the greater understanding of the place of sex in human life," and the development of proper health habits for sound mental and physical health. In assessing Plato's thought on the subject, Cahn explained that the early idealist saw health as a " 'dynamic equilibrium' between all inner and outer forces with the object of having an individual at harmony with himself and society" (1941, p. 289).

Recreation and Play.   The importance of recreation and play in an idealistic philosophy of education has seemingly not been fully understood or appreciated in the past, and the contributions that this area makes in the education of the individual should be the subject of scientific research in the light of future needs of our society. The self-expression theory of play appears to be quite compatible with idealism; that is, to the extent that the idealist can realize the eternal values through the choice of the right kinds of play and recreation, he or she should be progressive enough to disregard a dualistic theory of work and play.

This is not a new idea, but it has been largely disregarded by Christian educators until very recently. Plato, the first idealist, saw the value of play and recreation. He said that "the characters of future citizens are formed through their childhood games," and "play must be, therefore, most carefully utilized and supervised by the state" (Cahn, pp. 289–294). He believed further that "recreation, the activity of leisure, is a necessary alternate with toil to balance the daily life to permit the growth of the integrated man within society." Following this line of reasoning, an idealistic teacher of physical, health, and recreation education would therefore be challenged to use recreation and play to combat a deep-seated psychic disintegration that seems to be taking place in a society dominated by materialism. In this way, creative recreation could take on spiritual significance and could relate the person to all that is beautiful in life.

STRONG TWENTIETH-CENTURY INFLUENCES

In the course of the twentieth century there have been a number of strong attacks made against the traditional approaches. Even prior to World War I the idealism that had emanated from Kant had lost some of the prestige it enjoyed in the late 1800s. The defense of scientific investigation by Spencer and Darwin was a tremendously powerful influence. Pragmatism, under the influence of a number of early English and European scientists and philosophers—and, of course, the American triumvirate of Peirce, James, and Dewey—gathered much strength from naturalism and from the continued rise of scientific inquiry. Great emphasis was placed on the desirability of testing hypotheses through experience in order to gain "true" knowledge. In fact, it was stated that we couldn't even know the meaning of an idea before it was put into practice. In educational philosophy, the pragmatic approach became known as experimentalism, or pragmatic naturalism.

Philosophical Analysis

So-called philosophical analysis, with its numerous variations, emerged as the strongest philosophical influence in the Western world during the first seventy-five years of this century. Although various citizens of the West have engaged in philosophical thought for more than 2000 years, there is still an argument over the exact nature of the task. Since philosophy seems in some areas—for example metaphysics—destined to be superseded by science, many philosophers became concerned about the exact nature of their role. Some apparently concluded that philosophical activity does not result in knowledge after all—at least not *new* knowledge. And if science is becoming the be all and end all of scholarly endeavor, one might well ask what the justification is for an area of study treating such matters as values, truth, and ethics.

There have been three developments in the twentieth century that have sought to provide answers to this crucial question: (1) logical atomism, (2) logical positivism, and (3) ordinary language philosophy. The underlying tenet behind these approaches is that philosophy's function is analysis, but each one tended to view the subject of analysis somewhat differently. There was general agreement, however, that philosophy is to be approached through the medium of what has been called "language analysis" or "philosophy of language."

Logical Atomism.   This involved a new approach to logic as devised by Bertrand Russell (1872–1970) and Alfred North Whitehead (1861–1947) called *mathematical logic*. It had been thought that Aristotle's was the last word on this subject, but these two great philosophers developed a logic that was much broader in scope because of its inclusion of propositions rather than classes only. This more inclusive logical system involved the recommended greater relationship of mathematics to logic—ideas that were to a considerable degree brought to Russell's attention by the work of Peano, whom he met at the International Congress of Philosophy in Paris in July of 1900 (Russell, 1926, p. 191).

Russell's next step was to show that a language like English has essentially the same structure as mathematics. Because the language was not exact enough, however, it was thought that mathematical logic would help explain the components of language through sentences designed to offer "world facts." Carried through to its presumably logical conclusion, the philosopher would then be in a position to find out everything about the structure of the world by using this type of analysis to rearrange an ambiguous language so that the newly arranged, logical sentences would become crystal clear. This approach, which flourished for twenty years or more in some quarters, was thought to offer a new metaphysical system. It was eventually superseded by logical positivism, which carried mathematical logic a step further.

Logical Positivism.   In the 1920s a group subsequently known as the Vienna Circle came to believe that it was not possible for logical atomism to provide the world with a system of metaphysics. Their answer was logical positivism, which presented philosophy as an activity—

not as theories about the universe. They felt that philosophy's task was to analyze and explain what statements meant. Some statements would be able to withstand being subjected to the *verifiability principle*. This means that a sentence might be factually significant to a given person if he understands the observations that would enable him to accept or reject the proposition contained therein. However, a logically valid, factual sentence must be "confirmable" or "disconfirmable" if one really wishes to say "he knows what he is talking about." A statement's meaning is inextricably involved with the verification method (Feigl, 1949, pp. 9ff).

Thus, some sentences may be significant factually; others are not directly applicable to this world, although they appear to be analytically true; and a third group are nonsensical or nonsignificant. It can readily be seen how devastating such an approach to philosophical activity would be to traditional philosophical approaches. The usual philosophical statement of the past was definitely not empirically verifiable, which means—at least in the eyes of those employing this new approach —that the older efforts were typically mere conjecture and not really important. Philosophy was thereby awarded a new role—analysis of ordinary language statements into logical, consistent form. Then one could tell quite quickly whether a problematical question could be answered either through mathematical reasoning or scientific investigation. Philosophers do not therefore provide the answers; they analyze the questions to see what they mean.

Ordinary Language Philosophy. The third approach to philosophy involves a type of language analysis, but in a slightly different way. It was started in the 1930s by Ludwig Wittgenstein (?–1952), who had earlier been one of the originators and developers of logical atomism. In the period between the 1930s and 1952 (when he died), Wittgenstein decided it would not be possible to devise a language so perfect that the world would be reflected accurately. Accordingly, he came to believe that much of the confusion and disagreement over philosophy emanated from misuse of language in various ways. With this approach, the task of the philosopher was not to transpose the problems of philosophy into certain language terms; rather, it was to decide what the basic words and terms were and then to use them correctly and clearly so that all might understand. This is, of course, closer to semantics, the science of meanings. Wittgenstein was more anxious to learn how the term was used than he was to discover how people defined it. With such an approach it may be possible for philosophy to solve some problems through clarification of the meaning of certain terms that have been used synonymously (albeit often incorrectly). In this way we might gradually achieve certain knowledge, at least about our reaction to the world and how we describe it, through the medium of ordinary language philosophy—the newest of the three types of philosophical analysis sometimes called "philosophy of language."

Four Investigations. It must be granted that analytic philosophy has become most influential in the English-speaking world. Where these many achievements will lead remains open to question. Obviously, it is now clear that philosophers can use any language they wish, but they are obliged to make very clear the language rules they are employing (Carnap's "principle of tolerance"). Further, the newer mathematical logic, with its scientific base, offers infinitely greater possibilities of relating logic more completely to the technology of the computer, not to mention the development of an ideal language for philosophical endeavor based on synthetic statements (symbolic or mathematical logic). As Kaplan (1961, p. 83) indicates, this may provide us with a "rational reconstruction of the language of science," but where will we then find a philosophy to *live* by?

In the late 1960s and early 1970s, I was privileged to serve as thesis committee chairman for four men and women specializing in physical education and sport philosophy, all of whom used a different variation of philosophical analysis in an attempt to answer the requirements of their main problems and subproblems. Each of these investigations was in one way or another concerned with the meaning of some aspect of the term physical education. The first was an effort by the late Peter Spencer-Kraus to apply Austin's "linguistic phenomenology" to sport and physical education (1969). Spencer-Kraus found that "many of the problems recurring in that area [the philosophy of physical education and sport literature] were steeped in a confusion resulting directly from the equivocal use of the terms and idioms employed." He concluded that there was "a great need for consensus" in the matter of precise definitions of terms employed in sport and physical education, and he believed strongly that "the application of the Austinian technique might greatly improve the chances of arriving at that consensus" (pp. 56–57).

George Patrick's study was the second of the four projects, and it was entitled "Verifiability (Meaningfulness) of Selected Physical Education Objectives." An analytic description in terms of form and function of the stated objectives was made, and the normative part of the study was based on the descriptive analysis of the objectives and the kind of knowledge provided by logic, ethics, philosophy, and philosophy of education. Positivism's "principle of verifiability" was subdivided into two forms: weak or logical possibility of confirmation, and strong or operationally testable. Objective statements were viewed as informative, expressive, directive, and performative. Three functions of objectives were stated: (1) as slogans, (2) as guides to the educative process, and (3) as tests. It was found that objectives functioning as slogans were likely to be meaningless or verifiable in the second degree (weak); that objectives functioning as guides using informative-directive language were verifiable in the first or second degree; and that objectives functioning as a test must use the informative-directive mode of language before they could be considered verifiable in the first degree. Thus, "if physical educators wish to act responsibly, they should be able to state that for which they are accountable" (Patrick, 1971, p. 94).

The third investigation was carried out by Kathleen Pearson. It related to so-called conceptual analysis within what has more recently been called philosophy of language. She examined (1) the structure of the multiconcept "integration-segregation" as it pertained to male and female participants in physical education classes, and (2) the functional aspects of this multiconcept in the intentional, purposive, and responsible actions of persons engaged in the professional endeavor called physical education (Pearson, 1971, p. 2). After extracting the various meanings attached to the concept and describing their extensional features in the "structural analysis" phase, Pearson proceeded to a "functional analysis" stage, in which she delineated the reasons set forth for advocating the various "structures" or positions relative to the usage of the concept by writers in the available literature. She considered the assumptions implicit within each of the reasons and the empirical evidence available to support or cast doubt on the validity of the hypotheses underlying these reasons. Then the question was asked, "How might one be guided in making responsible decisions concerning the multiconcept in question?"

Pearson concluded specifically that physical educators attach many and varied meanings to the word "coeducation"; that the reasons set forth for this practice indicate a wide variety of objectives; that these claims or objectives have not been subjected to empirical research techniques; and that many contemporary physical educators still hold the dubious belief that jumping activities for girls and women cause injury to the pelvic organs. Generally speaking, she concluded that "the field is almost barren of empirical research to support or cast doubt on the advisability of integration-segregation of male and female participants in physical education classes" (pp. 213–214).

The final of the four thesis investigations was Robert Osterhoudt's encyclopedic study entitled "A Descriptive Analysis of Research Concerning the Philosophy of Physical Education and Sport" (1971). Building upon—and, in certain instances, subtracting from—a selected bibliography on sport and physical education that I had developed, Osterhoudt's efforts resulted in an organization of the body of knowledge in this area, and also offered "a reference for the classification and treatment of future works" (p. 227). He analyzed descriptively the selected literature of the twentieth century and, most important, reviewed major taxonomies for research prior to the development of a specific one for this particular investigation. The broad outline of this taxonomy had been suggested earlier in a paper by Pearson entitled "Inquiry into Inquiry" (unpublished) that had been investigated as a special project while studying with the author at Urbana. Once again, Osterhoudt built most effectively on this taxonomy when his detailed study of the literature warranted the institution of certain modifications. Basically, the literature was divided into three categories: (1) construct analysis, (2) system analysis, and (3) concept analysis. Interestingly enough—and the finding points up the significance of this inquiry into the "family resemblance" status for the term physical education—he found 138 studies he was able to classify as "the analysis of concept construction"! He urged that "a more abiding consultation with the mother discipline, with philosophy proper, is required, so as to avoid dogmatic espousals, with which the philosophy of physical education and sport has all too long been preoccupied" (p. 235).

Existentialism

During the past century still another philosophy, or at least approach to philosophy, has emerged as a significant force—*existentialism*. Prior to 1850 Sören Kierkegaard had become concerned about the many influences within society that were taking a person's individuality, indeed humanity, away. Since that time many others have felt a similar concern. Originally, existentialism was a revolt against Hegel's idealism, a philosophy stating that ethical and spiritual realities were accessible through reason. Kierkegaard decided that religion would be next to useless if we could reason our way back to God. Nietzsche wished to discard Christianity, since science had shown that the transcendent ideals of the Church were nonsense. In his opinion, therefore, our task is to create our own ideals and values. After all, we are responsible only to ourselves.

To write about the background and present status of existentialism is not a simple task because it is not one of the long-standing philosophic positions or schools. In fact, two writers who would admit to being existentialist in their orientation—or who might be included in a historical summary of this approach to philosophizing—might well be in rather complete disagreement on the majority of the main tenets of a philosophical stance. Thus, one existentialist is never a direct descendant or disciple of another, and it is often almost impossible to place them in what might be identified as a philosophic "family tree."

Certainly somewhere in the tradition of social philosophy, however, one can find specific ideas in the writings of the great philosophers of the West that have been echoed by advocates of existentialism, but the precursors within the modern era have been important thinkers like Pascal, Kierkegaard, and Ortega y Gasset. As Kaufmann indicates (1956, p. 11), "The three writers who appear invariably on every list of 'existentialists'—Jaspers, Heidegger, and Sartre—are not in agreement on essentials." He goes on to name others, such as Rilke, Kafka, and Camus, and explains that the "one essential feature shared by all these men is their perfervid individualism." How can this approach therefore be characterized as a philosophy?

MacIntyre (1967, pp. 147–149) provides one answer to this rhetorical question by relating all these people on the same family tree, so to speak, because he identifies six recurrent themes that are typically associated in a number of different ways. First, reality for the existentialist cannot be comprehended within a conceptual system. A second theme is that of a "doctrine of intentionality"—the idea that "the object of belief or emotion is internal to the belief or emotion" and cannot be explained in the naturalistic terms of the associationist psychologist. Third, one encounters time and again the thought that our existence is fundamentally absurd in a flawed universe that seems to be lacking basic purpose—although it is true that such a flaw does give us a guarantee of freedom of action. A fourth theme of existential philosophy is that "the possibility of choice is the central fact of human nature," and that we make choices through action or inaction (p. 149). Such choices are often controlled by criteria irrationally selected. Fifth, in our existence the concepts of "anxiety," "dread," and "death" loom very large because of this freedom and the "fragility" of our existence in the universe. Last, dialog and communication involving argument between reader and author using deductive logic will serve no purpose unless there is agreement on basic premises. Thus, plays and novels are often best employed as viable forms of expression by existentially oriented philosophers or authors.

As helpful as knowledge and comprehension of these six recurrent themes may be, the reader will still find it necessary to remain exceptionally alert whenever this term is employed in an article or conversation. The term existentialism seems unfortunately to have gone the way of other philosophic terms such as idealism, realism, pragmatism, and naturalism. In other words, *it,* like *they,* has been the victim of bastardization, and wherever it appears in popular literature care should be taken to examine the source and usage for authenticity. As DeMott says, "a foreign entry, heavy, hard to pronounce, fast in the forties, faded in the fifties. . . . Despite the handicaps, though, 'existential' is breaking through. Improving its place steadily, unfazed by cheapening, inflation, or technical correction, it's closing once again on high fashion" (1969, p. 4).

Despite these difficulties, which all terms from philosophy seem to encounter when they become jargon, it is relatively simple to explain a few basic "truths" about existential philosophy to teachers and to reasonably intelligent people. Many people recognize quite fully the long list of unanswered questions of the day. Church leaders have had increasing difficulty in answering many of these questions satisfactorily, and most college students have discovered that in the past few decades many philosophy professors haven't been trying to answer them in acceptable and interesting ways. Thus, it seems really important when a philosopher such as William Barrett of New York University explains:

> Existentialism is a philosophy that confronts the human situation *in its totality* to ask what the basic conditions of human existence are and how man can establish his own meaning out of these conditions. . . . Here philosophy itself—no longer a mere game for technicians or an obsolete discipline superseded by science—becomes a fundamental dimension of human existence. For man is the one animal who not only can, but must ask himself what his life means. (Barrett, 1958, p. 126)

Such an approach quite obviously makes this type of philosophizing potentially vital in our lives because we are actually offered a way of life. In contrast, other leading philosophical positions confront us with a depersonalized Nature, a transcendent Deity, or a State seemingly possessing both of these qualities. As Kaplan explains, "The meaning of life lies in the values which we can find in it, and values are the product of choice" (1961, p. 105). Thus, the direction of movement within selected concepts is *from* existence *to* choice *to* freedom.

Unfortunately (or fortunately—depending upon one's perspective), such seemingly wonderful freedom is not what it might appear at first glance. This opportunity for choice and freedom places an awesome responsibility on the individual man or woman: He or she is ultimately responsible for what happens to others too. In a sense "I am determining through my choice what all mankind everywhere is forever to become" (Kaplan, p. 108). Kaplan, in describing Sartre's position, explains that there are two kinds of people in the world (other than true existentialists, of course): "those who try to escape from freedom and those who try to deny responsibility—cowards and stinkers" (p. 109).

Such an outlook or life philosophy postulates no bed of roses for those who subscribe to it fully. Accordingly, we should choose our life patterns freely and with integrity; then we can become "authentic" persons only by accepting full responsibility for our choices. The beatnik blunder was to think that authenticity required freakish individuality. Actually, what is being offered is that we should responsibly choose one world or another for tomorrow; that we will have to be shaped so that we can somehow cope with such a world; and that each of us adhering to this process of living defines his or her own being and humanity—and that this is the only way this absurd world can acquire meaning!

The Nature of Reality (Metaphysics). The world of material objects extended in mathematical space with only quantitative and measurable properties is not the world we live in as human beings; our world is a human world, not a world of science. From the context of the human world all the abstractions of science ultimately derive their meaning. We are first and foremost a concrete involvement within the world, and we distinguish the opposed poles of body and mind. Existence precedes essence; we decide our own fate. Our self-transcendence distinguishes us from all other animals, and we cannot be understood in our totality by the natural sciences. Truth is expressed in art and religion, as well as in science. Time and history are fundamental dimensions of human existence. Our basic task is to blend the past, present, and future together so that the world—the *human* world—assumes meaning and direction. In this way we can be authentic. We stand open to the future, and the future stands open to us. Life's present conditions can be transformed so that responsible social action will result. (This basic material has been taken from William Barrett, *Irrational Man: A Study in Existential Philosophy.*)

Educational Aims and Objectives. It does not seem possible to refute the position that existential philosophy raises most serious questions about us and our life on earth. Consequently, considering the importance of education as a social institution, the problems raised by existential thought almost inevitably relate to schools and universities and the programs and experiences that are provided. As Langer has indicated, "In philosophy this disposition of problems is the most important thing that a school, a movement, or an age contributes. This is the 'genius' of a great philosophy: in its light, systems arise and rule and die. Therefore a philosophy is characterized more by the *formulation* of its problems than by its solution of them" (Langer, 1964, p. 16). Existential philosophy has most certainly confronted the problems of the age that we are facing generally and that we meet specifically in educational institutions at all levels. Many of these problems were critical thirty or forty years ago on a national basis at least, but now they must be resolved internationally—that is, if solution is still possible (for example, over-population, pollution). "Designs for the education of man living on the planet earth ought to produce diversity, for there must be many paths to this goal" (Redefer, 1974).

Does existential philosophy offer any implications of a positive and optimistic nature for education? If educators can bring themselves to accept Bedford's interpretations and conclusions regarding existentialism's implications, it would seem to be wise to give this philosophical stance serious consideration:

1. Man can always turn, reform, or rechoose.
2. Man has worth . . . either derived from God *or* he makes his own worth (value).
3. Each new person plays a decisive role in history.
4. Man is never permanently degraded.
5. Man can create meaning out of his existence no matter what its circumstances.
6. Man has everything to gain and nothing to lose by risking himself in life. (Bedford, 1961, p. 47)

Thus, an existentially oriented teacher and coach would be cognizant of the fact that the socialization of the student has become equally as important as a key educational aim (in this century) as purely intellectual development. He or she is most concerned because many of the educational theorists see us as "things to be worked over in some fashion to bring them into alignment with a prior notion of what they *should* be." Even the experimentalists could be challenged for their seeming failure to bring "the learner into a self-determining posture." Even if there is general agreement that a set of fundamental dispositions is to be formed as a result of the educational process, the existentially oriented *teacher* would inquire whether the criterion used for the evaluation of the worth of individual dispositions should be "public rather than a personal and private criterion." As Morris (1961) states, "If education is to be truly human, it must somehow *awaken awareness* in the learner—existential awareness of himself as a single subjectivity in the world." Students should "constantly, freely, baselessly, and creatively" choose their own individual patterns of education. The subjectivity of the existentialistically oriented learner can and should thrive in the arts (music, painting, poetry, creative writing), but it should not be forgotten that similar possibilities to study human motivation are available in the social sciences as well (and probably to a lesser extent in the natural sciences). (This material has been taken from Van Cleve Morris, *Philosophy and the American School.*)

The Educative Process (Epistemology). Great emphasis has been placed on the teaching-learning process, but it is indeed extremely difficult to describe the essential ingredients of the educative process. The language analyst would inquire whether (1) the subject matter was being considered; (2) the teacher's actions were being analyzed; (3) that which takes place within the student was being assessed; or perhaps (4) whether the end result was being evaluated.

Existentially oriented teachers would view the task in a less systematic manner and from a different perspective. For them, childhood is characterized as a "pre-existential phase of human life." About the time of puberty in the individual, there is an "existential moment" in the young person's subjective life. This is the time of the "onset of the self's awareness of its own existing." For the first time, the individual sees himself as responsible for his own conduct. Then, and only then, "education must become an act of discovery." The learners' experiences should be such that they become personally implicated in the subject matter and in the situation around them. Knowledge must be "chosen, i.e., appropriated, before it can be true for that consciousness." It is never something that is purely objective, nor is it somewhat purposeful in the person's life. Knowledge becomes knowledge "only when a subjectivity takes hold of it and puts it into his own life."

It could be argued, of course, that the existentialist has little to offer in the way of a method of knowing. And yet, whether logic, scientific evidence, sense perception, intuition, or revelation is being considered, "it is the individual self which must make the ultimate decision as to what is, as a matter of fact, true." Perceptually and cognitively, the individual is aware of the objects of existence, but there is something more—an "internal, subjective awareness"—that enables him to know that he knows. To the present time a case could be made for the position that psychology has given very few answers about this latter phase of the epistemological process. (Some of this material has been taken from Morris, *Philosophy and the American School,* and *Existentialism in Education.*)

Sport, Physical Activity, Health, and Recreation

What does all this mean for sport and physical education, not to mention health and recreation? Obviously, it is dangerous and possibly somewhat illogical to draw specific implications in this manner. On the other hand, it would be ridiculous to refrain from any consideration of possible implications. The field of physical education and sport—and the allied professions of health education and recreation—should strive to fulfill a significant role in the general educational pattern of the arts, social sciences, and natural sciences. The goal postulated for the individual should be *total* fitness—not just *physical* fitness, as important as this may be—with a balance between activities emphasizing competition and cooperation. The concept of "universal man" should be highly regarded as an educational aim, but it is absolutely necessary for the person to have the opportunity to choose for himself or herself based on knowledge, skills, and attitudes determined by self-evaluation. Somehow the child who is "authentically eccentric" should be made to feel at home in the physical activities program.

Further, there should be opportunities for youth to commit themselves to values and people in sport. An important question in sport and athletics, of course, is how to help preserve the individual's authenticity in individual, dual, and team sports where winning is so often overemphasized. It should be possible to aid the young man or woman athlete personally to select the values that are being sought in the activity. The young person is playing and taking part for actualization of self—that is, he or she is attempting to use sport for his or her own purposes. Because the opportunity for creativity is so important and should therefore be made available wherever possible to young people, physical activities such as modern dance should be given a prominent place in the program.

The educational process employed by the physical education teacher and sport coach should be as natural as possible under the circumstances; a give and take situation would be ideal. The student should be allowed to observe and to inquire freely. Freedom is very important, of course, but the teacher is needed since students cannot teach themselves competencies and skills as effectively as when they are under the guidance of an excellent teacher. Good teachers should show emotion, but they should not be strongly egocentric or too biased about a system or a point of view. If the aim of the program is students who are able to move their bodies with purpose and meaning in such activities as sport, play, dance, and exercise, the teacher should be absolutely dedicated to the search for truth in these aspects of life. It is vitally important that the end result be a "self-moving" individual, both literally and figuratively.

In existential philosophy the search for truth is typically an individual matter, but majority opinion should be tested when action is needed in a group situation. The student should strive to develop an "orderly mind" within an organism that seeks to move purposefully and with definite meaning. The student should be willing to debate issues, and should be encouraged to strive for creativity. A physical education program—as is the case with the entire educational program—should not be considered successful if the student becomes a "carbon copy" of the teacher. Such an inclusive methodology with accompanying specific techniques should characterize the existentially oriented physical educator's teaching and coaching.

In regard to health education and recreation education, professions that have been allied with physical education in the past, much of what has been stated above should apply in these fields as well. For example, the child must develop an awareness of the need for self-education about the various aspects of personal and community health. Controversial issues should never be avoided. All types of recreational needs—social, esthetic and creative, communicative, learning, and physical—should be met through a program of recreation education in the schools during the day and in the evening community school offerings. One function of play is most certainly personal liberation and release. All sorts of group recreational activities are important, and most certainly have a place, but opportunities for *individual* expression should not be downgraded and should be made available regularly. (Some of this material has been paraphrased from Zeigler, 1966, pp. 9–10.)

This first persistent problem—determining values as they might relate to life, education, and physical education and sport—has been treated philosophically, and to a slight extent historically, at somewhat greater length than most of the other persistent problems included in this text. So that the reader may continue to compare the philosophical stances of the major positions toward other persistent problems, approximately the same procedure will be followed in subsequent chapters.

The Influence of Politics [1]

THREE TYPES OF POLITICAL STATES

The history of the various world civilizations, and their accompanying educational systems, indicates that the kind and amount of education have varied in these societies depending on whether a particular society or country was (1) a monarchy, (2) an aristocratic oligarchy, or (3) a type of democracy or republic.

From the standpoint of sociology, government might be defined as a form of social organization. This organization becomes necessary as a means of social control to regulate the actions of persons and groups. Throughout history every known society seems to have developed some measure of formal control. The group as a whole has been termed the state, and the members are known as citizens. Thus, the state is made up of territory, people, and government. If the people eventually unify through common cultural tradition, they are classified as a nation. They develop a pattern of living, called social structure. Political organization is but one phase of this structure, but it exercises a powerful influence upon the other phases. A governmental form is usually a conservative force that is slow to change; inextricably related to the rest of the social structure, the political regime must adapt to changing social organization or anarchy results.

Aristotle's classification of the three types of political states, mentioned above, holds today as it did then. In a society where one person

[1] It should be understood that the word "politics" is used here in the best sense —as the theory and practice of managing public affairs. When we speak of a politician, therefore, the intent is to describe a person interested in politics as a most important profession, and not one who through "shady practices" might attempt to amass personal wealth and influence.

rules, it would seem logical to assume that he or she should have the best education so as to rule wisely. The difficulty with this situation is that there is no guarantee that a hereditary ruler is the best-equipped person in the entire society to fulfill this purpose.

If the few rule, then they usually received the best education. These people normally rise to power by demonstrating various types of ability. That they are clever cannot be doubted; it is doubtful, however, that the wisest and most ethical people become rulers in an oligarchy.

If the many rule through the power of their votes in democratic elections, it is imperative that the general level of education be raised to the highest degree possible. It becomes part of the ethic of the society to consider the worth of human personality and to give each individual the opportunity to develop his or her potential to the fullest. In return, in order to ensure smooth functioning of the democracy, the individual is asked to subjugate personal interests to the common good. Harmony between these two antithetical ideals would seem to require a very delicate balance in the years ahead.

Which Agency Should Have Control?   Whereas in a totalitarian state there is but one philosophy of education permitted, other types of government allow pluralistic philosophies of education to flourish. Under the latter arrangement the state could conceivably exercise no control of education whatsoever, or it could take a greater or lesser interest in the education of its citizens. When the state does take an interest, the question arises as to whether the state, through its agency the school, the family, or the church shall exert the greatest amount of influence on the child. When the leaders of the church feel very strongly that the central purpose of education is religious, they may decide to take over the education of the child themselves. In a society where there are many different religious affiliations, it is quite possible that the best arrangement is for the church and the state to remain separate.

The implications of this discussion for the professional in physical education and sport become immediately apparent. It is rather difficult in this instance to define the three major positions as objectively as we seemed to be able to do in the case of the persistent problem of values. It is possible to state that educational progressivism can flourish only in a democratic society, and that essentialism seemingly may exist in either a monarchy, an oligarchy, or a democracy. The key question, of course, is at what point essentialism and the objectives of a democracy conflict. Democracy itself means different things to particular educational philosophers; it is not possible to strike an absolute balance among the conflicting concepts of egalitarianism, freedom, sharing, and respect for individual dignity.

Experimentalism

To refine this line of thinking still further, experimentalism in education would be quickly eliminated in a totalitarian or fascist state. The same would seem to be true for Protestant Christian idealism, with its emphasis on cultivation of the individual personality and a higher loyalty to a Divine Being. The essentialistic Catholic Church has often been strong enough to withstand the onslaughts of a strong state, but it has been sorely pressed on many occasions.

In our specialized field within education, the experimentalist belief that physical education and sport can become an integral experience in the curriculum (according to the definition of educational values) would seem to be realizable *only* in an evolving democracy. The many objectives for physical education emphasizing the concept of "total fitness" can only be projected in a situation where individuals' progress toward these objectives is evaluated in terms of their own starting point. Such an educational climate is also necessary for the achievement of the experimentalist's goal for school health education—an individual capable of "living most and serving best"—and for recreation education.

Realism

Conversely, the realist can and does function under various kinds of regimes. Since physical education is regarded as education "of the physical," it is merely a matter of muscle strengthening and development of cardiovascular efficiency. Physical education yields to intellectual education, and sports can be a school for the development of loyalty and courage. In like manner, health is instrumental in achieving the higher purposes in life, and play and recreation are simply means to self-integration through reducing the psychic tension caused by life's stresses. Even here, however, there is the danger that organized sport (athletics of a highly competitive nature) tends to destroy the "play attitude."

Idealism

Idealism's position is not as straightforward. Physical development can take place in any kind of state, although it must be admitted that physical fitness appears to suffer in a laissez-faire democracy except when war becomes imminent. The development of the other aspects of human nature (for example, the idealistic goals of physical education prevalent during Greece's Golden Age) presupposes a society in which individuals and their needs and desires rank high. The intensive and continued participation in sport competition of many in the totalitarian state, or the focus of physical education on the development of strength and other physical attributes for purely militaristic purposes, negates the idealistic concept of the whole personality. The idealistic position in health education would not be jeopardized by the philosophy of state as it is now held, with the possible exception that for some citizens a particular type of political society might not view health as basic and valuable to all aspects of personality. The traditional position of idealism since the day of Plato on the importance of play and recreation has been similar to that of the realist. In some types of political society, the need of the individual for a balance between work and play might be slighted. This would disturb the idealist (and the realist as well!). We must also not forget that, for the idealist, the potential of play and recreation for spiritual development has never been fully explored. Thus, the "progressive" idealist would argue that the state should never curb individuality in the matter of creative recreational experience.

Existentialism

Initially, let us state that existentialist writers have not turned their attention to the question of the ideal political state. The existentialist would see the twentieth-century individual as a "homeless creature"; he or she appears to be seeking new and different kinds of recognition, inasmuch as the so-called earlier stability within society seems to have vanished. Since existentialists then are basically seekers, they would feel out of place within a totalitarian regime that demanded unquestioning obedience and negated the development of individual personality and rights. On the other hand, life in the variety of democratic states extant leaves much to be desired. The problem of an exploding population in so many countries, democratically oriented or otherwise, tends to make us more lonely than ever—even though we may be "rubbing shoulders" with the masses daily. The era of the "organization man" within our democratic, capitalistic society has further destroyed our identities as individuals. The democratic ideal within a republic does offer us an opportunity to be vocal, enlightened citizens, but somehow few seem to take advantage of this chance for individual expression that almost guarantees the taker immediate recognition and identity.

Transposed to the educational scene, the existentialist is once again disturbed by the failure of our programs to produce young men and women who show evidence of "self-determining posture." How can we awaken the awareness of learners so that they will demand a more individualized pattern of education? This should be possible within the pluralistic framework of education in the United States. Specifically, how can we help the child who is "authentically eccentric" to feel at home in our typical physical education program? Insisting that he or she measure up to physical fitness norms does not appear to be any solution to the problem. Self-evaluation and self-motivation could well be the key to this dilemma, but how can this be realized in large classes where there is insistence upon standardized routines both in physical fitness drills and in sport skills? Existentialists are well aware that we don't yet have the answer to this problem, and they don't see much evidence of concern about it either.

PHYSICAL EDUCATION UNDER VARIOUS SYSTEMS

The implications of state involvement in education concern both progressivist and essentialist. The progressivist, who is concerned with social reform, would favor a democratic state in which the individual could choose social goals on a trial and error basis. The basic question remains, Which agency—the school, the family, or the church—should exert the greatest amount of influence on the child? In a totalitarian state the answer is obvious. When the church decides to educate the child, because it believes the central purposes of education are primarily religious, the role of physical, health, and recreation education tends to decline for both philosophical and economic reasons. In a totalitarian state, the church will be restrained in the achievement of its objectives, but a realistic type of physical education and sport may flourish. In a society where pluralistic philosophies exist and where the federal government perhaps adopts a laissez-faire attitude, the resultant educational product in our specialized area will tend to be quite uneven. The matter is that simple, and yet that complex!

The Influence of Nationalism

In the English language the word "nation" is generally used synonymously with country or state, and we think of human beings who are united under a type of governmental rule. These individuals, members of a political community, are usually considered to possess a certain "nationality" within a definable period of time. The word "people," having a broader and somewhat ambiguous connotation, normally refers to the inhabitants of several nations or states as an ethnological unit.

The word "nationalism" itself might apply to a feeling, attitude, or consciousness that persons might have as citizens of a nation—citizens who hold a strong attitude about the welfare of their nation, about its status in regard to strength or prosperity. Carlton J. Hayes in *Nationalism: A Religion* (1961) refers to patriotism as "love of country," and nationalism as a "fusion of patriotism with a consciousness of nationality." Nationalism might be defined as a political philosophy in which the good of the nation is supreme. The word is often used incorrectly as a synonym for chauvinism.

HISTORICAL BACKGROUND

Thus defined, nationalism has been evident throughout the history of civilization from the relatively simple organization of the tribe to the complex nation-states of the modern world. Some scholars regard nationalism as a term of relatively recent origin, however, because until the modern period no nations were sufficiently unified to permit the existence of such a feeling. But the European heritage reveals many examples of "nationalism." We have only to think of the Greek and Roman cultures with their citizenship ideals and desires to perpetuate their culture. Then, too, the Hebrews believed that they were a people selected by God for a unique role in history, and the Roman Catholic Church developed far-reaching loyalties over a significant period of time.

During the course of medieval history, and into the Renaissance, many rulers and their nobles struggled with the Church for control. Eventually people began to think of themselves as German, or French, or English. As some sort of representation on parliamentary bodies became possible for those persons or groups known as the middle class (and in the nineteenth century for the lower class), it is reasonable to assume that they would develop a new type of patriotism, and that this feeling would in time blossom into nationalism.

Nationalism got an early start in England, and the English developed what could be called a truly national life. This more "pure" type of nationalism was brought to America by many of the new settlers, although then and now it has periodically erupted into a concept that might be called irrational. Nationalistic feeling was evident in France even before the revolution with the development of absolute monarchies and the gradual breaking away from the Church's domination. It has been intimated by some that nationalism is a necessary step in the development of internationalism.

German nationalism was stimulated greatly after the crushing defeat by Napoleon at the Battle of Jena; the German people were forced to take stock of their political organization and to suggest remedies for improvement and subsequent return to power in central Europe. Linking nationalism with the concept of power rather than with freedom, however, has often encouraged a type of chauvinism characterized by dislike and even hatred of other nations and peoples. Such a fusion has occasioned untold hardship and disaster to evolving civilization.

The Industrial Revolution stimulated nationalism through the economic doctrines of mercantilism. And the rejection of free trade did much to hold back the progress of *all* peoples, both in developed and underdeveloped lands. Individuals were exhorted to follow a pattern of blind allegiance to a country whose leaders in many cases equated greatness with military power. Thus it was perfectly logical that individual freedom would be subjugated to the "greater glory of the fatherland." Unfortunately, these strongly nationalistic beliefs helped to develop an unreasoning fervor that caused people to accept racist theories blindly—beliefs that have resulted in unbelievable acts by so-called civilized persons even in the twentieth century. Thus, balancing the world's hopes for a broader concept of internationalism was this ruthless nationalism, raised to the status of a religion in certain countries of the world. Certainly nationalism, and nationalistic education, has its place in the political spectrum, but every effort must be made to preserve the higher goal of individual freedom.

NATIONALISM IN EDUCATION

Reasoned and controlled nationalism has allowed the educational aims of the Church to coexist with its own, probably because their efforts were in somewhat different spheres. But when nationalism has grown disproportionately, it has swept everything in its path aside. Thus, during wartime the very roots of our democratic republic here in the United States have been visibly shaken by an unreasoning nationalism—necessary, perhaps, under the circumstances but very damaging to our national ideals. Obviously, the more totalitarian a state is, the better nationalism thrives; conversely, it is quite difficult for strong nationalism to develop in a pluralistic state. People living in a democratic society would not be satisfied with a nationalistic education dictated by a minority, but if it were possible for nationalism in education to emanate from the goals of a free people, the common good would then be served. A democracy that is far enough advanced to consider sharing its culture with other countries is well on the way to a concept of internationalism. This stage of advancement, if achieved by the majority of nations, might well prepare the way for the existence of "one world"—an idea regarded as an unrealizable dream by a number of conservatives, but, according to many liberals, the only method of ensuring permanent peace.

NATIONALISM IN AMERICAN DEMOCRACY

The influence of nationalism on our field is readily observable. If a strong state is desired, the need for a strong, healthy people is paramount. We need only think of the Medes and the Spartans or, in our own time, Nazi Germany and the USSR. The situation in the United States, viewed historically, has been discussed by H. J. VanderZwaag (1965). He points out that the United States underwent various stages of nationalism in the nineteenth century—from "national and sectional feelings" to a more firm nationalism after the Civil War, with leanings toward internationalism by the turn of the century. VanderZwaag also indicates that it was quite natural for people to become concerned about an *American* system of physical education as the ties with other cultures were lessening; and this was, in fact, what the resultant merger represented. Then he asks whether nationalism has been the dominant force shaping our physical education policies. His conclusion: Physical education has not been cultivated for purely nationalistic purposes; rather, "by 1920, it was evident that the United States had evolved a program of physical education which was characterized by informality and an emphasis upon national sports."

IMPLICATIONS OF EDUCATIONAL PHILOSOPHY
FOR PHYSICAL EDUCATION

Experimentalism (and reconstructionism) can flourish only in a democratic society. In our country at present the individual states and the local systems can promote just about any type of program in physical, health, and recreation education for which they can gain support. The federal government, through the President's Council on Physical Fitness, is attempting to place what might be called a nationalistic emphasis on the *physical* fitness of youth, but it has absolutely no power to enforce its recommendations unless a specific community desires to proceed along these lines. Even if federal funds are made available to our field under the Elementary and Secondary School Act of 1965, it is still questionable whether communities applying for these funds would feel themselves wholly restricted by governmental regulations. Enforcement of these laws is, of course, complicated by the possibility of various interpretations. Thus, it is almost impossible to promote nationalism in health and physical education when it must emanate from the goals of a free people. If our government should attempt to dictate in this matter, as it has done in wartime, the basic educational objectives of our democracy would be threatened.

The realist, conversely, can and does function under various philosophies of state, but the idealist may run into difficulty in a political system in which the state begins to encroach on the individual's needs and desires. In a progressive system the state will tend to accentuate the socialistic goals of education. The more totalitarian a state becomes, however, the more control it exercises over the educational system and over each individual in planning for the national welfare.

Existentialists would not be particularly disturbed by the presence of what might be called a "healthy" type of nationalism in a society, but they would be rather violently opposed to the overriding nationalism that destroys individual human aspirations. They would argue that it is up to us to make something out of ourselves, that we must choose our own values in order to give life meaning.

Language analysts would approach this problem from a completely different perspective. At the outset they would point out that nationalism is really a very vague concept, and that it is not possible to discuss the influence of a social force on a social institution if we haven't accurately defined what we mean when we use the term "nationalism" today. Some have stated that nationalism is a thing of the past. Others have questioned whether a person must forego all nationalistic tendencies when he or she becomes an internationalist. What is the difference between a regionalist and a nationalist, or a regionalist and a universalist? What specific forms of nationalism are we seeing at present? If there is only one form of nationalism evident in the United States today, what might *that* form of the phenomenon mean for the conduct of education (and, of course, the conduct of physical education and sport)? In this way the language analyst would attempt to get at the very root of the problem.

CONCLUDING STATEMENT

Nationalism as a persistent historical problem is still with us and will probably continue to exert an influence on physical education. Even the most advanced states supposedly on their way to internationalism are still exhibiting nationalistic behavior. If nation-states can achieve a relatively stable world order, each one possessing its own "healthy" or creative nationalism, professionals in physical education and sport will not have to worry about the goals of their profession being warped and distorted by overly aggressive nationalists.

The Influence of Economics

Broadly interpreted, economics as a field is concerned with what we produce and the formal and informal arrangements that are made concerning the usage of these products. Economists want to know about the consumption of goods that are produced and who takes part in the actual process of production. They ask where the power lies, whether the goods are used fully, and to what ends a society's resources are brought to bear on the matter at hand.

The long-established social order was greatly disturbed by the advent of the machine age and the factory. Men left their homes and their private enterprises, and in the course of our century women followed them. Even the farmer became an entrepreneur and, from simple bargaining at the outset, the complex structure known as the "market" developed. In time transportation became cheaper, and trading areas were consequently greatly enlarged.

With the progress of the machine age, the division of labor was tremendous, and families were often no longer self-sufficient. Industrial organizations mushroomed, and the articulations among these various groups were often disorganized. New inventions and products became part of the evolving culture and in turn created new demands. As a result of all of this, people seem now to be seeking stability—or at least a reasonable semblance of order. Such stability is not yet in sight; paradoxically, change has become the only relatively certain factor in life. Such social forces as automation, small wars and possible large wars, space travel, the exploding body of knowledge in all areas, to name only a few, are continually disturbing the economic organization within, between, and among societies. Other influencing factors within the field of economics itself have been organization in the production of goods, mass production, organized research, and the general organization of business, labor, and consumers.

HISTORICAL
BACKGROUND

For thousands of years people lived in small, relatively isolated groups, and their survival depended on their own subsistence economies. Early civilizations had to learn how to create surplus before any class within the society could have leisure for formal education or anything else that might be related to the "good life." Athens, for example, did not have a golden age until it became a relatively large commercial and cosmopolitan center. Although the Romans amassed great wealth and developed an extensive educational system, their education remained basically of instrumental, rather than intrinsic, value to that culture. When the empire declined politically and economically, educational decay set in as well. Then it was necessary for the Roman emperors to subsidize education from the central treasury.

During the early Middle Ages, education suffered as the economy again became agrarian in nature. Later, with the surge in trade and industry, vocational education was provided for the sons of middle class merchants. The gradual intellectual awakening and then the rise of a spirit of scientific inquiry during the Renaissance, coupled with more profitable commerce and industry, revived education still further. However, only a very small portion of the population ever had enough wealth to gain the leisure necessary for education and cultural pursuits.

The Industrial Revolution brought about marked social and economic changes; as group after group gained wealth, they demanded recognition in government. Gradually the masses, supported by educational theorists, clamored for more educational opportunities, and elementary and secondary education became increasingly available on a variety of bases. Class-structured education remained a problem in many countries of Europe despite the existence of steadily improving economies. It is now possible, but still somewhat difficult, for a boy or girl to rise above the social and/or economic level of the family. However, the truly brilliant young people do have this chance.

The United States has now reached a stage where approximately 40 percent of its young people go on to some form of higher education. There are still many obstacles to be overcome, as a portion of the population is still disenfranchised because of poor educational and family backgrounds. Our economy has now reached a point, however, where young people are being urged to stay in school to avoid glutting the labor market. Very soon compulsory attendance beyond the age of sixteen may be required in many states. This will be possible only because automation is giving us increasingly the type of surplus economy in which a smaller number of people will have to work fewer hours to provide life's necessities. As more people achieve a greater amount of leisure, the challenge to education and our specialized field becomes very great indeed.

In summary, therefore, education has prospered when there was a surplus economy and declined when the economic structure weakened. Thus, it may be said that "educational cycles" of rise and decline seem to have coincided with economic cycles. Despite these developments, historically formal education has rarely included programs of study about economics that could be described as significant and thoroughgoing— particularly in general education curriculums. Similarly, it has been traditional to regard vocational areas of study with less esteem than the liberal arts or humanities.

Educational aims will tend to vary depending upon how people make their money and create surplus economies. There is not much time for schooling in the typical agrarian society, because people have to work long and hard. If commerce is added to the agrarian base in a country, education will advance still further as people will ask more from it to meet the needs of the various classes involved. The modern industrial economy has made still further demands on education and has produced the monies so that it can be obtained.

THE PROBLEM IN A MODERN SOCIETY

Advancing industrial civilization has brought many advantages, but it has created many problems as well. One of these has to do with specialization in function—some people manage and others labor, and this results in an uneven distribution of wealth. Of course, there has always been specialization of function of one sort or another in societies, and the leaders have invariably seemed to end up with the lion's share of the good things of life. The labor movement is striving mightily to reverse this result to a reasonable degree (although there is certainly no general consensus as to what the word "reasonable" means in this context). The seemingly inevitable existence of classes has had a definite effect on the educational structure. People with more money have been able to afford longer periods and different types of education for their children. It is not difficult, therefore, to understand why the social welfare state concept has been popular with the middle and lower classes and, incidentally, why the Democratic party, which has traditionally designated itself as the party of the people, has more registered voters in the United States than its rival. Although this is a great oversimplification, there is undoubtedly enough truth in it to warrant further consideration.

Essentialistic education has tended to preserve the culture of the past—the cultural heritage—and its advocates would not be striving for the same sort of change, and certainly not at the same rate, as progressivists. If it is inevitable that there will always be classes of society sharply divided and that those who work with their hands will be considered inferior (really a most unfortunate connotation), the only hope for the masses is probably in increased educational advantages made possible through continued technological advancement and automation. Much has been written in the United States about the possibility of a classless society, and certainly many of the advantages of the good life are increasingly being made available to all. Some educational philosophers predict the coming of a day when all people will profit from a general education—an education that will enable them to participate more fully as individuals and as members of a democratic society. We in the United States have sought to recognize talent in any person no matter of what socioeconomic status, and to give him or her the opportunity to realize his or her potential. One of the unfortunate outcomes of this trend has been that the cream has been skimmed off many of our less fortunate communities—the ghettos—and we have developed no means to put it back again.

What does this mean to us in the field of education? It means that we have to make a choice as citizens as to which type of economic society we wish to promote. If we feel that this is a world in which people exhibit varying talents and should be educated accordingly, an uneven distribution of wealth will continue. Such a realistic appraisal and approach will undoubtedly encourage the continuation of educational opportunities being available to those who are able to pay for it. This has meant traditionally that cultural education will rank much higher than mere job training. On the other hand, the social progressivist will encourage the development of a type of state that will make its many educational advantages increasingly available to all to the limit of their potential.

IMPLICATIONS FOR PHYSICAL EDUCATION AND SPORT

Professionals in physical education and sport rarely give much consideration to the influence of economics until they begin to feel the pinch of economy moves. Then they find that some segments of the society consider their subject matter area to be less important than others, and the people representing these groups decide that physical education or varsity athletics, for example, should be eliminated, or at least sharply curtailed. Such a move often comes as a distinct shock, and it is frequently rationalized by our claim that athletics is being used as a lever to pry more funds from a recalcitrant and pleasure-seeking public who would not wish to see its spectacles discontinued.

Physical education, especially as it connotes education of the physical, has a good chance for recognition and improvement under either type of economic system. In largely agrarian societies physical fitness normally results automatically through hard work. An industrial society, on the other hand, must prescribe programs to ensure a minimum level of physical fitness for all, either through manual labor or some other type of recommended physical activity. If the distribution of wealth is markedly uneven, the more prosperous groups might achieve their physical fitness through a variety of means, artificial or natural. In a welfare state, where a person would enjoy a relatively longer period of educational opportunity, society would have to decide to what extent it can or should demand physical fitness of all its citizens and how to achieve its end. Here the major philosophical positions in education would dictate value structures; physical education and sport would be accorded a higher or lower rank depending on which educational philosophy prevails.

Health Education

Health education within the schools, with its subdivisions of health services, health instruction, and healthful school living, has developed tremendously in the United States during the twentieth century, and it is now generally recognized that through the educative process youth will develop wholesome health attitudes, habits, and skills.

The same health problems that arise in a democracy could obviously occur under a different political regime; the more influential factors here are climate, geography, and state of economic development. Health standards, generally speaking, are higher in those countries in which scientific investigation is at a higher level and in which the attitudes of the people act to create a more healthful environment. Such advancement usually means that more money has been made available for research, for environmental change, and for improved public health and school education programs.

A welfare state would be more concerned about meeting the health needs of people through democratically approved taxation funds to government agencies and to schools and through donations of interested individuals and groups to private agencies dedicated to the improvement of national health. An economy with an uneven distribution of wealth would be inclined to spend a lesser amount on the health of the masses, with the best health care going to those who can best afford it. This is true to a degree even in the United States, although people in the lower income brackets can often get fine medical attention if they have the patience to wait in line at a clinic. It is the ever-expanding middle class that many times is "priced out of the market" unless these persons have the foresight, or are forced, to enroll in one of the many private health insurance plans.

It should be pointed out in passing that the rising tide of nationalism throughout the world in the so-called underprivileged countries will undoubtedly bring about improved health education, since leaders will see to it that the populace is strong and healthy whether or not public opinion is entirely favorable to the necessary expenditure. The developing concept of internationalism through UNESCO and related agencies holds great promise for the improvement of health standards around the world. In addition, since the onset of the cold war, East and West are often found vying with each other to give (or to lend) money for the adoption of health measures in many countries.

Recreation Education

The first condition for recreation education is leisure, and leisure comes about only in a surplus economy. The amount and types of recreation education for school-age youth, and for other age groups as well, depend a great deal on the prevailing philosophy in an educational system. In the United States some leaders have predicted that automation will force our society to prepare people for improved use of expanding leisure. In a society in which uneven distribution of wealth is not curbed, the wealthy will have the most expensive recreational pursuits, while the masses will have less time for play and recreation, even of an educational nature. In such an economic system, past experience has shown that cultural education is rated much higher than vocational education. Granted that the educational realist, and many of the idealists as well, views cultural education *as* education for leisure as well as transmission of the social heritage, this would still mean that the masses would receive less cultural education. Thus, the larger part of the population living in such a society would be deprived of knowledge and skills for recreational enjoyment.

In a state in which interest in social welfare is high, however, both cultural and vocational education are accessible to all once a surplus economy is attained. Special features of this system include community recreation and adult education. With more people enjoying leisure as they see fit, recreation educators can only hope that the standard of living will continue to rise and that educational and recreational opportunities will meet the challenge. In order to ensure this, economists must be encouraged to devise improved methods of preventing economic cycles and material wealth must not be allowed to spoil us and jade our senses as to what a *high* standard of living might really mean. Finally, scientists must discover substitutes for the natural resources that are steadily being dissipated.

The Influence of Religion

Religion may be defined broadly as "the pursuit of whatever a man considers to be most worthy or demanding of his devotion" (Williams, 1952, p. 350). To be completely religious, therefore, an individual would have to devote herself completely to the attainment of her highest aim in life. The more usual definition of religion explains it as a belief in a Supreme Creator who has imparted a spiritual nature and a soul to us and who may possibly guard and guide our destiny. Because there are so many types of religion in the world, and these are in various stages of development, it is almost impossible to present a definition that would be meaningful and acceptable to all.

FOUR STAGES OF RELIGIOUS DEVELOPMENT

In order to understand the evolution of religious thought, we may trace four successive stages: (1) animism, (2) animatism, (3) polytheism, and (4) monarchism (Champion and Short, 1951, pp. 1–5). *Animism* is described as primitive peoples' realization that there were many natural occurrences in the world over which they had no control. Powerful spirits or beings seemed to cause these catastrophes and hardships. What were they to do in order to stop or lessen the effects of these unpleasant happenings? The best course of action seemed to be appeasement of these angry spirits.

The second, more advanced stage, is designated as *animatism*. People had gained more knowledge about natural phenomena; some of them they learned to control to a certain extent, or at least were able to make some adaptation to that made them less vulnerable to adverse effects. The idea of nature spirits in stones and trees lessened, and people began to conceive of greater, less personal influences. Seasonal change came to be regarded as the "work" of a very powerful "God."

There is a division of opinion as to what happened next. Some scholars believe that monotheism was the next stage. This happened when a particular tribe accepted a tribal deity. Subsequently, certain tribes were organized into larger groups, according to this theory, and they compromised by accepting each tribe's god and developing a pantheon of many deities. In this way it is theorized that a third stage, known as *polytheism,* developed naturally as the gods became increasingly more important and powerful. Of course, it is conceivable that both monotheism and polytheism were occurring but in different periods of time and in tribes far distant from one another.

The fourth stage is generally considered to be *monarchism.* This was an approach in which the high priests (and perhaps subsequently the people) selected one god as the greatest of all. The other gods would then tend to become less powerful and important. Since the group's own social organization was hierarchical, it was only natural for people to see such a hierarchy among the gods. It followed therefore that this greater god was right much more often than lesser deities. If he were all wise, it stands to reason also that he would tend to be just in his dealings with people. The bad people would eventually be punished, and those who were good would be rewarded.

At some stage in this development people became concerned about where gods live. Hallowed places (shrines) were constructed which later took the form of churches and temples. Certain groups in particular societies believed further that the various gods needed a place where they could live together—a separate world at some distant point up in the sky.

Eventually it was not sufficient for gods merely to visit their temples. So the idea gradually spread that gods could return to earth and thereby become involved with human problems. A further refinement of this belief was the concept that it was possible for God to become embodied in human form—the idea of *divine incarnation.* Still another method whereby God could establish a most intimate relationship was considered to have taken place. It was called *immanence*—a situation in which God was present somehow within the very structure of the earth and the universe.

In the course of this development from animism to monarchism, people came to believe that God had three aspects: (1) He was eternal, existing endlessly apart from the world he created; (2) He had the power to take the form of a man (incarnation); and (3) He was an omnipresent Spirit dwelling in all things. It now becomes quite understandable how the doctrine of the Trinity (Father, Son, and Holy Ghost) grew and was subsequently expressed in the creed of the Christian Church.

Along with the concept of God came a self-concept, distinguishing human beings from other creatures. They had something in their makeup that animals didn't have—a soul that was believed to be immortal and separable from the body at death. Although people could not describe it accurately, they felt that this entity was the animating principle of life.

Now we had a God—one God—who possessed infinite power, holiness, wisdom, and foreknowledge. Here was a concept achieved through tremendous endeavor and struggle, although many were unwilling to accept it. Upon this concept were founded the major religions of the world; in the West Christianity and Judaism subscribe to this belief, although there is much disagreement among the various branches of both faiths.

Many persons do not give assent to the more orthodox religious beliefs. *Skepticism* holds that absolute truth and knowledge are not available to us, although partial knowledge may be possible. *Agnosticism* seems to go one step further in positing that knowledge of the ultimate origin of the universe is impossible. Last, there is *atheism.* a position in which there is complete disbelief in a God or Supreme Power underlying the cosmos.

We have followed the approach that there have been four stages in our religious development; now, however, a fifth position has emerged that some regard as an extension of the fourth. We have looked at reality, which we may call God, and have conceived of some sort of partnership. Some consider God to be a friendly partner, if we work according to his physical laws. Recently many church leaders and religious scholars, as an extension of the "friendly partner" position, are postulating the idea of a rather democratic, cooperative God as a foundation for a new world order. Religious liberals find difficulty in accepting this position. Although recognizing their debt to Christianity and Judaism, they are uniting on a "free-mind principle" instead of any common creed. Some of this group—those who believe in natural order and evolution and who spell man with a capital "M"—have been designated as naturalistic humanists by themselves and others. Religious liberals then are free spirits who give allegiance to the truth as they see it; they seek to communicate with all liberals no matter to which of the world's twelve great religions they nominally belong.

Another significant reaction to orthodox religion during the past hundred years has been existentialism. This philosophy has been discussed under our first persistent problem; here let it suffice to say that, on the religious plane, existentialism stressed our ultimate dependence on God to reveal himself rather than our finding God through reason. For many, though, God had already ceased to exist; our task, therefore, was to create our own ideals and values, inasmuch as we were responsible only to ourselves. Twentieth-century atheistic and agnostic existentialists (and it should be stressed that there are Christian existentialists as well, who view all of this differently) are striving to further the existentialist view of human beings as unique historical animals making a valiant attempt to look at themselves objectively in a world in which God may be, and probably is, dead.

In the pages above, designed to trace in broad outline our religious experience, no attempt has been made to indoctrinate the reader. The premise here is that *each and every educator* should work out this problem individually, inasmuch as the decision will undoubtedly have an influence on his or her development as an individual and as an educator.

THE INFLUENCE OF RELIGION ON EDUCATION

The Christian contribution to the history of the world, and especially to education, has been enormous. For the first time (in the Western world at any rate) the ideas of a universal God and of brotherhood took hold. In addition, the Christian emphasis on the afterlife entailed a strict moral preparation. Actually, the basis for universal education was laid with the promulgation of Christian principles emphasizing the worth of the individual.

The early Church was concerned with moral reformation. The previous, strongly pagan centuries of the Roman Empire had introduced vices that were difficult to obliterate. The Christians set up many types of schools to accomplish this purpose, and for a long period the main concerns of monastic life and education were asceticism, chastity, poverty, and obedience. It wasn't until later that the monastic school became interested in the expansion of knowledge and became more tolerant of inquiry. Scholasticism aimed (1) to develop faith and (2) to discover truth through the method of logical analysis. Thomas Aquinas (1225?–1274), like Aristotle, shared the spirit of the realist. After serious consideration, he stated his belief in the reality of matter as the creation of God. He saw God as the first cause—an Absolute with eternal and infinite qualities.

The Protestant Reformation influenced education greatly while lessening to a considerable degree the all-powerful position of the Catholic Church. The authority of the Bible was substituted for that of the Church, and individual judgment was to be used in the interpretation of the Scriptures and Christian duty. This outlook required the education of the many for the purposes of reading and interpreting God's word. Thus the groundwork was laid for democratic universal education in place of the education of the few for leadership.

In the United States, as the educational ladder extended upward toward the middle of the nineteenth century, religious education was removed from school curriculums because of many conflicts. Catholics felt so strongly about the need for religious instruction for their children that they began their own system of education. Protestants, however, went along with the secularization of the schools, a great boon for the country but perhaps not for Protestantism in the long run. The home has done reasonably well in the inculcation of morals, but with rising materialism and the seeming decline of the family as an institution, certain problems have arisen. Many parents no longer seem qualified, nor do they seem to have the desire, to pass on the Christian tradition. One hour a week of Sunday school instruction does not appear to be doing the job adequately. Protestantism's neglect of religious education may in time threaten its very survival, and some argue that this has occurred simply because of a democratic approach to church government. To be fair, it should be pointed out that many Catholics are concerned about the lasting effect of their system of religious education as well.

The position of Catholic realists must be clarified: They still believe that the Catholic Church has the primary role in the education of children and that secular control *cannot* be the only jurisdictional power in such a basic responsibility. This belief includes the explicit idea that salvation is achieved through God's grace *and* through good works following Christ's example and teaching. The implications for education are straightforward: If there are unchanging educational objectives, we on earth must concern ourselves with the means necessary to achieve this ultimate union with God. This view of education as preparation means that the child must be prepared for an eventual life of reason; obviously, the three Rs are basic along with science, literature, geography, history, and perhaps a foreign language. Character training is tremendously important in elementary education and, at the secondary level, every young person should have a greater or lesser amount of general education and preparation for life through the learning of a trade (if he or she is not going on to a university).

A separate educational system is supported by Catholics at considerable hardship, since they pay taxes for public schools too. Apparently they feel very strongly that the civil government does not have the right to educate the child—in certain areas at least. However, the goal of educating every Catholic in a full-time Catholic school is at present unrealizable. If a Catholic school is available within reasonable distance, parents are encouraged to send their children to it. What is really important, of course, is that the child receive religious instruction from qualified teachers. In a situation in which religious orientation is so important, and in which it can become a reality so naturally within the atmosphere of a Catholic school, it is understandable that the Catholic would consider moral training not properly dealt with in a public school.

Discussion often arises concerning (1) which agency shall educate the individual—the home, the church, the state, or some private agency; (2) whether or not any agency is capable of performing the task alone. In a democracy each agency would appear to have a specific function to perform in completing the entire task. In Nazi Germany the state attempted to handle the majority of the responsibility. In the United States the Catholic Church combines with the home to perform this all-important function and has succeeded to a great degree. Experimentalists would certainly not agree with much of Catholic methodology and curriculum content. They would tend to place the major responsibility on the home and the school, whether this school was sponsored by the local community and the state or by some private institution. Some under the progressive banner—certain Protestant Christian idealists—believe that the church has a definite task to fulfill in educating the spiritual nature of the individual, but the pragmatic experimentalists can visualize this function being carried out successfully by the school alone. In the United States today, however, parents must decide for their own children whether religious values, broadly or narrowly conceived, *will* be inculcated, and in what way.

History has shown that public schools have not been hostile to religion as such. Sectarianism during the modern period has made it difficult to teach the Christian religion in the public schools. In the United States there has been continuous concern about the inculcation of religious and moral values in the public schools despite the separation of church and state. With at least eleven major religous groups in the world, it does seem that some sort of comparative religious education should be taught. That has happened only rarely, because it is so difficult to find an instructor who would be acceptable to the various factions concerned.

Increasingly, world opinion charges that society in the United States is wholly organized on the basis of materialism, and not religious principle. There appears to be a low level of public morals, much political corruption, many dishonest business people, a large amount of income tax evasion, an increasing rate of juvenile delinquency, an increase in all sorts of crimes including forcible rape, and thousands killed annually by guns and on the highways. This is a harsh indictment of American life. We must ask ourselves what role religion is to play if we hope to build the spiritual core of our country to meet the urgent problems we face in the second half of the twentieth century. Clearly, if organized religion is to survive, it must become more interested in problems of social change—and quickly. Our society needs a unique type of social institution that is flexible and capable of a high level of intelligent self-direction on the part of its adherents. Can the church meet the challenge, or will the school gradually become the social organization that will effect beneficial social change?

RELIGION AND PHYSICAL EDUCATION AND SPORT

Relatively few significant historical studies have been conducted within our field relative to the influence of religion on physical education and sport, although there is some evidence that this situation will be changed shortly. Other historians have occasionally provided insight into this question, and with their help we can turn to many fine sources still available. It is true that in the early cultures the so-called physical and mental education of the people could not be viewed separately. Many ancient rituals and ceremonies included a variety of types of dance and physical exercise that may well have contributed to physical endurance and skill. The development of these attributes may have been incidental, or it may have been by actual design on the part of the priests and elders

Various early religions placed great stress on a life of quiet contemplation, and this may well have contributed to the disesteem of certain bodily activities of a physical nature. Continuing emphasis on intellectual attainment for certain classes in various societies must have strengthened this attitude. Yet the harmonious ideal of the Athenians had esthetic and religious connotations that cannot be denied, and physical education and sport ranked high in this scheme. The same cannot be said for the practical-minded Romans, however, where the "sound mind in a sound body" concept meant that the body was well trained for warlike pursuits and other activities of a similar nature.

Despite considerable writing in our field to the effect that the Christian Church was responsible for the low status of physical education, recreation, and athletics in the Western world, some evidence to the contrary is now accumulating. It is seemingly true that Christian idealism furthered the dualism of mind and body—a concept whose effects have been detrimental to physical activity ever since. Furthermore, the doctrine of original sin, with the possibility of ultimate salvation if asceticism were practiced, tended to negate the fostering of the Greek ideal for well over a thousand years. H. I. Marrou (1964, pp. 185–186) is of the opinion, however, that "physical education was quite dead in the

Christian era and that its death had been a natural one, unaccompanied by any violent revolution—history would have told us if there had been anything of the kind." He believes that the Church Fathers limited their harsh criticism to professional sport, not to amateur sport or physical education. This thesis is borne out by Ballou (1965), who comes to the conclusion that "early Christianity taught that God cared about bodies as well as souls in contrast to a position suggested by physical literature that God only cared about souls." He explains further that the "body is evil" approach was generated by proponents of heretical movements later rejected by the Church. Ballou concludes, however, that the Christian Church "failed to exert leadership in the area of the games by not reorienting them to a Christian perspective." Until further corroborative study clarifies this matter from different aspects over a longer period of time, we may tentatively conclude that the earlier blame placed upon the Church itself will have to be tempered.

The fact still remains, however, that physical education and "the physical" did fall into disrepute until certain humanistic educators revived the Greek ideal during the Renaissance. The mind-body dichotomy has plagued both this field and the entire theory of education. Even today, when the unity of the human organism has become common knowledge and is continually being substantiated by new evidence, this unfortunate situation persists. Insofar as the churches are concerned, however, the situation has been gradually improving in the past hundred years. It could be argued that spreading materialism has weakened the influence of religion and that church leaders are acceding to the popularity of physical recreation in order to maintain their congregations. It seems reasonable to conclude, however, that organized religion, and certainly specific denominations within the major organized religions, are becoming increasingly aware of the role that physical recreation can play in the promulgation of the Christian idealistic way of life.

To substantiate this statement, a few examples will be presented. Bennett (1962) pointed out that The Church of Jesus Christ of Latter-Day Saints, of all the various religions and denominations, appears to be taking the strongest position in regard to the care of the body, inasmuch as "the Mormon faith teaches that the spirit and body are the soul of man. It looks upon the body as a non-evil component of the eternal soul of man. . . ." Bennett, himself a Presbyterian, believes strongly that recreation under religious sponsorship can help the American people improve moral and ethical standards; except for the Mormons, however, he sees few significant signs of encouragement among most Protestant churches.

Still further, organized Christianity has taken the role of sport much more seriously in recent years as well. Another indication of Christianity's new interest in sport has been the establishment and rapid development of the Fellowship of Christian Athletes. This is an organization that "exists to serve Christ and the Church. Its concern is to draw athletes in particular and youth in general into the realm and experience of vital Christian commitment within the Church" (Bennett, 1962).

One further statement made by the late Pope Pius XII (1945) shows the type of support he gave to athletics: ". . . Now, what is primarily the duty and scope of sports, wholesomely and Christianly understood, if not to cultivate the dignity and harmony of the human body, to develop health, strength, agility, and grace?"

CONCLUDING STATEMENT

Thus, it appears that various religious leaders at different stages in the world's history have exerted a variety of influences on health education, physical education, recreation, and sport. It is evident, however, that much more careful study of this question is in order, especially since modern psychology has placed increasing emphasis on indivisibility into mind and matter. The more essentialistic philosophies of education have typically established a hierarchy of values ignoring the importance of a well-rounded education, despite the fact that lip service is regularly paid to the necessity for physical, as well as mental, culture. Interestingly enough, even many pragmatic naturalists and experimentalists do not in practice accord physical education and play what they claim are their rightful places in the education of youth. Yet those of us in this field professionally should not despair; we are making definite progress in so many ways, and scientific evidence is accumulating to such a degree that value systems may in time be changed, or at least altered considerably. It seems reasonable to say that Christianity and Judaism have hampered the fullest development of physical, health, and recreation education, but it is true also that many religious leaders are revamping their earlier positions as they realize the potential of these activities as spiritual forces in our lives.

The Influence of Ecology

The influence of ecology has only been felt in a recognizable and significant way for the past five or ten years by North American society, so it is not unusual that very little attention has been paid to the environmental crisis by those in the field of sport and physical education. Our field cannot be especially criticized for this failing; as a matter of fact, the large majority of people conduct their lives in a manner which quite clearly indicates that they still do not appreciate the gravity of our situation. This topic can also be considered a persistent problem to the field in the same way as the other five social forces of values, politics, nationalism, economics, and religion. Although the problem has not been with us over the centuries in similar fashion, now it seems here to stay. No longer, as it has almost always been possible in the past, can we simply move elsewhere to locate another abundant supply of game to hunt, water to drink, or mineral resources to exploit when natural resources are depleted.

Ecology is usually defined as the field of study that treats the relationships and interactions of human beings and other living organisms with each other and with the natural (or physical) environment in which they reside. Until very recently very few scientists were known as ecologists; they were identified either as biologists or zoologists. Now many of these scientists are being asked to consider our situation (plight?) in relation to the environment in a much broader perspective than that in which an experimental scientist typically functions. The outlook must of necessity become macroscopic rather than microscopic—and very few people are prepared to make this transition in such a relatively short span of time.

For a variety of reasons we can no longer proceed on the assumption that our responsibility is to "multiply and replenish the earth." In the past we have been exhorted to both increase the population and develop an economy to cope with the various demands. Now there are close to 4 billion people on earth, and approximately four babies are being born somewhere in the world every second. It has become starkly obvious to reflective people that strong attitudes favoring population control must be developed, or it is quite possible that some version of the Malthusian law will soon be operative on a massive scale. (Although there are some who disagree with such a statement today, the reader will recall that Malthus theorized in 1798 that the population tends to increase more rapidly than the food supply—a question of geometric progression as opposed to arithmetical progression. This idea still seems valid today, with the only possible checks being war, disease, natural catastrophes, famine, and birth control.)

Moving more directly into the realm of economics, it has been pointed out that the United States—as opposed to Canada, for example —has some extremely difficult choices to make in the next few decades; in fact, a number of these choices may be made because of the severe crises the nation will encounter. Those who look ahead optimistically seem willing to allow a continuous growth economic system, whereas those who will undoubtedly be classified as pessimists argue for a no growth system (Murray, 1972, p. 38). It is imperative for us all to understand that the forecasting models developed by economists and ecologists quite typically differ sharply—that is, the consequences of their recommendations, respectively, are completely different. Certainly all are aware of contradictory economic theories that appear in the daily press, but it is also obvious that very few people, relatively speaking, are aware of the collision course seemingly being taken if the ecologic models have any validity at all.

In an article entitled "The Ecologist at Bay," Grahame Smith explains: "The decline in quality of this planet and the precarious aspect of continued existence of life on Earth are largely the results of this comfortable shell of consumer technology with which each American is surrounded" (1971, p. 69). Thus, ecologists find themselves in a situation in which they comprehend fully the dangerous position in which *some* people on earth—a relatively few million as a matter of fact—are. However, for ecologists to cry out in alarm to the general populace in the favored countries any more vigorously, and to have them truly understand the reality of the precarious approach being followed, is to risk being ridiculed and branded pessimists and doomsayers. Nevertheless, the problem is definitely here, and it cannot be escaped by closing our eyes. As Pogo, the cartoon possum, has stated—and it is a remark we must accept ruefully—"We have met the enemy, and he is us!"

In an effort to consider this problem more carefully and in the process to place it in some perspective for all educators—and specifically those involved with sport and physical education—we will (1) offer a few definitions, (2) present a brief historical background, (3) highlight the problem as it is faced in modern society, (4) analyze it from a particular philosophical perspective with implications for education generally and for sport and physical education specifically, and (5) offer a concluding statement.

DEFINITIONS

As a result of the development of ecology and what has been called "environmental science," many new words and phrases have been added to our vocabulary. Ecology itself is "the science of the mutual relations of organisms with their environment and with one another" (Huxley, 1963, p. 6). Or, to be somewhat more precise, Murray states: "ecologists study competition between individuals and between populations for resources, the growth of populations and the movement of materials (e.g., water and minerals) in ecological systems (eco-systems)" (1972, p. 36). It is not possible or pertinent to define even the most common terms usually employed in this area of study here, but it should be understood that we have polluted the earth—and are doing so now and may continue to do so in the future—in both the biosphere (the zone of life) and in the remainder of the atmosphere. This includes the area from 35,000 feet up to perhaps 600 miles above the eatrh. The biosphere is "that envelope made up of the Earth's waters, land crust, and atmosphere where all organisms, including man, live" (Kunz, 1971, p. 67). An eco-system is "an integrated unit or 'system' in nature, sufficient unto itself, to be studied as a separate entity—e.g., a rotting log in the forest, a coral atoll, a continent, or the Earth will all its biota" (*Ibid.*). Fortunately, many of these common terms are already recognizable, and their continued use in the various communications media should make them part of everyday vocabulary. A few of these terms are as follows: allowable release level, biodegradable, biota, carcinogen, coliform bacteria, compost, decibel, demography, effluent, energy cycle, green revolution, greenhouse effect, herbicide, atmospheric inversion, nonrenewable resource, recycling, smog, sonic boom, symbiosis, thermal pollution.

BRIEF HISTORICAL BACKGROUND

There are now approximately 4 billion people on earth. At the beginning of the Christian era that figure was only 250 million. By the time America was settled by Europeans, the figure had been doubled to about 500 million, in a period of only 1600 years. By 1830 the figure had increased twofold again to 1 billion people in somewhat less than two hundred years. In the next hundred years, the amount doubled again to 2 billion, and now, in about only *fifty* years, the total number of men, women, and chldren on earth is approaching four billion. As Huxley says, "By the year 2000, unless something appalling bad or miraculously good should happen in the interval, six thousand millions of us will be sitting down to breakfast every morning" (1963, p. 2). To make matters worse, it is in the underdeveloped countries that the rate of increase is so much higher than the average. It will presumably not be possible for such nations to move ahead to full industrialization because of the inevitable drain on their resources caused by such rapid growth.

In another realm—that of poor husbandry insofar as land and animal use are concerned—our careless and ignorant abuse of the planet probably goes as far back as 8000 years ago when we first began to farm the land. There are today innumerable archeological sites that were once thriving civilizations. For a variety of reasons, including poor use of land, most of these locations are now dusty and desolate ruins. An example of such an area is North Africa, which was once exploited extensively by the Romans. Here, valuable topsoil was eroded by poor farming techniques, incorrect grazing of livestock, and flagrant abuse of timberland. One can go back to ancient Greece to find another example of once fertile land with an abundant supply of water and forested hills. Now much of the area seems blighted, with rocky hills and barren lowlands denuded of topsoil. Wildlife is almost extinct as well.

Much the same story can be related about Turkey. Early port cities, such as Ephesus and Tarsus, offer no evidence today of their history as trading ports. The Fertile Crescent of biblical times has long since gone, and the "land between the rivers" (the Tigris and the Euphrates) shows almost no evidence of its former luxuriant vegetation. Thus, turn where one will—to areas desolated by fifteenth-century sheepraisers in Spain, to the pre-Columbian American civilization on Monte Alban in Mexico— one is apt to find examples of poor management and land and forest degradation. Obviously, some peoples have managed their resources wisely—The Netherlands (Holland) and Japan, for example—but they are rare exceptions in an otherwise bleak picture. The discussion that follows will describe concisely why the coming century will need to be characterized by a concern never before shown.

THE PROBLEM IN MODERN SOCIETY

What then is the extent of the environmental crisis in modern society? Very simply, we have achieved a certain mastery over the world because of our scientific achievements and technology. We are at the top of the food chain because of our mastery of much of the earth's flora and fauna. Because of the exponential (geometric) explosion of the human population, increasingly greater pressures "will be placed on our lands to provide shelter, food, recreation, and waste disposal areas. This will cause a greater pollution of the atmosphere, the rivers, the lakes, the land, and the oceans" (Mergen, 1970, p. 36).

All this has been explained graphically by the National Geographic Society in a chart entitled "How Man Pollutes His World" (1970). Here the earth is "divided" into air, land, and sea. It is vital to understand that this satellite is self-sustaining; is possessed of only a finite quantity of oxygen, water, and land; and it has no means of reconstituting itself with further natural recources once the present supply is exhausted. This means that we must give immediate attention to the effect of supersonic jet aircraft on the atmosphere at various levels; to what increasing urbanization will mean insofar as strain on the physical environment is concerned; to how significant the stripping of vegetation is to the earth's soil supply and to its ability to produce oxygen; to how dangerous the effects of mercury waste, harmful pesticides, chemical fertilizers, and trash and sewage disposal are to the natural environment; and to what the oil spills and dumping at sea will mean to the earth's great bodies of water and their ability to sustain fish, bird, and bottom life. We need to ask ourselves questions about the extent to which nature's self-renewing cycles are being disturbed. To repeat a point made earlier, what sort of a world will the more than 6 billion people of the year 2000 inherit?

In the United States alone, many rivers, lakes, and streams are being used as sewers; the air in some cities is so polluted that one might as well be smoking a pack or so of cigarettes daily; New York City alone is estimated to have as many rats as it has people (more than 8 million); 3.5 billion tons of garbage are produced each year; more than four-fifths of the original forests have been converted for other purposes, as have 280 million acres of crop and range land; at least 3000 acres a day are covered with concrete and other substances. And, of course, many other nations in the world are following the same path. Further, if all this sounds a bit melodramatic, as these words are being written there are stories in the press explaining how "a global network of international agricultural research centers, none of them more than twenty years old, is facing an 'explosion' of demands from individual nations for help in increasing food production to meet rapid increases in population" (*The New York Times*, 1975, p. 20). And still further, "air pollution plagued several large and populous areas along the Eastern seaboard today, causing serious potential hazards for people with respiratory or other health problems and at least some discomfort for countless others" (*Ibid.*, p. 37).

This diatribe could be continued, but hopefully the point has been made. Certainly the gravity of prevailing patterns is recognized by many, but such recognition must become knowledge to a great many more people who are in a position to take positive action in the immediate future. Interestingly enough, "a group of Protestant theologians asserted . . . that Christianity had played its part in provoking the current environmental crisis and that any solution to it would require major modification of current social and religious values" (*The New York Times*, 1970). At a conference whose theme was the theology of survival, it was stressed that typical Christian attitudes toward nature "had given sanction to exploitation of the environment by science and technology and thus contributed to air and water pollution, overpopulation, and other ecological threats"(*Ibid.*). The participants agreed that the desirable changes would have to be brought about by local, regional, national, and international political action, but such improvements would never be realized without radical alterations in our fundamental attitudes (values) toward nature. All these thoughts and ideas are encouraging, of course, and one can only hope that positive, concerted action will be forthcoming. However, when an ecologist decries the "fragmented approach that we tend to take in seeking solutions" (Smith, 1971, p. 69), and when noted scientists like Paul Ehrlich assert that the President's Council on Environmental Quality is "dodging the crisis" through its inability to make available the best scientific advice to the president (Ehrlich and Holdren, 1970, p. 73), one cannot be criticized for shaking one's head somberly.

PHILOSOPHICAL ANALYSIS

How does one approach a question such as the influence of ecology or the environmental crisis philosophically? Presumably no one philosophical position or stance would actually include any tenets designed to bring about an end to life on earth as it has been known. Of course, some particularistic approaches might be so despairing and pessimistic about the future that the inevitability of our consciously or unconsciously destroying ourselves is a distinct possibility.

In an interesting article, however, Holmes Rolston has asked what to many might seem like a contradictory question—"Is there an ecological ethic?" (Rolston, 1975, pp. 93–109). He inquires whether an environmental ethic—the values that we hold about our environment—is based simply on a specific ethical approach (within a philosophical position) or whether there is actually a built-in naturalistic ethic in the universe. Commencing from the position that the dividing line between science and ethics is definite if one but accepts the philosophical categories of descriptive law and prescriptive law as being separate and distinct, Rolston explains that descriptive law, presented in the indicative mood, is employed in science and history. Prescriptive law, on the other hand, is used in ethics, and the imperative mood is involved implicitly or explicitly. Thus, in moral philosophy the quickest way to be accused of committing a naturalistic fallacy is to blithely assume an "ought" from an "is"—at least in the eyes of philosophers with a scientific orientation. Transposed to the discussion of ecological ethics, environmental science should tell us what we think we know through observation, experimentation, and generalization about the environment. Environmental ethics, on the other hand, means presumably that we have applied one or another set of ethical values to our understanding of and relationship to the environment.

Those who argue for ecological morality have differences in opinion that divide them into two groups: (1) those who equate homeostasis with morality, and (2) those who appear to go even further by arguing that there is "a moral ought inherent in recognition of the holistic character of the ecosystem" that results in an ecological ethic (Rolston, 1975, p. 94). In treating the first group, Rolston seeks a "moral translation" from the paramount law in ecological theory—that of homeostasis (a closed planetary ecosystem, recycling transformations, energy balance). Paul Sears is quoted to the effect that "probably men will always differ as to what constitutes the good life. They need not differ as to what is necessary for the long survival of man on earth. . . . As living beings we must come to terms with the environment about us, learning to get along with the liberal budget at our disposal . . . we must seek to attain what I have called a steady state" (Sears, 1969, p. 401).

Here the argument appears to be as follows: if you wish to preserve human life—and you ought to want to do so—the ecological law (that the life-supporting ecosystem must recycle or all will perish) indicates that technically you ought not to disturb the ecosystem's capability to recycle itself—and according to moral law (which equals natural law) you ought to assist such recycling wherever possible. With this approach, values are not strictly inherent in the makeup of the world; they are ascribed to it by us attempting to employ careful husbandry with what we have assumed to be our possession (the earth). Rolston argues that we can call the balance of nature (and the ends which we seek that are presumably compatible with an ecosystemic balance) "ultimate values if we wish, but the ultimacy is instrumental, not intrinsic" (Rolston, 1975, p. 98).

The other major claim referred to above allows one to use the term ecological ethic without quotation marks, because the assumption is that "morality is a derivative of the holistic character of the ecosystem"

(p. 98). Rolston recognizes that this is a radical idea which will not receive ready acceptance. It endows nature and its integral ecosystem with value. This is obviously a proposal for the broadening of the concept of value—nature in and of itself would have value whether anyone was here to appreciate it and employ it or not. The leap is made from "is" to "ought" because "the values seem to be there as the facts are fully in" (p. 101).

Because of past philosophical and religious speculation, not to mention the so-called philosophy of science, it is extremely difficult to find a logical place for a primary ecological ethic in which the long-standing classical ought "has been transformed, stretched, coextensively with an ecosystemic ought" (p. 104). Are intelligent human beings ready to agree that "egoism should be transformed into ecoism" (p. 104)? Thus, the self would be identified with Nature as one of its components, as part of the ecosystem. It would not be human beings *and* nature; it would be human beings *in* nature with such a transformation of outlook. Then we would have a much stronger obligation to preserve nature's balance, because we are truly a part of the world—and the world is a part of our bodies.

With such an outlook, we would create what might be called the ecological person, and such a person might be able to postulate an authentic naturalistic ethic:

> Man, an insider, is not spared environmental pressures, yet in the full ecosystemic context, his integrity is supported by and rises from transaction with his world and therefore requires a corresponding dignity in his world partner. Of late, the world has ceased to threaten, save as we violate it. How starkly this gainsays the alienation that characterizes modern literature, seeing nature as basically rudderless, antipathetical, in need of monitoring and repair. More typically modern man, for all his technological prowess, has found himself distanced from nature, increasingly competent and decreasingly confident, at once distinguished and aggrandized, yet afloat on and adrift in an indifferent, if not a hostile universe. His world is at best a huge filling station, at worst a prison or "nothingness." Not so for ecological man; confronting his world with deference to a community of value in which he shares, he is at home again. (Rolston, 1975, pp. 107–108)

IMPLICATIONS FOR EDUCATION

Even though the difficulty of moving from an "is" to an "ought" has been recognized in the realm of science and ethics, there are quite obviously many scientific findings classified as environmental science that should be made available to people of all ages whether they are enrolled in educational institutions or are part of the everyday world. Simply making the facts available will, of course, not be any guarantee that strong and positive attitudes will develop on the subject. It is a well-established fact, however, that the passing of legislation in difficult and sensitive areas must take place through responsible political leadership, and that attitude changes often follow behind—albeit at what may seem to be a snail's pace. The field of education must play a vital role in the development of what might be called an "ecological awareness." This is much broader than what was called the conservation movement within forestry and closely related fields that was bent on the preservation of this or that feature of nature. Now ecology (or environmental science) places all these individual entities in a total context in which the interrelationship of all parts must be thoroughly understood.

Sound educational planning should take place at all levels, from early childhood education through the free tuition courses now being offered to many older citizens by certain universities. As Mergen states, "The knowledge that has been accumulated is vast, and ecological principles should be made part of the educational menu for economics, city planners, architects, engineers, the medical profession, the legal profession, religious groups, and all people concerned with the public and private management of natural resources, as well as politicians and governmental employees" (1970, p. 37). Obviously, those concerned professionally with physical education and sport, health and safety education, and recreation and park administration from the standpoint of professional education have an equally important stake in this total educational process. As a matter of fact, these three professions are more concerned than most with us *and* with our relationship to the total environment, whether natural or artificial.

Presumably the usual struggle will take place among those who will want to introduce a new subject into the curriculum, those who will demand that environmental science be taught incidentally as part of existing subjects within the educational program, and those who will see no need for the study of environmental interrelationships to be in the basic curriculum. Further, some will want the subject matter taught as facts and knowledge in a subject-centered curriculum based on a logical progression from the simple to the complex, whereas others will stress that interest on the part of the learner should dictate if and how the subject should be introduced, because this is the way people learn best. The urgency of the ecological crisis would seem to warrant an approach that veers neither to the right or left of center. The point would seem to be that a literally devastating problem is upon us, and that we should move ahead rapidly to see that some of the basics of environmental science are made available to all. These issues have been with us for so many centuries that they will not be solved tomorrow no matter how the crisis is resolved—or how we *attempt* to resolve it.

It is difficult to state that certain information and attitudes should be taught to the population of a pluralistic society—and then to look forward confidently to the effective execution of such a pronouncement throughout the land. This is simply not the way things happen in countries like the United States and Canada, for example, where educational autonomy prevails in the individual states and provinces. All that can be hoped is that knowledge about the several positions regarding economic growth will be made available fairly to the people as a controversial issue. What should be made known is that certain ecological and economic theories and recommendations are diametrically opposed and that which should be followed and how far is something the people must soon decide.

B. G. Murray, an ecologist, makes it quite clear that citizens of the United States are definitely being placed in a position where a decision will have to be made between a continuous growth economic policy or a no growth one (1972, p. 38). Immediately it is apparent that most citizens are not even aware that some scholars are recommending such a thing as a no growth policy. Is this not the land of capitalism and democracy, where a steadily increasing gross national product is a certain indicator of economic prosperity? One wonders whether it is a case of the optimists saying, "full speed ahead, if we ever hope to reduce poverty in the United States," and the pessimists responding with the idea that "population and economic growth must certainly strive for steady-state by the next century (if that is not too late)." Whoever heard of such nonsense as a steady-state situation? This is the most difficult task educators face as they attempt to explain and carry forward the various forecasting models developed by scholars in both the natural and the social sciences.

In a comparison of conflicting ecological and economic models, Murray examines the concepts of growth, movement of materials, and competition. In regard to growth, he explains that all types of biological growth follow a characteristic pattern that in time reaches a steady state or equilibrium in which as many organisms are dying as are being born into the system. In United States business, however, the high standard of material living has been reached by continuously increasing GNP to meet the needs and demands of a continuously increasing population. Question: How long can this growth curve be maintained—and at what cost to all (including the rest of the world)? It is explained further by Murray that continuous growth curves are not unknown in biological and physical systems (p. 38). However, the result is usually disaster—death of the host organism as when uncontrolled cell growth takes place in cancer, or even when the chain reaction of fissioning uranium-235 nuclei results in the inefficient use of energy in nuclear explosions (p. 39). The rule of the ecologist here implies that a system will eventually collapse unless it stops growing at some point and *recycles*.

The second concept discussed is the movement of materials, and here reference is being made to the biogeochemical cycles operative within nature—"the movement within ecosystems of minerals, water, oxygen, carbon dioxide, and other nutrients essential for life" (p. 39). One example of this process, of course, is that which carbon dioxide follows on its cyclic path between the earth's atmosphere and the many organisms that inhabit this planet. Interestingly enough, the recycling that takes place is not completely efficient, with the result that the process known as "succession" results in a somewhat different makeup based on the ecosystem's chemical composition. The serious difficulty created by human beings is that both food requirements and the demands of technological progress are simply not recycled in such a way as to sustain even a steady-state situation indefinitely. In other words, the movement of materials is all in one direction—for the temporary service of an expanding population that is increasing in number exponentially.

Third, and last, the other fundamental rule of ecology is discussed: Sooner or later competition excludes some of the competing species. Practically this means that, if two organisms are competing for an exhaustible resource (and which one isn't in a closed system?), one of the competitors will be dispensed with by its rival "either by being forced out of the ecosystem or by being forced to use some other resource" (p. 64). Thus, there exists a basic contradiction between the economic theory that competition is supposed to maintain diversity and stability of systems, and the theory based on the ecological model described above.

By now it should be readily apparent that this issue of conflicting models and resultant theories should have an overriding priority for inclusion somewhere, somehow, and very soon in the educational system. We need to know what all this means for such cherished concepts as increasing growth, competition, capitalism, and advancing technological revolution. The merging of tenable principles of environmental science with altered values and norms into acceptable and highly desirable educational theory and practice is an immediate challenge for all educators in programs that have either a disciplinary or professional education orientation.

IMPLICATIONS FOR PHYSICAL EDUCATION AND SPORT

If the field of education has a definite responsibility and strong obligation to present the various issues revolving about what has rapidly become a persistent problem (or social force) in North American society (and especially in the United States), this duty obviously includes the teaching professionals at all educational levels who are specialists in all the subject matter areas taught in the curriculum. The primary concern in this context is, of course, with those who teach in physical education and sport (and/or some combination of health and safety education and recreation and park administration). (The reader will appreciate immediately that these three fields are now designated as *allied* professions, even though many physical educators and coaches get involved with certain duties that often are carried out by the professional practitioners in one or both of the other two allied fields. The same can be said, of course, for personnel functioning in each of the two allied fields.)

Physical educators and sport coaches, like those practicing in the other two allied professional fields, quite naturally have a certain general education responsibility to all participants in classes or community recreation programs. Thus, they are directly concerned with our relationship with ourselves, our fellow human beings, other living organisms, and the physical environment. Responsible citizens and educators will have an understanding of worldwide population growth and what problems such growth will present. Granted that there are conflicting views on this matter, students should at least be able to expect that instructors will have a reasoned position about this controversial issue. The physical educator and coach should also understand how continuous growth economic theories contradict basic ecological theory. There can be no argument about the fact that both population growth *and* advancing technology—the latter with the capability to improve the material living standard of all to the extent possible—seem to be leading earth's population to a position at which some fundamental changes in attitudes and practices will probably *necessarily* result (or *ought* to change, at any rate). Although attitudes toward improved international relations have waxed and waned over the decades, the responsible physical educator and coach will realize that the quality of life cannot be steadily improved in *some* countries on earth without due consideration being given to improving the conditions of *all* people everywhere. Finally, the informed citizen and educator will be aware of the urgent need to take care of the manifold ecosystems on this "closed" planet and will do all in his or her power to assist with the necessary recycling so that a "reconstituted" earth will be transmitted to future generations.

Now we must consider whether there are any *specific* implications for physical educators and coaches as they face their own professional task. As matters stand now, they are confronted daily with the fact that for a variety of reasons modern, urbanized, technologically advanced life in North America has created a population with a very low level of *physical* fitness, with a resultant decrease in overall *total* fitness. What makes matters so extremely difficult is that the large majority of the population has been lulled into a false sense of complacency by what Herbert Spencer over a century ago called a "seared physical conscience" that is unable to "monitor" the body properly and accurately (1949, p. 197). As a result of this presumed sense of complacency, there is an unwillingness to lead a life that may be characterized as "physically vigorous." What we have created, therefore, is a ridiculous situation in which people on this continent are to a large extent overfed and poorly exercised, whereas a multitude of people on many other continents are underfed and often quite strenuously exercised! All of this adds up to a world situation that may well bring disaster to us all before the twenty-first century.

Although many professions will undoubtedly be focusing in on this dilemma soon, it is the profession of physical education and sport that is *uniquely* responsible for the exercise programs that will enable men and women "to be rugged animal[s] fit to withstand the excessive wear and tear that life's informal and formal activities may demand" (Zeigler, 1964, p. 55). Additionally, it is this same physical educator who gets involved with health education courses in which nutritional practices and habits are discussed. As Spencer indicated, "generally, we think, the history of the world shows that the well-fed races have been the energetic and dominant races." He explained further that animals can work harder when they are fed more nutritiously. The point he wishes to make is that a sound diet is necessary for both energy and growth (1949, p. 191). What this adds up to is that the physical educator/coach is also in a situation in which he or she teaches about nutrition at least indirectly in daily practice—and quite often directly in classroom situations. Thus, he or she can to some extent advise students about the correct food to eat for a physically vigorous life, as well as which amounts of what food will ensure adequate nutrition to maintain normal health—not to mention advice about how to keep from being overweight or underweight.

A vigorous exercise program and correct nutritional instruction relate quite directly to two aspects of the ecological crisis discussed earlier —that is, the pollution of the earth and its atmosphere, and adequate nutrition for the children born on this earth. Without getting involved in the moral question of birth control, physical educators and coaches should do all in their power to curtail pollution because it will in a short time—and in a variety of ways—make it increasingly difficult for us to exercise vigorously and to maintain physical fitness. When the air we breathe and the water we drink become increasingly impure, how then will we maintain the fitness of all?

Second, there is the matter of adequate nutrition for the rapidly increasing population in the countries least able to feed their offspring. Although some may believe that the Malthusian principle should be allowed to take effect and that the favored nations should take care of their own needs, it would seem more humane to keep the world's hungry people as adequately supplied with staples as possible. But at the same time we in physical education should redouble our efforts to make certain that young people learn correct eating habits to guarantee relatively lean and fat-free bodies that are capable of vigorous exercise to ensure physical fitness. There is so much food wasted on this continent that our moral sense should be affronted. For example, how many people could be kept alive with our garbage? Or to view the question in another way, is it quite so necessary that millions upon millions of dogs and cats be sustained when human beings are dying of malnutrition?

In addition, people at all stages of life show evidence of a variety of remediable physical defects, but there is typically an unwillingness on the part of the public to make exercise therapy programs readily available through both public and private agencies. Many physiotherapy programs are available briefly after operations or accidents. Such assistance is typically helpful and fills an important need. But our concern here is with the unavailability of exercise therapy programs in the schools and certain private agencies under the supervision of qualified physical educators after a physician prescribes exercise.

Keeping in mind the ecological principle that "competition kills competitors," it would appear to be the direct responsibility of physical educators and coaches to involve *all* young people in a vigorous program of physical activity—human movement in sport, dance, and exercise— that can be characterized as interesting, joyful, and exuberant. In this way it is quite possible that interest will be maintained throughout life. The society could then be characterized as a nation of fit people able to meet the necessary first condition for the maintenance of independence and prosperity, *physical* fitness within a concept of *total* fitness (Spencer, 1949, p. 177). (In the process we should presumably direct young people away from such "sporting" activities as the use of snowmobiles and speedboats and auto racing, which pollute the environment, tend to destroy the ecosystemic balance, and provide a mechanical means for propelling the body from one point to another.)

Physical education and sport can play an important role in the social and psychological development of the individual. As important as the element of competition may have been in the past—and may continue to be in the future—it is now time to place at least equal emphasis on the benefits to be derived from *cooperation* in the various aspects of sport competition. Most certainly the future of life on this planet will present all sorts of opportunities for cooperative effort both at home and abroad. A wholesome balance between competition and cooperation in a child's education can develop highly desirable personality traits, while at the same time offering numerous occasions for the release of the overly aggressive tendencies seemingly present in so many individuals.

As indicated earlier, those teaching physical education and sport skills often get involved directly or indirectly with health and safety education and/or recreation education. These instructors have some contact with practically every student in the school. Thus, they have great potential for conveying knowledge and assisting in the formation of correct attitudes about all three allied fields through effective teaching. Additionally, the physical educator/coach can set an example personally for all young people to follow. For example, the area of health and safety education provides innumerable ways to demonstrate safety practices; personal hygiene; and attitudes (and practice) toward the use of alcohol, tobacco, marijuana, and what presumably are the more harmful drugs. Wholesome attitudes and practice in the area of sex and sex education are also extremely important—the whole area of family life education, for that matter, should be taught well both by precept and practice.

Similarly, the area of recreation education offers many opportunities for education in ways that will promote improved ecological understanding. In the first place, a change in leisure values—at least as they have now been established—should take place. Through recreation education it should be possible to promote an understanding of and respect for the world's flora and fauna, not to mention the whole concept of ecosystemic balance. Even though our so-called post-industrial society is not reducing working hours at the rate predicted earlier and many in leadership roles are putting in even longer hours, there is still an urgent need to promote the concept of creative leisure. We need a return to what used to be considered the simple recreational pleasures— perhaps with a few variations to satisfy the young. The physical educator/coach should promote the concept of physical recreation for all, of course, but by precept and example the idea of the young person getting involved with esthetic and creative activities and hobbies (involving learning recreational interests) should be fostered as well.

CONCLUDING STATEMENT

The influence of ecology is now such that it must be included as a persistent problem along with the other social forces of values, politics, nationalism, economics, and religion. Although there is a dividing line between science and ethics, perhaps morality should now be viewed as being derived from the fundamental, all-encompassing nature of the ecosystem. This plea for the broadening of the concept of value—perhaps a truly naturalistic ethic—would have both direct and indirect implications for education, which could play an important role in the development of an "ecological awareness." The physical educator/coach, and those in the allied professions, has a unique role to play in helping individuals to develop and maintain *physical* fitness within a concept of *total* fitness based on a goal of international understanding and brotherhood.

PROFESSIONAL CONCERNS III

Whereas the earlier problems presented can be classified as social forces influencing the whole field of education, those included in this chapter have a much greater professional orientation. Of course, these problems have also been influenced by social forces.

Curriculum

Any educational curriculum has been, and is continually, influenced by a variety of political, economic, philosophical, religious, scientific, and technological factors. In curriculum instruction, therefore, a primary task is to determine which subjects should be included because of their *recurring* interest among educators and people. Today, as always, decisions must be made as to how a curriculum is selected. Shall its construction be based on the philosophy of state and its function; on the demands of nationalism; on whether it will help the individual to make a better living; on whether it will help him or her to stay alive and healthy; on the need for reduction of tension in a troubled world; on human nature; or according to the way in which an individual learns best Or is there perhaps a predetermined set of values that dictates educational aims? We must ask ourselves further whether the educator's task is to transmit the cultural heritage; to help youth develop skills for problem solving; or to provide a miniature society in which students may enjoy living at its best so that they will have an example to follow after their school days are over. If we view the curriculum as a means of disciplining the mind, we will tend to stress certain time-proven subjects. If, on the other hand, we want to help youth develop a number of habit patterns that will be effective in their social environment, certain other subject matter areas or experiences will be included. The curriculum has developed and expanded at a fantastic rate on this continent over the past two centuries, and many people insist that this trend must be reversed so that the "essential" subjects can be taught adequately.

HISTORICAL BACKGROUND

A brief history of physical education and sport is included at this point to lay the groundwork for the subsequent philosophical analysis of the various persistent problems (for example, curriculum, use of leisure) that will be presented. (For a more detailed historical treatment, see the volume on the history of physical education and sport in this series.

Physical Culture in Early Societies

Primitive and Preliterate Society. In primitive society there appears to have been very little organized, purposive instruction in physical education; education was usually incidental, a by-product of daily experience. The daily activities of labor, searching for food, dancing, and games were essential to the development of superior bodies—and thus to survival. In addition to promoting physical efficiency, these activities helped strengthen membership in the society and served as a means of recreation.

Egypt. Physical education in early Egypt was not part of any formal educational system; rather, it was simply instrumental in completing daily work activities. The development of certain social institutions had influenced the types of physical activity engaged in by people of different social classes, either through direction or by choice. The upper class received educational advantages not available to others. Sports and dancing were popular with the nobility, but such opportunities were limited even for them except during times of religious observances or when the inundation of the Nile took place.

The masses in Egypt had to master a variety of physical skills to earn their livelihood. These were acquired through varying types of apprenticeship, such as weaving or nail-making. When the Nile flooded, even the masses got relief from life's typical heavy labor and could take part in leisure activities. As was often the case throughout history, fishing, hunting, and fowling were engaged in for pleasure by some and as business by many. Furthermore, pictorial evidence of all sorts of games abounds, especially the kind played by children and youth.

When the army became a distinct class of society, men acquired physical skills that prepared them to do battle. There were all sorts of military exercises and maneuvers that would prepare young men to use a bow, to wield a battle ax, and to hurl a lance. Wrestling was a most popular activity, and many evidently acquired a fairly high degree of skill. Swimming became a common skill as well. Some persons became so proficient that they can be designated as professionals—the soldier, of course, but also dancers, acrobats, wrestlers, and bullfighters. It can also be assumed that many people engaged in sports for the sheer pleasure it gave them. This tends to correct an earlier impression, probably accepted erroneously from the really sport-conscious Greeks, that the Egyptians were actually not concerned with such pursuits to any extent at all.

Babylon and Assyria. These cultures were quite similar to that of Egypt in their development of social institutions. Thus, the physical activity available was usually appropriate to the station of the individual concerned. Workmen taught their trades to their sons. Women did the household work, and their daughters learned how to fulfill the same function through informal apprenticeship. Not much information is available about sports and recreational activities for the lower classes, although there must have been occasional opportunities for dancing, music, informal games, and rudimentary hunting and fishing. We do know, for example, that fishing was usually a regulated business· rather than an idle pastime.

One chief business was the fighting of wars, and this meant that soldiers received a great deal of physical training along these lines. The infantry was usually composed of soldiers from the lower classes; the charioteers and horsemen possessed greater social status. Archers were said to have come from the mountainous areas.

The Early Hebrews. For the early Hebrews there was again really no organized physical training and sport; physical culture was demanded primarily for the purpose of military defense. Certain health safeguards, for example, dietary regulations and the promotion of cleanliness, were looked upon as religious obligations. Wholesome activities were promoted especially on the Sabbath—"a time for recreation of mind and body; but idleness was condemned" (Woody, 1949, p. 106).

China. In the ancient Chinese civilization, formal physical education had little if any place. The major aim was to preserve and perpetuate the existing social order—an order that could only be classified as nonprogressive. Even the military motive, present in the other early cultures, was nonexistent here. As a type of classical civilization evolved and various religious influences were felt, even less emphasis was placed on physical development. Health standards were poor indeed. In later Chinese history, soldiers received military training. Judging by the nature of the combat, this was definitely rigorous.

With all the emphasis on academic excellence, there appears to have been little understanding of the possibility of using physical recreation to relieve intellectual strain. In the early times it is true, however, that sons in upper-class families did have an opportunity to learn dancing, and then later on, as young men, they received instruction in archery and charioteering. At the beginning of the third millennium, an early emperor, Fu Hi, evidently encouraged his subjects to hunt and fish and saw to it that they received instruction.

India. Although India has been known as the "sickest nation in the world," and although the climate and the religious philosophy forced a certain rejection of physical activity, there does appear to be evidence that the matter of individual and communal health received considerable attention in ancient times. Hygienic rules and ritualistic dances in accordance with religious beliefs were common among the Hindus. Archeological finds point out that many sports and amusements were part of the early life, and the early Vedic hymns praised such attributes as strength, health, and bravery. There is no doubt that soldiers, farmers, and artisans engaged in strenuous physical activity as part of their occupations, and there is continued mention of the importance of proper diet. The primitive Aryan conquerors, on the other hand, were not concerned about the health and physical training of the populace.

Much later, Buddha himself is said to have neglected "manly exercises"; his prohibitions against exercises and games indicate that people typically took part in all sorts of games, tumbling, wrestling, boxing, swordsmanship, and riding. The unique Indian practice of yoga has continued from ancient times down to the present day and involves systematic exercises in posture, stretching, and breathing—an interrelationship of mind and body in which fifteen "postures" are still commonly accepted today.

Still further, the horse, the war chariot, archery, wrestling, and a chivalrous code of conduct are referred to on numerous occasions in early Vedic and later literature. Later a more distinct warrior class was established, of which there were six subdivisions under one governing body. One army, for example, was said to have numbered as high as 400,000, and was composed of admiralty, transport, infantry, cavalry, war chariots, and elephants.

Iran. The Persians developed an admirable educational tradition in keeping, of course, with the mores and customs of the time. Moral training in obedience and truthfulness was inculcated by the wise men of the society. However, this education, provided only for the children of upper-class families, totally neglected literary and general intellectual attainment.

The three major classes in Persian society were priests, soldiers, and tradesmen. The latter received a type of physical training through apprenticeship in farming, trade, and mechanics. The soldiers, of course, received careful and thorough training at arms. According to Herodotus, boys had to know the fundamentals of horsemanship and archery, and throwing the javelin was also an essential skill in this militaristic society.

Other elements of training that assumed significant importance were hunting (from prehistoric times of great value in all early societies), wrestling and hand-to-hand combat, the events of the Pentathlon, and polo (or chugan, as it was called).

Crete.   In this island culture hunting with the bow and arrow seems to have been prominent and very popular. Bull-grappling was also a well-developed art or profession, in which women and men engaged while performing fantastic gymnastic maneuvers. Wrestling and boxing are depicted on artifacts, as are various types of gladiatorial contests. There appears also to have been a religious quality to some sports like that which was attached to music and dancing. The fact that the Cretans were surrounded by water means that they had to learn to swim, and some remains show evidence of the breaststroke and an overhand side-stroke with a type of flutter kick. There is disagreement as to whether Cretans took part in or were influenced by Greece's great athletic festivals. As yet, however, there is no evidence that organized training in sport existed.

Greece.   There is universal recognition of the fact that physical education was highly valued in ancient Greek society. From 1100 to 700 B.C., the Homeric Age, athletic sports held a prominent place in the culture. As a society of individualists, the Greeks sought to develop physical and intellectual excellence in their citizens—to produce a man of action.

The goal of Spartan society was the development of devoted citizens and fine soldiers. Obviously, physical training was the chief educational tool. Young Spartans' training was exactly what one might expect—a strict regimen, firm discipline, and strenuous activity, all designed eventually to produce a hardy, courageous young man. When the exercise program was in session, everyone was expected to be active at all times.

It is noteworthy that specialization in competitive athletics was not encouraged. This was especially true if it tended to interfere with the primary goal of turning out hardened, seasoned warriors. However, games and exercises that would contribute to the basic goal, such as wrestling, boxing, archery, hunting, riding, and other similar activities, were not lacking. Running, especially the race with full armor, had an important place in the training regimen. It was in these activities that the Spartans excelled at the Olympian games on numerous occasions.

Harmonious development of body, mind, and spirit was of paramount concern to Athenians, the first time in recorded history that physical education was valued so highly in the development of the ideal man. Although we tend to forget that these opportunities were available only to freemen, we still remain astounded by the degree to which Athenian society did succeed in producing the "all-around" citizen.

The physical education of boys took place in a palaestra, an institution for wrestling and gymnastic activities, which was typically private and probably frequented by the sons of well-to-do families in the afternoons. It is possible that some sort of a rotational scheme was devised to keep the facilities in use during the daylight hours. These structures, supervised by trainers called paidotribes, were more or less elaborate, depending on the economic status of the particular community in which they were built. The boys were divided into age groups and received training in exercise, games, diet, posture, combative sports, and track and field events. There is evidence that swimming and dancing, at least for some, were integral parts of the curriculum.

After the period at the palaestra, probably concluding with the fifteenth year, the sons of the wealthier families received competitive athletic instruction in the various public gymnasia. Since these were public facilities, however, it is quite likely that the more gifted warranted special attention despite their financial status. Training in warfare skills, and dancing for those involved in the chorus and other religious festivals, was stressed. A point of interest is that the paidotribe may be compared to today's general physical educator, while the gymnast, often a specialist. may be likened to our coach, a man who becomes proficient in the development of a boy or young man in a specific sport or gymnastic activity. The director of the gymnasium, known as a gymnasiarch, was usually a man of wealth performing a public service. It was his responsibility to supervise and to train athletes for special festivals, and he also directed the work of the various lesser officials and maintenance men of the gymnasium.

When training at the Ephebic College was added, a training that appears to have been informal in nature before it received official status in the fourth century, it was instituted for young men between the ages of eighteen and twenty. It appears that this training became compulsory and state-organized only after the defeat at Chaeronaea by the Macedonians in 338 B.C. The society could no longer allow itself the luxury of a militia characterized by individual freedom; instead its young citizens had to prepare to staff the patrolling units and the fortresses. The young men learned how to fight in battle armor and how to employ the spear, javelin, bow, and catapult. Undoubtedly, such activities as running, boxing, wrestling, swimming, horse riding, chariot driving, and various types of forced marches were included in the training regimen. It has been argued that the Macedonians were professional soldiers, and the Greeks soon learned that their amateur soldiers could no longer compete on even terms. This must have been a painful period for the Athenians—a period in which they learned the hard way that their idealistic educational aim had to be subverted in the face of an impending encounter with highly trained opponents supported by improved technology of warfare.

The Greeks recognized sports and games for many reasons. From a realistic standpoint, they knew that these activities served a utilitarian purpose—preparation for the very important business of war. In addition, there is evidence that they understood full well that strenuous training developed strength, power, and endurance. They realized also that it was possible to stave off some of the effects of growing old by continuing to "play the game." Thus, the relationship between physical culture and vigorous health was apparent to them. Furthermore, the men of letters and those with creative artistic talents praised the realization of many of the innate drives that led persons to aspire to noble words and deeds. And the various sociological and physical factors of the culture and geography combined to produce a vigorous, active life. Mortals envisioned the gods they created as possessing these desired traits to the highest degree; so they tried to imitate their gods, and they praised them through the medium of athletic contests and festivals while simultaneously honoring their own dead. All types of festivals developed, which included a wide range of religious, artistic, and sporting activities. The Great Panathenaea games, for instance, celebrated the earlier unification of Attica under the city-state of Athens and were held for an eighty-day period every four years. The legendary Olympic Games, the most famous of the Panhellenic festivals, were presumably first held in 776 B.C. at Olympia, a sacred spot in Ellis on the River Alpheus.

The great importance of the games and festivals in Greek life, the early amateur ideal, the gradual change in the character of the events through professional influence, and the eventual excesses of the worst type are quite well known to most readers and cannot be discussed at length here. That the changing political scene exercised a direct effect on the character of the games appears to be self-evident, a point that cannot be overemphasized. The national games of Greece served the people's religious needs; they helped the Greeks realize their kinship with one another; they aided them in the pursuit of excellence; and they provided these fascinating ancients with release, fun, and excitement.

Rome.   There is evidence that children in the early Roman culture had all sorts of games to play and that these games were employed to serve ends other than play as the children grew older. Although the well-known *mens sana in corpore sano* is Latin, it does not express the Roman ideal—to prepare a citizen to bear arms for his nation, not to promote a harmonious development of spirit, mind, and body (as had been the case in Athens). The same basically natural activities were employed in this society as in all the others described previously—they ran, jumped, hunted, boxed, wrestled, rode horseback, and learned to use the tools of war. Both boys and girls learned to swim, but dancing and music had little if any place, except occasionally in religious and public celebrations, such as triumphs of war. Competitive sports were limited largely to games that prepared for war. It is true that the circus games were early introduced into Roman life, but they were never carried to an excess— even broadly speaking—until the later days of the republic.

A vigorous life was encouraged by the hard work on the farms and the subsequent military training. The Romans were most certainly warlike, strong, aggressive, courageous, durable, and well disciplined; and their ability as warriors increased as they learned from experience. Although the Romans did adopt much from the Hellenic culture, they never seemed to capture the spirit of the Greek athletic contests. One obvious reason for this is that the glory of the earlier athletic festivals had undoubtedly degenerated by the time the Romans conquered Greece, and the practical-minded victors couldn't envision any benefit to be derived from such activities. When they became "city folk," however, toward the end of the republic, palaestras and gymnasia appeared in increasing number. The gradually increasing importance of such facilities may be noted thereafter throughout the days of the empire.

Subsequently, Roman emperors built magnificent public baths and provided all sorts of extravagent games and entertainment to gain the approval of the populace. But, despite these developments, intellectual leaders took every opportunity to mock and repudiate the Greek system of active participation in gymnastics, music, and dancing. The Romans understood that man should be restless and active and that such activity contributed to the individual's health and strength; in fact, Cicero, Sallust, and Quintilian all stressed the utility of physical exercise. They were simply unwilling to grant it a respectable status in Roman education and may well have equated it with the degeneracy they saw taking place. Seneca indeed strikes a harsh blow at physical education; his advice was to exercise rapidly, get tired, and return to the more important aspects of life.

Many historians do affirm, however, that the Romans were strongly interested in recreation and play. This was probably more true before their wealth increased, when individual freedom was at its height and the military demands of the empire nonexistent. It could be argued, of course, that the urge to play is an innate need for re-*creation* and refreshment present in all men. In any case, the Romans enjoyed various games, both of an active and a sedentary nature. Gambling was extremely popular, especially with the wealthy classes, and there were all sorts of games similar to chess and checkers. Ball games were played by all classes, but, strangely enough, the idea of striking a ball with a stick or racket does not seem to have gained acceptance to any considerable extent. They did have a number of differently sized balls and admired ambidextrous performers. Swimming and boating were popular recreations and often served a utilitarian purpose as well. Hunting and fishing were work for some and play for others—a distinction previously noted in other early societies.

The relationship of exercise to health was recognized by the Romans and should be discussed briefly here. Rome's geography seems to have invited disease and epidemics. And when the hardy, vigorous life of the early republic gave way to the luxury of the empire, degeneration set in. Romans' eating habits, for example, grew worse steadily, and their diseases seemed to have become much more complex. Celsus and Galen, physicians of the day, recognized the need for "medical gymnastics" and devised extensive remedial systems. Scorning the experience of the Greeks, they developed specializations of their own, of which a great deal was quackery. Eventually, though, improved community health services were made available. Early medical science did make significant progress despite the hindrances posed by charlatans and the so-called saint cures promulgated by the Christian and Gnostic sects.

The story of Rome's decline, its disastrous misuse of leisure, the passion for degrading entertainment that developed, and the horrible examples of inhumanity and cruelty to beasts do not need reiteration. Did these excesses bring about the decline of Rome, or were they symptomatic of a declining Rome? At any rate, two factors should be obvious: The type and extent of physical education programs were dependent on the political system, and changing political and social conditions produced a culture that could not cope with its leisure time. These developments should be of interest to us in America today.

The Middle Ages

The Dark Ages. The Visigoths began their successful invasion to the south in A.D. 376, and the end of the Roman Empire is commonly dated at A.D. 476. The period following has been typically, but perhaps incorrectly, designated as the Dark Ages, a time when most literature and learning came to a standstill and would have been completely lost save for the newly organized monasteries. "Ill blows the wind that profits nobody" is a proverb that applies to this era. The Visigoths did possess splendid bodies, and it is often argued that it was just this addition of new blood that made possible the development of the later medieval and Renaissance cultures.

Christian Influence on Physical Education.   As the immoral society of the declining Romans became a mere memory, Christianity continued to spread because of the energy, enthusiasm, and high moral standards of its followers. The Church managed to survive the invasion of the barbarians, gradually became an important influence in society, and continued to expand on all fronts. Although Jesus Christ was in many ways anything but an ascetic, the early Christians envisioned the individual's moral regeneration as the highest goal. They became most concerned about their souls and possible eternal happiness. The physical was of this world, and consequently evil; affairs of the soul were of God. This way of life, known as asceticism, saw the summum bonum in subduing the desires of the flesh, even by means of torture if necessary. Many churchmen were opposed to the idea of physical activity in sport and games because the Roman sports and games had led to so many evils and excesses, and also because athletic festivals had been associated with the earlier pagan religions. Certain Catholic historians and educators have stated that the Church has been unjustly maligned on this point. Professor H. I. Marrou makes it quite clear that, in his opinion, physical education "simply died of old age." He maintains that it was the above-mentioned "passion for athletics" that was criticized so sharply (1964, p. 185).

And so for hundreds of years during this period of the early Middle Ages, there was no training or cultivation of the physical. Work in the fields and around the grounds of monasteries was probably the only activity that kept the monks physically fit. When such work was transferred to the laity and more intellectual pursuits became the rule for them, even this basic physical fitness was lost. As is so often the case, the pendulum had swung too far in the other direction.

The Age of Chivalry.   Physical education was revived to a degree in the age of chivalry. Feudal society was divided into three classes: (1) the masses, who had to work very hard to support the other classes and eke out a bare subsistence for themselves; (2) the clergy, who carried on the affairs of the Church; and (3) the nobles, who were responsible for the government of certain lands or territories under a king, and who performed the necessary military duties. In this period a physical and military education of the most strenuous type was required of the knight along with prescribed training in social conduct to enable him to serve his feudal lord, the Church, and all women. Such an ideal was undoubtedly better in theory than in practice, but it did set higher standards than those which had previously existed. The aim of physical education was certainly narrow, and health standards were usually frighteningly poor by present standards. With the loss of the Greek ideal, physical education once again served a most practical objective—that of producing an individual well trained in the art of hand-to-hand combat, possessing all the necessary physical attributes (strength, endurance, agility and coordination). With the subsequent invention of war machinery, the enemy was not always met at close range. As a result, death in battle became to a certain degree accidental and was not necessarily the result of physical weakness. Naturally, some divergence resulted in the aims and methods of military training and those of physical education.

A Transitional Period. With the decline of feudalism and the rise of an early type of nationalism, trade became more vigorous and towns grew up. A stronger middle class gradually arose with a resultant demand for an improved educational system designed to prepare youth for its lifetime occupations. During this time some physical education of an informal nature contributed to the social life and recreations of young townspeople, as well as to their military training. Games and sports were accompanying features of frequent religious holidays.

The Renaissance

The historical period that followed feudalism became known as the Renaissance. It was natural that learned people should begin to look back at the periods in history in which similar societies had existed. The Church was solidly entrenched, and there was much enthusiasm for scholarship in the professions of law, theology, and medicine. The scholasticism of this period, with its emphasis on intellectual discipline, found little if any room for physical education, however. Unorganized sports and games were the only activities of this nature in the cathedral schools and universities. In the late fourteenth and fifteenth centuries, however, a philosophy called humanism developed; scholars rediscovered old Greek and Latin texts that sang the praises of the individual. Thus, once again, after many centuries the physical side of the human being was not overlooked. Most humanistic educators appreciated the value of the earlier Greek ideal and emphasized the care and proper development of the body. Vittorino da Feltre, at the court of the prince of Mantua in northern Italy, set an example in physical education methods in his school. His aims were to discipline the body so that hardship might be endured with the least possible hazard; his pupils were someday to bear arms and had to know the art of war. Sports and games of an individual and group nature were included because of the recreative value of such activity. He believed further that the ability of youth to learn in the classroom depended somewhat upon the physical condition of the individual involved.

Early Modern Period

As the schools lost their original aim and concentrated exclusively on the study of the classical languages and neglected the other aspects of these civliizations, there followed once again a decline in liberal education. The importance of physical education also declined, as preparation for lifework was crowded out of the curriculum by preparation solely for university education. When the spirit of Italian humanistic education finally spread over all Europe, the Greek ideal of physical education had lost strength and was realized only by relatively few individuals. The Protestant Reformation did nothing to encourage physical education activities—with the possible exception of Martin Luther himself, who realized a need for the physical training of youth. Certain educators did rebel against the narrow type of education that had come into vogue, but they were the exception rather than the rule. Rabelais satirized contemporary education by his depiction of the typical Latin grammar school graduate; his Gargantua was a "dolt and blockhead," who subsequently became a worthwhile person when his education became more well-rounded. Michel de Montaigne, the great French essayist of the sixteenth century, believed that education should not be divided into two parts—that of mind and that of body. Other educators, such as Locke, Mulcaster, and Comenius, also recognized the value of physical exercise and attainments. In the seventeenth century, character education was the primary aim, but health and physical fitness were stressed as underlying needs. Locke, for example, stressed the importance of recreation for youth, an idea that unfortunately was not accepted as the ideal in a society characterized by a variety of social classes.

**From the Eighteenth Century
to the Present**

Eighteenth-Century Europe. The eighteenth century was a period of change to what would today be called more up-to-date political, social, and educational ideals. In France, Voltaire denounced both the Church and the state. Jean Jacques Rousseau decried existing social and educational patterns; he blamed social inequality and civilization itself for a great deal of the unhappiness in the world. His solution?— a "back to nature" movement that would eliminate the degeneration caused by human beings and contrived societal groupings. In his famous educational work, *Émile,* he portrayed what he considered the ideal education for a boy. From the age of one to five, the only concern should be for the growth and physical welfare of the child's body. From five to twelve years of age, the idea of natural growth was to be continued as the sturdy, healthy youngster learned something about his environment. Rousseau considered the individual to be an indivisible entity and was firmly convinced that lifelong growth was possible. For him it was difficult to determine when an activity lost its physical value and possessed intellectual worth alone.

The opinions of both Rousseau and Voltaire, combined with other social influences, did lead to the ruination of the existing social order and helped to bring about its reconstruction in the next century. For example, Johann Basedow started a naturalistic school in Dessau according to the ideas of Rousseau. This school, called the Philanthropinum, was the first school in modern Europe to admit children from all social classes and give physical education a place in the daily curriculum. A number of other prominent educators expressed themselves on the proper place of physical education in the educational curriculum and helped influence public opinion in the late eighteenth century. Outstanding among these men were GutsMuths, Kant, and Pestalozzi. Friedrich Froebel, who ranks along with Pestalozzi as a founder of modern pedagogy, offered the first planned program of education through the medium of play.

Emerging Nationalism.   Physical education in modern Europe has been closely connected with emerging nationalism. Both the French and the American revolutions sparked feelings of national loyalty in many parts of the world. Gradually education was recognized as a vital means for promoting citizenship and thus, indirectly, economic and political stability. The development of national interest per se appears to have been useful in bringing about necessary social reform; now, however, as we think more in terms of a world government, we must seek to place greater stress on the cultural contributions each nation has to make. Physical education and sport typically have been used to promote physical fitness and the desire to excel in competitive sports. Now, however, the cooperative as well as competitive aspects of physical education and sport should be stressed. Let us compare our systems with pride but not strive to beat our opponents into the ground on the field of friendly strife. Competition in a wide variety of sports among nations can be thrilling, adventurous, and educative. But to overemphasize it to the extent of maintaining that we must win to prove our way of life is best merely defeats our purpose.

Germany.   The German gymnastic societies (Turnvereine) originated in the first decade of the nineteenth century. Friedrich L. Jahn, a staunch patriot of the time, is considered the father of this movement. He wanted his people to become strong enough to throw off French domination. Jahn believed not only that exercise was a means of growth and development for the individual, but also that there was a certain mental and moral training to be derived from experience at the Turn-platz. Prussia's War of Liberation (1813) undoubtedly owed its success in some measure to his work. Turnen underwent periods of popularity and disfavor during the next forty years, and the Turnverein only reluctantly accepted the games and sports of the modern period.

Adolph Spiess did a great amount of work in planning and develop-ing school gymnastics, as he strove to have physical training included as an important part of the child's education. In 1849 he established normal classes in gymnastics at Darmstadt, and his influence was subsequently felt in the various school systems of Germany. In contrast to Jahn's informal, leisurely approach to gymnastic training, Spiess emphasized its formal aspects. Down through the years there have been efforts to broaden the scope of physical education in keeping with changing educational phi-losophies and political regimes. The National Socialists, of course, gave a strongly militaristic flavor to physical education and used it as an im-portant means of glorifying the supremacy of the state. Such use of phys-ical education and sport deserves most careful study.

Great Britain. Great Britain's isolated position in relation to the Continent made rigorous training for warfare and national defense some-what less necessary and tended to foster the continuance of interest in outdoor sports. In feudal England archery was the most popular sport; in the fifteenth century it was rivaled by golf, an activity that was soon banned by law because of the disturbance it created. A little later, how-ever, it became quite popular with the nobles. Field hockey, cricket, bowling, quoits, tennis, rugby, hammer throwing, and pole vaulting had their origins in the British Isles. Many other traditional sports originated elsewhere but were soon adopted by the English people.

In the early nineteenth century, an urgent need for systematized physical training was felt. Clias, Ehrenhoff, Georgii, and Maclaren were some of those who introduced varied methods of physical education to the British people. The new interest in systematic school gymnastics and the movement for improved health do not seem to have interfered with participation in sports, however. Down through the years Great Britain has encouraged active participation by all schoolchildren and avoided overtraining the few. This has been evidenced by the stress on team games as a means of socialization and of developing desirable personality traits. Other European systems of physical education have periodically received attention in Great Britain (for example, Swedish gymnastics), but it can be fairly said that Britons have never neglected the educational aspects of physical education in the twentieth century nor the fundamental prin-ciples of exercise to promote health and physical fitness.

Sweden. The development of modern physical education in the Scandinavian countries has been significantly related to the nationalism so evident throughout Europe as a whole. Sweden, like many countries in Northern Europe, underwent periods of conflict, resulting eventually in severe delimitation of its once extensive empire; Russia's conquest of Finland in 1808 left Sweden with approximately two-thirds of its former territory. It is no wonder, therefore, that the Swedes felt a desire to regain their prestige—much in the same way that the Germans did after the victories won by Napoleon.

Per Henrik Ling (1776–1839) is credited as the man who gave the greatest impetus to Swedish physical education. Having studied in Denmark under Nachtegall, he brought his newly found knowledge and experience back to his homeland. With his characteristic drive and enthusiasm, he secured acceptance of a program of gymnastic activities designed to improve the physical fitness of Sweden's military forces. In addition, he saw that properly designed exercise programs could do much to improve the health of the entire populace. Known as "medical gymnastics," this aspect of Ling's total educational program was designed to produce a well-balanced organism.

Those who followed Ling temporarily lost sight of his broad aims, but twentieth-century Swedish physical educators have regained the balance that seemed so basic to him—a balance that can be characterized as an essentialistic approach, leading ultimately to both physical and mental health. All types of sports are encouraged, especially those that lend themselves to the climate of this geographical area. Conscious development of character through participation in team sports has received less attention.

France. The French Revolution of 1789 overthrew an absolute monarchy in which the citizens had little or nothing to say about the determination of their own destiny. In each of the thirty-two provinces an Intendant representing the king exercised absolute power. The economy was not stable, and the system of law was not uniform. The actual crisis of the revolution was preceded by loss of territory in 1763 and many poor administrative decisions by a weak Louis xvi. Such social reformers as Montesquieu, Voltaire, and Rousseau helped to establish the intellectual climate for a rebellion.

With the revolution came the establishment of the First French Republic. Austria and Prussia, themselves monarchies, attempted to restore the king's ever-weakening power. But the momentum of the revolution proved too great; after the execution of Louis xvi and Marie Antoinette, a coalition of adjoining powers attempted to conquer France. It was then that Napoleon Bonaparte (1769–1821) came to power. His successes in battle strengthened a weakened French national pride.

Through centralized governmental administration he was able to give the situation stability. He improved the system of French law and developed an educational system that extended from the elementary school through the University of Paris. Further struggles lay ahead, however, and for a time it appeared that the French would defeat all their adversaries. After a truly disastrous Russian campaign, a defeat at Leipzig in 1813, and a subsequent loss in battle at Waterloo, Napoleon was banished. At Vienna in the years 1814–1815 the map of Europe was redrawn by the diplomatic representatives of England, Prussia, Russia, Austria, and other less important states.

French physical education development during these years was the result of the work of such foreigners as Francisco Amoros and Phokion Clias. The program was formal in nature and was designed to produce strong, active bodies for the military units. Later on, after the Revolution of 1848, the status of physical training declined until France suffered further loss of prestige in the Franco-Prussian War. At this point efforts were made to introduce sports and games into the lives of youth in order to develop the requisite qualities for a strong and vigorous citizenry. Such names as de Coubertin, Hébert, Demeny, and Simon are today recognized for vigorous leadership in the early part of the twentieth century.

Olympic Games Revival. At the end of the nineteenth century, Baron Pierre de Coubertin of France brought about the revival of the Olympic Games (1896). Despite the fact that two world wars, and many lesser wars, have been fought since the advent of the modern Olympic Games, the world looks forward with great interest and a feeling of international good will to these games every four years. The public and the various communications media have persisted in keeping unofficial team scores, although performance is on an individual basis. As a result, winning records in recent years have had definite political overtones. Yet there is no doubt that sports and games for both men and women have become increasingly popular in most of the countries of the world, and a certain amount of improved international understanding has resulted from sports competition.

The United States. Finally let us consider the role that physical education and sport has played in the educational pattern of the United States, since this is of immediate importance to us, and how physical education activities have adapted themselves to changing economic, political, and social conditions.

As the population of colonial America was mostly rural, organized gymnastics and athletics found no place in the daily lives of people. Most of the colonists, presumably with the exception of the group known as the Puritans, engaged in the games and recreational activities of their motherlands as time permitted. The significance of play and its possibilities as an important phase of the educational process were not comprehended; in fact, those who determined educational policies were opposed to the idea of physical education and sport.

The national history of the United States is mirrored, to a degree, in the history of the academies. These schools aimed to prepare youth to meet the many challenges of life, an emphasis that naturally upgraded the position of physical education in the curriculum. Some of the early academies, such as Dummer, Andover, Exeter, and Leicester, were founded and incorporated before 1790. This movement reached its height around 1830 when there were approximately 800 such schools throughout the country.

Many early American educators and statesmen advocated the idea that both the body and the mind needed attention in our educational system. Captain Alden Partridge, one of the early superintendents of the United States Military Academy at West Point, crusaded for the reform of institutions of higher education. He deplored the neglect of physical training. Other crusaders included Benjamin Franklin, Noah Webster, Thomas Jefferson, Horace Mann, and Henry Barnard. Through such men as Charles Beck, Charles Follen, and Francis Lieber, German gymnastics came to the United States in the early nineteenth century. At this time, however, the people did not appreciate fully the value of these activities.

The Turnvereine influence made important contributions to physical training shortly before the Civil War. The Turners advocated that mental and physical education should proceed hand in hand in the public schools. The greatly increased enrollment of the elementary and high schools soon made them the outstanding agency for the improvement of national health and physical welfare. Turners were leaders in the physical education movement around 1850 in the cities of Boston, St. Louis, Rochester, and Cincinnati. Two other contemporary leaders were George Barker Winship and Diocletian Lewis. Winship was an advocate of heavy gymnastics and did much to convey the notion that strength and health were completely synonymous. Lewis, who began the first teacher-training program in physical education in the country, a crusader in every sense of the word, desired to improve the health of Americans through a system of light calisthenics. He believed his system would develop grace, flexibility, and agility as well. His stirring addresses to many professional and lay groups did much to popularize gymnastics and to convey the idea that such exercise was more for the weak than for the strong.

After the Civil War, the Turnvereins continued to stress the role of physical education in the educational system. Influencing hundreds of thousands of people through direct or indirect contact, they have always opposed purely military training as a substitute for physical education. In addition, the modern playground movement found the Turners among its strongest supporters. The Civil War had clearly shown the need for a concerted effort in the areas of health, physical education, and athletics. The Morrill Act of 1862 laid the foundation for the establishment of the land-grant colleges. Because of the stress on military drill, however, physical education did not gain acceptance at this time. An extremely differentiated pattern of physical education existed in the post-Civil War era.

American sports, as we now know them, originated in this period of internal conflict. Baseball and tennis became popular in that order. Golf, bowling, swimming, basketball, and a multitude of other so-called minor sports made their appearance in the latter half of the nineteenth century. American football started its rise to popularity during this period. The Amateur Athletic Union, organized in 1888, gave invaluable service toward the promotion of legitimate amateur sport.

The Young Men's Christian Association, which traces its origins back to 1844 in London, when George Williams organized the first religious group, has as its underlying theme that physical welfare and recreation significantly aid moral welfare. Some of the early outstanding leaders in physical education in this organization were Robert J. Roberts, Luther Halsey Gulick, and James Huff McCurdy.

It was at this time also that many colleges and universities initiated programs which indicated the concern of administrators and teachers about the health of their students. The University of Virginia was the first to have a real gymnasium, and Amherst College followed in 1860 with a two-story structure devoted to physical training. President Stearns urged the governing body to start a department of physical culture whose primary aim was to foster sound health practices. Dr. Edward Hitchcock headed this department for a period of fifty years until his death in 1911. Yale and Harvard erected similar buildings, but their physical training programs did not receive adequate support until somewhat later. Dr. Dudley Allen Sargent, who took charge of Harvard's Hemenway Gymnasium, led his university to a preeminent position in the field of physical education. His program, later adopted by many Midwestern colleges, stressed physical education for the individual and the attainment of a perfect structure (harmony in a well-balanced development of mind and body). From the outset, colleges took the position that games and sports were not necessarily a part of the educational program. Interest was so intense, however, that the wishes of the students could not be denied. They were anxious to demonstrate their abilities in the various sports against young men from other institutions; thus from 1850 to 1880 the rise of interest in intercollegiate sports was phenomenal. Rowing, baseball, track and field, football, and later basketball, were the major sports. The colleges soon found that these athletic sports needed control, as evils began to creep in and destroy the values originally associated with the games.

The years from 1880 to 1890 undoubtedly formed one of the most important decades in the history of physical education in America. The colleges, the Christian Associations (YMCA and YWCA), the Turners, and the proponents of the various systems of gymnastics all made noteworthy contributions during this decade. The Association for the Advancement of Physical Education was founded in 1885, with the word "American" not being added until the following year. This professional organization was the first of its kind in the field, and it stimulated improved teacher education. The next step for the young field was the promulgation of a planned, organized program of physical education—a program the aims and objectives of which were in accord with the existing educational pattern. Then began the long, slow struggle to bring about the widespread adoption of such a program. Early state legislation for physical education did result before the turn of the twentieth century.

During the late nineteenth century efforts were made in the area of organized recreation and camping for children in the larger cities. The first playground was started in Boston in 1885, followed closely by similar developments in New York and Chicago, as the ill effects of the Industrial Revolution began to be felt. This was the meager origin of the present burgeoning recreation movement in our country. Private and organizational camping got its start before the turn of the century as well and has flourished since that time.

In the early twentieth century, Americans showed renewed enthusiasm for discussing the question of educational aims and values. Early American education had been religious in nature but gradually became secularized by an emerging nationalism. As America came into its own economically speaking, educational aims veered from the purely political to the economic. The tremendous increase in high school enrollment forced a reconsideration of these aims at all levels of the system, and the application of scientific methods facilitated this task. In particular, social scientists attempted to state our aims in the light of sociological implications. For the first time, education was conceived in terms of preparing the individual for a role as a citizen of an evolving democracy. John Dewey's writings encouraged the viewing of the curriculum as child-centered rather than subject matter-centered. The progressive education movement, an outgrowth of his thought, placed great emphasis on individualistic aims but countered them by a demand for social rather than purely individual welfare.

The relationship between health and physical education and our educational system developed rapidly during the first quarter of the twentieth century. Health education in all its aspects was viewed seriously, especially after the implications of the draft statistics of World War I were fully comprehended. Many states passed legislation regarding the teaching of physical education in the schools. National interest in sports and games grew at a phenomenal rate in an era when economic prosperity prevailed. The basis for school and community recreation was well laid.

As physical education began to achieve maturity through its introduction by law into a great many schools, the struggle between the inflexibility of the various foreign systems of gymnastics and the individualistic freedom of the so-called natural movement was being waged with increasing vigor. The rising interest in sports and games made the conflict quite unequal, especially after the concept "athletics for all" began to take hold in the second and third decades of the century. The natural movement was undoubtedly strengthened by findings of certain natural and social scientists and thinkers, particularly John Dewey, and the newer method appeared to be more effective in the light of the changing ideals of an evolving democracy. It is certainly also true that the influence of idealism, with its emphasis on the development of individual personality and the possible inculcation of moral and spiritual values through the transfer of training theory applied to sports and games, remained strong.

Health education likewise made rapid progress during this period. The scope of school hygiene increased, and the importance of the medical examination grew. School health education was gradually recognized as including three major divisions: health services, health instruction, and healthful school living. The need to develop and expand in this area was seen by many, and during this period the tendency began toward some separation between health and physical education. Many physical educators began to be concerned with other aims and were also devoting a great amount of time to athletic coaching duties. The expansion of direct and indirect health education of the general populace through the medium of many private and public agencies tended to draw those more directly interested in the aims of health education away from physical education and athletics.

Progress in the recreation field was significant as well. The Playground Association of America, organized in 1906, was one response to the recreational need. At this time, however, there was still an extremely close relationship between physical education and recreation because of the keen interest in the aims of recreation taken by a number of outstanding physical educators. Many municipal recreation centers were constructed, and some of the schools served as after-hours recreation centers. People began to see that recreational activities of all types served an important purpose in a society undergoing basic changes. Some recreation programs developed under boards of education; others involved joint sponsorship of school boards and municipal governments; and a large number of communities placed recreation under the direct control of the municipal government. In the last case, school facilities were rented when possible, or municipalities gradually developed recreational facilities of their own. To trace the recent development of the field of recreation and park administration would be beyond the scope of this volume. Recreation has now become a separate profession with many challenging opportunities and rewards to the dedicated professional practitioner. Certainly professionals in physical education and sport should work together cooperatively with people in this allied field as they work toward the achievement of jointly held aims and objectives.

The period from 1930 to 1970 is so close to the present that it is almost impossible to gain the perspective needed to assess these years accurately. The depression of the 1930s, World War II and its aftermath, the Korean conflict, the developing "cold war" in general, and then the struggle in Vietnam have been such strong social influences that aims and objectives in physical education and sport were either dominated by them, or at the very least directly influenced by their presence.

It would be elementary to say that physical educators and coaches want more and better physical education and sport programs; that school health educators feel that more and better health and safety education would be valuable to students; and that those involved in recreation see their area of concern becoming more vital to the future of our society and are making every effort to professionalize themselves. Yet this is probably an accurate thumbnail description of the present state of affairs. The energetic American Alliance for Health, Physical Education, and Recreation, a department of the National Education Association, has accomplished a great deal through the efforts of its many thousands of professional members. The profession has struggled valiantly to coordinate its various allied movements within the framework of public education and seems to have made real progress. Unfortunately there are also many additional thousands of young professionals who do not join the alliance at the state, district, or national levels.

In the 1960s a specialist trend developed in the field of physical education that subsequently drained off a number of physical educators with quite high degrees of scholarly competence in the various subdisciplinary areas into quite separate disciplinary societies. Of course, in light of conflicting educational philosophies, it is no simple matter to determine what is educational or what is scholarly—or if one is different from the other—and what appears to be respectable for one segment of the profession as opposed to another. A sort of caste system appears to have developed among physical education teachers, sport coaches, elementary specialists, university scholars, teacher educators, and graduate professors. This is where much of the difficulty lies. There is also the problem all professions have—developing truly dedicated professional practitioners of any type who view their field as a vocation or calling.

We have seen teacher preparation strengthened through the media of national conferences, accreditation, and self-evaluation. The dance movement has been a significant development. A great deal of progress has been made in physical education and sport research, especially in the physiological area of exercise science and in sport and physical education history. Furthermore, it has been possible to separate the concepts of physical education and military fitness in many people's minds. The national interest in sport and competitive athletics has continued unabated —indeed, has actually grown! Finally, the recent demand for physical fitness improvement that began in the 1950s with encouragement at the federal level has stimulated the raising of program standards. That there are encouraging signs is self-evident, but the value struggle within the field will only intensify unless we can bring about greater consensus. Such agreement and understanding will only come through a deeper study and application of scientific and philosophical methods. Since the professional educator has a key role, he or she needs to be more fully informed in this regard.

PHILOSOPHICAL ANALYSIS

As indicated earlier, the values that are held in a society will quite obviously be reflected both directly and indirectly in the curriculum most students are asked to study. In general educational philosophy during the twentieth century, there have been two major viewpoints on educational values: they are either subjective or objective. The educational progressivist tends to view educational aims as relative and experimental in a changing world. Specific educational objectives emerge as life goes on, and presumably we learn from experience. The educational essentialist, conversely, looks upon educational values as objective and intrinsic in the universe. They are there because that's the way things are in this world. Consequently, on the essentialist's scale of values, intrinsic values take precedence over any possibly instrumental values. The fulfillment of our inherent potentialities overrides any and all other subsidiary educational objectives.

When educational values are recognized and accepted, the next step is obviously to determine how such educational aims and/or objectives are to be realized. (It helps in discussing this subject if the reader views aims as being long-range goals, perhaps not attainable, and objectives as short-range goals that may be accomplished within a specified period of time. This approach is not intended to be arbitrary in any way, but it has proved useful in past experience.) The word "curriculum" means a runway or course based on its Latin derivation, and thus it is reasonable to assume that we proceed along a course—a "course of study"—to achieve our educational goals. As Brubacher has stated, "one may well say that the curriculum is nothing more than aims or values writ large in expanded form" (1969, p. 155). The further assumption is, therefore, that the curriculum should be so designed as to bring the educational values espoused to fruition.

For experimentalists, the general aim of education is more education. In the broadest sense, education consists of the changes that take place in people as a result of the experiences they have. Students should have an opportunity to participate in the formation of educational aims and objectives; this type of involvement goes a long way in helping to generate the all-important interest needed to make the entire educational process successful. A general aim of education might be called social efficiency, as defined by John Dewey. Pupil growth is a paramount goal in the final analysis, with the individual being placed at the center of the educational experience.

Experimentalists are much more interested in promoting the concept of total fitness rather than physical fitness alone. Further, they believe that physical education should be an integral subject in the curriculum. Students should have the opportunity to select a wide variety of useful activities, many of which should help them to develop *social* intelligence. The activities offered should bring natural impulses into play. Basically, physical education classes and intramural sports are viewed as more important to the large majority of students than interscholastic or intercollegiate athletics and deserve priority if conflict arises over budgetary allotment, staff availability, and use of facilities. This does not mean, however, that experimentalists will not give full support to team experiences in competitive sports involving opportunities for both cooperation and competition. These can be vital educational experiences for those concerned if properly conducted.

For reconstructionists, a position that has been viewed by some as "utopian experimentalism," social self-realization is the supreme value in education. The realization of this idea is most important for individuals in their social setting—a world culture. Positive ideals should be molded toward an evolving democratic ideal by a general education that is group-centered and in which the majority determines the acceptable goals. Education by means of hidden coercion is to be scrupulously avoided. Learning is explained by the organismic principle of functional psychology. Social intelligence acquired teaches us to control and direct our urges as we concur with or attempt to modify cultural purposes. Reconstructionists concur with the concept of total fitness within an educational design pointed toward the individual's self-realization as a social being. In our field there should be an opportunity for a selection of a wide variety of useful activities. Instruction in motor skills is necessary to provide a sufficient amount of physical fitness activity. The introduction of dance and art can contribute to creative expression. Intramural sports and voluntary recreational activities should be stressed. This applies especially to team competition, with particular stress on cooperation and promotion of friendly competition. Extramural sport competition can be introduced when there is a need; striving for excellence is important, but it is vital that materialistic influences be kept out of educational programs. Relaxation techniques should have a place, as should the whole concept of education for leisure.

For realists, the educational aim is to acquire "verified knowledge of the environment." There is recognition of the value of content as well as the activities involved in learning. Consideration is given also to what might be called "the external determinants of human behavior." When a person is educated, he or she has acquired the art of utilizing knowledge. Thus, the primary task of education is to transmit knowledge, without which civilization cannot continue to flourish. Whatever human beings have discovered to be true—because it conforms to reality—must be handed down to future generations as the social or cultural tradition. (Some holding this philosophical stance believe that the good life emanates from cooperation with God's grace and that the development of the Christian virtues is obviously of greater worth than the learning of so-called verified knowledge—or anything else.)

Realists believe that education "of the physical" should have primary emphasis in our field. They are concerned with the development of physical vigor, and believe that such development should have priority over the recreational aspects of physical education. Many holding this position recommended that all students in public schools should have a daily period designed to strengthen muscles and develop bodily coordination. Physical education must yield, of course, to intellectual education. Qualified approval is given to interscholastic athletics since they do help with the learning of sportsmanship and desirable social conduct if properly conducted. But all these aspects, with the possible exception of physical training, are definitely extracurricular and not part of the regular curriculum.

For idealists, education is the process whereby the developing organism becomes what it latently is. All education may be said to have a religious or moral significance, which means that there is a moral imperative, so to speak, on education. As we strive to realize ourselves, there is the possibility of realization of the Absolute within the individual mind. Education should aid the child to adjust to the basic realities (the spiritual ideals of truth, beauty, and goodness) that the history of the race has furnished us. The basic values of human living are health, character, social justice, skill, art, love, knowledge, philosophy, and religion.

Idealists are extremely interested in individual personality development. They believe in education "of the physical," and yet they affirm the concept of education "through the physical" as well. Nevertheless, although physical education is important, it does occupy a lower rung on the educational ladder. Idealists believe that desirable objectives for physical education include the development of responsible citizenship and group participation. In competitive sport, they believe that the transfer of training theory is in operation in connection with the development of desirable personality traits, but sports participation should always be a means to an end.

For existentialists, socialization of the child has become equally as important as so-called intellectual development in this century's educational aims. There should be concern, however, because many educational philosophies imply or assume that children are to be fashioned so that they will conform to a prior notion of what they *should* be. Even the progressivists seem to have failed in their effort to help the learner "posture himself." Further, even if it does become possible to get general agreement on a set of fundamental dispositions to be formed, should the criterion employed for such evaluation be a public one, rather than personal and private? Education should seek to "awaken awareness" in the learners—awareness of themselves as single subjectivities in the world. Increased emphasis is needed on the arts and social sciences, and students should "constantly, freely, baselessly, and creatively" choose their own pattern of education.

The existentialist in the field of physical education should strive to fulfill a role in the general education pattern of arts and sciences. The goal is *total* fitness—not only *physical* fitness—with a balance between activities emphasizing competition and cooperation. The concept of universal man is paramount, but we must allow individuals to choose their physical education and sport activities based on self-knowledge—that is, what knowledge and skills they would like to possess. We should help the child who is "authentically eccentric" feel at home in the physical education program. The educator, and this includes the physical educator, of course, should help youth find ways to commit themselves to values and people. A person should be able to select a sport according to the values he or she wishes to derive from it. This is often difficult today because of the extreme emphasis on winning in this culture. The physical educator should also include esthetic and creative activities such as modern dance in the program for both sexes.

Section Two

Methods of Instruction

In an advanced culture, values are generally converted into educational aims and objectives. The next step is to develop an appropriate curriculum. Keeping in mind that curriculum and method should go hand in hand if effective education is a desired end product, the next professional concern (or persistent problem) to be discussed is methods of instruction. One generally expects such a topic to revolve around what the teacher "does" to a subject matter, but this approach is probably somewhat naive. We should undoubtedly be aware of the subject matter (for example, tennis); how the teacher teaches tennis; what takes place within the learner as he or she seeks to learn tennis from the instructor; and, finally, what the end result is (that is, what a learner does when he or she has learned to play tennis).

Further, as Brubacher explains, the question should be clarified both from the standpoint of the epistemological aspects and the axiological aspects (1969, pp. 221–274). Epistemologically, we ask whether students will learn best and most quickly if the tennis skills, for example, are presented authoritatively in logical order (from simple to complex). Or should these skills be introduced in what has often been called a "psychological order"—that is, a problematic approach that proceeds according to the interest of the learner? Second, from an axiological standpoint, it seems to be true that the technical questions regarding teaching and learning recede when a psychological order of learning is employed and the value component of the structure of knowledge becomes readily apparent. Thus, we soon become involved with the social setting in which learning will take place, as well as such other matters as student motivation and the evaluation of educational achievements (Brubacher, 1969, p. 253).

BRIEF HISTORICAL BACKGROUND

Primitive and preliterate peoples undoubtedly learned through imitation and through trial and error. When writing developed in the early civilizations, memorization played a large part in the educational process. Tradition and custom were highly regarded, and the importance of precept and proper example were very real aspects of both physical and mental culture. Testing in early societies was carried out through various initiatory ceremonies designed to give the young man (and occasionally the young woman) the opportunity to test himself in the presence of peers and elders. Most of the education seems to have been informal, however, and different systems of apprenticeship were employed in all phases of life's activities. The educational pattern was prescribed, and young people were expected to follow the same traditions and customs from generation to generation. The practical aspects of life were learned by doing them repeatedly, and strict discipline was often employed if the child was lazy or recalcitrant.

In early Greece many of the same methods were used, and motivation was supplied by introducing elements of rivalry as well as by narration of various tales and myths of the great heroes of the past. In Spartan Greece, boys were taken from their homes at the age of seven years, and their training in the barracks was in the hands of very strict captains. The educational program was severe and exacting, as the ultimate aim was the production of a brave and hardened soldier. Officers of the state examined these boys and young men regularly. Incompetence and cowardice were grounds for punishment by flogging, and there is no doubt that the element of fear can encourage a certain type of learning.

The educational methods of the early Athenians were similar but, according to popular belief, not quite as strict and harsh as those of the Spartans. There was no question, however, that lax methods would produce poor results. Attention was given to the grouping of young men according to capacity, and there was evidently careful matching for the various contests that were sponsored regularly. Overemphasis on coaching and the development of certain specialized techniques became a distinct problem in later Athens, and this trend was often criticized by philosophers and other educational leaders.

Roman education was extremely utilitarian in nature. In the early Roman period education was centered in the family, although its ultimate goal was service to the state. Children learned by precept and example from their parents and elders. Obedience was at times exacted through an extremely rigorous discipline. Parents gave their children regular supervision and made every effort to set fine examples for them; the child was expected to "do the thing that was to be done." The cultural aspects of the educational process, so evident in later Athenian education, were almost completely lacking in early Rome. Later, as the need for higher intellectual attainments developed, the task of educating the child often fell to Greek slaves. Thus the Romans made no significant innovations in educational method and indeed failed even to appreciate two areas where the Greeks had excelled—music and gymnastics.

The Christian Church dominated the educational scene in the early Middle Ages. Although Jesus of Nazareth is generally regarded as a great religious leader and a fine teacher, many of those who followed him employed less exciting teaching methods. Jesus is said to have taught with enthusiasm and authority. He had a commanding knowledge of Jewish history and lore, and yet he dealt with the controversial issues of the time. He welcomed questions from his audience, and he made full use of his excellent powers of persuasion. Many less capable Church leaders in the early Middle Ages, however, evidently employed a great deal of formality and dogmatism in their teaching. St. Augustine (A.D. 354–430) attempted to put more life into his teaching methods and those of his associates, but educational methods generally seem to have been dominated by asceticism and severe discipline. However, the training of monks and knights necessarily included a fair share of realism and practicality.

Educational methodology is said to have improved considerably toward the end of the Middle Ages when the universities were gaining in power and prestige. The Catholic Church made an effort to combine the best of Aristotle's approach to teaching with the better methodology employed in Christian education. Thomas Aquinas placed great stress on what might be called the self-activity of the learner. Debating techniques and Aristotelian logic were employed to stimulate interest and to promote sound learning. Of course, the lecture method was still prominent, as printing had not yet been invented. Subsequently, the idea of the dissertation was introduced—the hypothesis and the findings were defended orally.

With the onset of the Renaissance, there was greater recognition of individual differences. Vittorino da Feltre, who conducted the school at the court of the prince of Mantua, encouraged the idea of small classes in which the child's needs and capacities were considered. To him, self-activity was very important, as well as consistent use of constructive criticism and praise. The whole spirit of this period was humanistic, and it is not surprising that innovations were employed to make the process more interesting to all concerned. The reader should not be misled, however, into thinking that schoolwork had become fun; lectures and disputations were still the most frequent teaching methods at the university level, and the students at the lower levels were largely involved in memorization and emulation.

This discussion of the historical background of educational methodology could be prolonged indefinitely. Many famous educational leaders since the Renaissance have made significant contributions, but their influence was often short-lived and they themselves were often dominated by social forces beyond their immediate control. For us as physical educators it is important to understand that the concept of a mind-body dualism has prevailed in many quarters down to the present day, despite the evidence from psychology about the unity of the human organism. Fortunately, gradual realization has come that people learn in many ways, not just intellectually; but observations of various classes on all levels even today are often discouraging in this regard.

In the eighteenth and nineteenth centuries, educators like Rousseau, Froebel, Pestalozzi, and Herbart, working with preadolescents, set the stage for the investigations and subsequent innovations of the twentieth century. Unfortunately, most of us still do not teach as well as we know how, either in the classroom or in the gymnasium and the pool. The social forces at work today have resulted in a new drive toward the mastery of facts and knowledge, and at the same time in physical education we are exhorted to provide physical fitness so that a "sound mind can be superimposed on a sound body." Thus, we continue to come full circle to the question of educational philosophy, and whether chemistry, for example, is essential in the curriculum and physical education is nonessential. Some would argue that we should take advantage of the current trend of essentialism and stress the physical *training* aspects of our work in order to ensure our place in the daily school program.

Is physical education "curricular," "cocurricular," or "extracurricular?" Your answer to this question may well depend upon your position on the educational philosophy spectrum (see **Figure 5, Chapter II, Section I**). Thinking about the entire field of physical, health, and recreation education (and this includes safety and driver education, as well as intramural and interscholastic athletics), the experimentalist will see it as "curricular"; the realist, as "extracurricular," with the possible exception of a daily physical training period; and the idealist, as "cocurricular."

Having taken this stand, we must come to a decision about the influence that content has on method. Shall physical, health, and recreation education (or whatever part of it you would include in the curriculum) be taught formally, semiformally, or informally? Our primary concern as teachers is motivating the student so that the learning process will occur most easily and the material will be remembered most thoroughly. Or looking at it another way, what are the most effective means whereby the teacher can get students to perform a physical skill most efficiently in keeping with their potential? From still another standpoint, what is the best way for the teacher to arrange the learning situation so that students may modify their ways of behaving and truly understand what they are doing? In offering some answers to these questions from various standpoints on the educational philosophy spectrum, we should keep in mind that teachers generally, no matter what their philosophy, have been increasingly sensitive to changes in psychological learning theory.

PHILOSOPHICAL ANALYSIS

The experimentalist is chiefly concerned with aims that emerge out of the educative process; objectives and teaching methods must go hand in hand to be effective. Experimentalist teachers should be characterized by a social outlook that is broad, by special consideration for the learner, by a fine background of educational preparation, and by teaching techniques that are planned specifically for the teaching situation at hand. A physical education program that is interesting and significant to students is the only way that their attention can be guaranteed. With this in mind, therefore, teachers should begin at the students' level and give them as much freedom as they can use wisely. This will mean that there will be opportunities for changes in plan and program involving student choice.

If we involve students in purposeful activity just as soon as possible, the learning experience will be greatly improved. Disciplinary measures, if necessary at all, should arise spontaneously from the actions of the class. Experimentalists reject measurement of student progress by an absolute standard; they are vitally concerned, however, with evaluation of individual pupil growth, and especially with the student's self-evaluation of the success or failure of the whole educational venture.

Authoritative use of texts and preplanned lectures do not fit into the experimentalist teaching program, one of the reasons being that experimental problem solving involves a considerable measure of contingency. An experimentalist teacher guides students in such a way that they will use their reasoning abilities in the realization of the technical, associated, and concomitant learnings available to them as they learn the various sport skills.

Before we move toward the center and right side of the educational philosophy spectrum, let's take a quick look at the reconstructionist teaching method. As you will recall, this has been designated by some as the "extreme" progressivist position. Typically, this is a group-centered approach to education in which majority decisions prevail. The main aim of education is to "reconstruct" society and to "internationalize" the democratic ideal throughout the world. With this approach, therefore, all teaching methods should be geared to the realization of the agreed-upon goals. Learning is a cooperative venture, and the interest of the student is obtained by providing purposeful activity consistent with the educational goals. Teachers assume the role of democratic leaders as they guide students who must assume responsibility if progress toward social self-realization is ever to be made. Discipline, if and when necessary, comes from the group. Tests are shared efforts; awards and prizes are not made to individuals, as the emphasis is on group accomplishment; and in place of necessarily subjective grades is a conference to evaluate the student's total growth.

A consideration of the realist teaching method brings us to the essentialist side of the educational philosophy spectrum. Here there are typically two orders of learning: a logical or "essential" order, and an order in which the teacher starts with the child's interests and then works back to ensure adequate coverage of the subject matter. Generally speaking, "learning is a process of acquiring objective knowledge by the scientific method." One essentialist stresses that education is more than a matter of merely acquiring knowledge, since it must be used practically for subsequent enjoyment of life. The naturalistic realist typically practices a problem-solving approach to classroom learning, whereas for the rational humanist, the greater the amount of reasoning required to learn a subject, the more important is that subject in the curriculum.

Realists support the theory of transfer of training; rational humanists and perennialists (scholastic realists) believe that this takes place through the transference of disciplinary values, which have a functional application to any situation. Furthermore, when a new learning situation presents itself, it is quite apt to contain a number of identical elements that had appeared earlier in another learning circumstance.

Interest is desirable but subordinate to effort, and prizes and awards may be used by the teacher to stimulate students to achieve the greatest amount of excellence in their efforts. The curriculum, logically and sequentially arranged, presents little opportunity for electives; and drill, needed to perfect patterns of habit formation, especially at the lower learning levels, may, however, be varied and correlated with other teaching techniques.

The realist teacher will find it legitimate to indoctrinate; the teacher is a "person of authority who transmits the truth and wisely guides immature minds." Another assessment of the teacher's role is that "the teacher should be the voice of science; clear, objective, and factual." Realist teachers rely on proven methodology, and the application of research and measurement to physical education is most important. They believe that there should be a physical education requirement throughout the years of the formal education system—or at least until certain objective standards of performance are met.

Realists believe in the use of required texts that include all the necessary knowledge to be learned (of a theoretical nature). Quizzes and examinations are needed to convey to the student information about the caliber of his or her performance. Objective grades give students a clear appraisal of their progress and relative position in regard to others.

Much of what has been said about the realist teaching method applies to the classroom situation, of course, and implications for physical training can be logically assumed. The teacher should organize the gymnasium period to guarantee muscle development, improvement of circulorespiratory efficiency, and increased coordination. The achievement of these objectives will require careful attention to the methodology discussed above. In the teaching of physical skills, furthermore, careful analysis will be necessary, as the whole process must be broken down into its elements and the interrelations perceived. The realistic teacher should be a movement analysis expert.

Idealists subordinate method to objectives; they are apt to state that they follow no one method wholly, but that they determine the method as they progress toward the realization of the immediate educational objective. Even Plato stressed that teachers should not be particularly conscious of whether or not they were using a specific technique. Rather, he believed that teachers should use reason and should base the selection of a particular activity or technique on a foundation of sound scientific investigation with demonstrated validity and proper psychological methodology.

Idealists typically believe that students, with careful guidance, should choose their objectives, activities, topics for reports, and even their textbooks. Objective and subjective data should be used for individual guidance and for group planning. They are also strong advocates of the use of the lives and works of great leaders to provide enrichment for the curriculum of the younger generation. Because children are imitators, such a technique will encourage them to strive for high attainment.

Interest is most important, but the idealist has discovered that it alone will not suffice to accomplish all the necessary educational objectives. Although a play attitude is especially good with children, the instructor should not forget the proverb that "the hard is the good." Furthermore, when discipline is invoked to cause students to respond with effort, they may well discover that their interest has been aroused.

An idealist believes that bodily development is limited to the unfolding of what is given the individual by birth, since education cannot augment the nerve cells of the brain. It can, however, fully develop any capacities for which there is potentiality within the student. For this reason it is important to help children get the right start in health and physical education. They should become as skillful as possible, have a reasonable amount of success, and have a lot of fun in physical activity.

The idealistic coach will point out to aspiring young athletes that they will have to make certain sacrifices if they hope to be successful and worthy team members. Interscholastic sport competition provides a dramatic means of contributing to individual development, as it develops traits of perseverance, courage, and respect for law and order. The coach should eventually step into the background as the students achieve maturity. The goal is not glory for the coach; it is presumably to help the participants achieve their inherent selfhood. The coach with a truly idealistic philosophy will make every effort to keep from succumbing to the materialistic demands of the public. In athletics we should do all in our power to avoid extreme specialization within the educational system, because the development of the whole personality of the participant is apt to suffer when the performance of the skill becomes most important.

Idealistic teachers of physical education should not only be able to teach specific skills; they must be aware of ever-present opportunities for developing related interests. The rigidly formal physical education class, the stereotyped, dull team practice, or the gymnasium activity that is often merely poorly organized informal recreation will be avoided if the teacher uses a method that creates some suspense for the student—suspense to be resolved only by his or her own decision or active effort.

In physical education theory or health instruction in the classroom, teachers would be wise to use an "informal dialectic" that encourages the student to think about the problem under discussion. Some lecturing and experimenting can be useful along with the discussion technique. Idealistic teachers must constantly remind themselves that their influence is making an impact on mind and spirit and that, accordingly, their teaching should serve human needs and help others understand Christian principles.

The existentialists' teaching method is difficult to conceptualize. In the first place, they are primarily concerned that the young person should have the opportunity to grow in an environment of freedom—no choices should ever be forced on the student! They would agree, for example, that a democratic learning situation is better than an essentialist one; yet, even in the democratic environment a person may be deprived of the opportunity to make individual decisions. Any design for education that is superimposed on developing students tends to rob them of the chance to be themselves.

Thus, the very fact that teachers are provided in the school situation means that they must employ extreme care in the educational methodology that they practice on the often unsuspecting child. As the existentialist sees it, it is up to the teacher to insert a moral dimension into the child's education. This is *not* meant to imply that the teacher should make any moral decisions for the child. To the contrary, the essential task is merely to give the child an awareness of himself in relation to the world, to provide an impartial background for decision making. He should not be made to fit into some preestablished system of what is right or wrong, or be told how he should solve the problems he will encounter in an overly socialized environment.

Professional Preparation

Based on historical investigation and philosophical analysis carried out over a period of thirty years, I believe that there have indeed been contrasting philosophies of professional preparation for physical education in the United States since its beginnings in 1861. Additionally, and more specifically, it is now hypothesized that these contrasting philosophies or positions can be classified roughly as progressivist, essentialist, or *neither* within the departmental or subdisciplinary entity known as educational philosophy (Zeigler, "Historical Perspective on Contrasting Philosophies, etc.," 1975).

Here, a brief historical review of professions in general, and teaching in particular, is presented. Then a summary of professional preparation for physical education in the United States is given, with emphasis on selected persistent problems. Third, it seemed desirable to enumerate the selected problem areas in teacher education in physical education that seemed to imply adherence to specific stances within educational philosophy. Next, there is a comparative analysis of the philosophical stances underlying the contrasting positions within professional preparation for physical education. Last, six recommended criteria for a "complete" or "adequate" philosophy of professional preparation for physical education are enumerated.

HISTORICAL BACKGROUND

Even though the idea of professions and rudimentary preparation for this type of work originated in early societies, it seems that the term "profession" was not used commonly until relatively recently (Brubacher, 1962, p. 47). However, centers for a type of professional instruction were developed in Greece and Rome as bodies of knowledge became available. In medieval times universities were organized when the various professional faculties banded together for convenience, power, and protection. The degree granted at that time was in itself a license to practice whatever it was that the graduate "professed." This practice continued in the Renaissance, at which time instruction became increasingly secularized. Further, in England especially, training for certain professions (for example, law) gradually became dissociated from universities themselves (Brubacher, 1962, pp. 42–56).

An unabridged dictionary offers a number of different meanings for the term "profession," but it is usually described as a vocation that requires specific knowledge of some aspect of learning in order to have the practitioner accepted as a professional person. The now legendary Abraham Flexner recommended six criteria as being characteristic of a profession as far back as 1915 in an address to a group of social workers. A professional person's activity was (1) fundamentally *intellectual,* and the individual bears significant personal responsibility; (2) undoubtedly *learned,* because it is based on a wealth of knowledge; (3) definitely *practical,* rather than theoretical; (4) grounded in technique that could be taught, and this is the basis of professional education; (5) *strongly organized* internally; and (6) largely motivated by *altruism,* since its goal is the improvement of society (Flexner, 1915, pp. 578–581). The crucial aspect of this analysis was, however, "the unselfish devotion of those who have chosen to give themselves to making the world a fitter place to live in" (p. 590) and the presence or lack of this "unselfish devotion" will tend to elevate a doubtful activity to professional status or lower an acknowledged profession to a venal trade.

Professional preparation of teachers, at least to any considerable extent, is a fairly recent innovation. In early times the most important qualification for the position was a sound knowledge of the subject. If the subject matter was deemed important, the status of the teacher rose accordingly. For example, when a larger percentage of the populace acquired a knowledge of reading and writing in the later years of the Greek period and in the Roman era, the status of children's teachers declined, but those who taught the more complex subjects were highly respected, although not rewarded highly with money (Brubacher, 1966, pp. 466ff). Over the centuries public esteem accorded teachers has been highest when they have prepared students for what were considered to be the more important demands of life.

The medieval university, with its emphasis on the learned professions of theology, law, arts, and medicine, elevated the function of the teacher in the eyes of the public. Teachers who possessed background knowledge in the seven liberal arts—knowledge that ordinary people could not comprehend—were considered qualified to perform this art. At this time there was no such thing as professional education prior to becoming a teacher, at least in the sense that state or provincial certification is needed today on this continent in order to teach in publicly supported institutions at certain levels. During this period there was, however, a type of professional teacher organization similar to that of the medieval guild. According to Butts, "In the thirteenth century a career in university life became so important that it began to challenge a career in church or state as an outlet for the energies of able young men" (Butts, 1947, p. 179).

There were evidently not enough good teachers at the secondary level up through the period of the Renaissance. Despite this fact, the status of teachers remained low up through the eighteenth century. This can probably be attributed to a considerable degree to lack of development of what might be classified as a science of education. It was generally recognized that teaching was an art (a belief that still prevails in many circles today), and this belief led to the position that the individual either had this ability inherently or not. During this period the Catholic Church made some progress in turning out good secondary teachers, but competent instructors were in very short supply, and conditions were even worse at the elementary level (Brubacher, 1966, p. 472, quoting from Edmund Coote's *English Schoolmaster*).

In the late eighteenth and early nineteenth centuries, it was in Prussia that the most headway was made in improving teacher education. The government gave strong support to this development under Frederick the Great. The teaching methods of Pestalozzi were later introduced to strengthen the program still further, and the system was copied extensively in America. The advancements made in the theory of pedagogy based on Pestalozzi's approach to the child's nature were truly significant. These developments were "the product of the reform movement in education which tended *toward realism and away from classicism*—an effort which had for its object the practical education of the masses, the fitting of youth for citizenship and the practical duties of life" (Luckey, 1903, pp. 27–28).

The United States. The status of teachers in the colonial period in the United States depended largely upon whether a teacher taught at the college level or in the lower branches of education. Once again it was a question of knowledge of subject matter, with no emphasis on theory of pedagogy. The advancement that was made in the nineteenth century came in the type of professional education offered to elementary school teachers through the rise and growth of the normal school idea.

Gordy reports that elements of the German pattern were adopted in the first normal schools in the United States, but that much originality on the part of the early advocates was also evident (1891, pp. 20–21).

The years between 1830 and 1860 witnessed the struggle for state-supported schools, and by the end of this architectural period, the American educational ladder as a one-way system was fairly complete. Once the various types of schools were amalgamated into state systems, attention was turned to the quality of teacher engaged for the educational task. Although there was a steadily larger number of state normal schools, improvement in the status of teachers came slowly. By the end of the nineteenth century, the normal school was a well-established part of the American educational system. However, the transformation of this type of institution from secondary status to college-level rank did not occur until the beginning of the twentieth century. With the tremendous growth in the number of public high schools, it became absolutely imperative for the normal schools to become normal colleges and to graduate men and women with degrees that would be accepted by accrediting associations as being roughly comparable to university degrees. (Interestingly enough, colleges and universities were uncertain about the role they should play in the technical phases of teaching in the nineteenth century; thus, so-called professional education for teachers was quite often no better than normal school training.)

The Twentieth Century.   This century has witnessed a number of significant developments in teacher education, but primarily for elementary and secondary school teachers. Normal schools became normal colleges and were subsequently designated teachers' colleges. During the 1950s and 1960s most of these institutions were elevated to university status by state legislatures. In a number of cases the declaration was undoubtedly premature, because the "scholarly writing and research" component of many of these universities has been very slim indeed. Also, a full component of schools and colleges representing the many disciplines and professions has been lacking.

Education as a professional area of study has gradually made an inroad in most of the well-established leading colleges and universities, but it has yet to justify the disciplinary status that is claimed by many. Yet there was such a demand for secondary school teachers that it seemed unreasonable for these institutions not to make some provision for such programs in their educational offerings. Thus, despite the fact that colleges and universities did not require that their professors present evidence of course work in professional education leading to certification, more than 500 institutions of higher education added such programs between 1900 and 1930 to help prospective teachers meet the teacher certification requirements imposed in the various states.

PROFESSIONAL PREPARATION FOR PHYSICAL EDUCATION

Professional preparation for physical education in the United States began in 1861 when Dio Lewis started the first ten-week diploma course (Lewis in Barnard's *American Journal of Education*). The Normal School of the North American Turnerbund began in 1866 in New York City (North American Turnerbund *Proceedings, 1866*). In many instances these early schools were owned by the individual or society sponsoring them, but eventually the normal schools underwent a distinct transformation. Names were changed; curriculums were expanded; staffs were increased in number; degrees were offered; and eventually affiliation with colleges and universities took place (Zeigler, 1962, pp. 116–133).

The field has been influenced by a variety of social forces as the American scene changed. Foreign traditions and customs held sway initially, but gradually a fairly distinct American philosophy of physical education emerged. If there was indeed a fairly distinct image, it has since become blurred as it became possible to delineate the various educational philosophical trends (Zeigler, 1964, chaps. 5, 7, 9, 11). Such occurrences as wars and periods of economic depression and prosperity have typically brought about sweeping changes.

In the period from 1900 to 1920 educators began to take the place of physicians as directors of professional programs (Elliott, 1927, p. 21). In addition, many publicly supported colleges and universities had entered the field and were awarding baccalaureate degrees upon the completion of programs with majors in physical education. Specialized curriculums were developed in schools of education, but they were organized independent of professional education schools as well as in several other patterns. The subsequent establishment of separate schools and colleges of physical education within universities has had a truly notable influence on professional preparation and on the status of the field as a whole (Zeigler, 1972, p. 48).

In the twentieth century many leaders have urged that a stronger "cultural" education be provided for prospective physical education teachers. The need for an improved background in the foundation sciences was expressed. Until recently there was a definite trend toward increasing the so-called general professional education course require-ment. A number of studies have indicated a lack of standardization in course terminology within the specialized professional education area, as it was typically designated, of health, physical education, and recrea-tion (for example, see *Professional Training in Physical Education,* 1928, p. 41).

In the decade after World War I, a conflict that exerted a tremen-dous influence on the field and forced a flood of state health and physical education laws, some 137 colleges and universities joined those already in existence to offer professional education in health and physical educa-tion (Zeigler, 1950, p. 326). As a result, school health education and physical education were interwoven in the curriculum in a somewhat confusing manner. In addition, courses in recreation, camping, and out-door education were often introduced. Gradually separate curriculums in school health and safety education and recreation leadership were developed in many of the leading universities. A series of national con-ferences helped to bring the various curriculum objectives into focus (for example, see the *National Conference on Undergraduate Professional Preparation in Physical Education and Recreation,* 1948). The present strong trend toward specialization of function may take the present three areas still further apart (and this seems to include dance and athletics as well). The American Alliance for Health, Physical Education, and Recreation, the largest single department of the National Education Association, has been a great unifying force in the total movement, but nevertheless the differences among the various philosophies of education are almost impossible to overcome.

There have been many attempts to improve the quality of profes-sional preparation through studies, surveys, research projects, national conferences, and accreditation plans. In the 1950s, Snyder and Scott recommended careful consideration of the "competency approach" as a means of improving the entire professional preparation process in phys-ical education (1954). Influences such as the need for a disciplinary ap-proach and economic pressures (accompanied by the introduction of higher education boards at the state level) have had a marked effect on colleges and universities offering professional programs in the field. The leaders in the field are currently moving carefully, often with great intro-spection, as they look to the future. The current shakedown taking place in higher education may yet prove to be beneficial to physical education, but only if wise leadership and dedicated professional effort are able to influence the rank and file of the profession to raise their standards higher than they appear to be at the present.

SELECTED PROBLEM AREAS IN
PROFESSIONAL PREPARATION

Since the early development of teacher education in physical education, a great number of developments have either solved specific problems or created new areas of concern. In a study published in the late 1920s, five "outstanding developments in professional training" were listed as follows: (1) The philosophy of physical education has undergone a change; (2) educators take the place of physicians as directors; (3) academic degrees are granted for major units in physical education; (4) specialized curriculums in physical education are offered in schools of education; and (5) the organization has become very complex (Elliott, 1927, pp. 16–23). In the process of this investigation, however, Elliott found that many interesting problems presented themselves for further study:

1. An investigation of the qualifications and functions of the physical educator.
2. The need of a selective process in the admission of students to professional curricula which will not only determine mental and physical fitness, but personality and leadership qualifications.
3. The organization of a professional curriculum, with a greater freedom of election than is now in practice, which will provide the necessary and desirable professional preparation in physical education, as well as the cultural background.
4. The organization of courses, especially in the foundation sciences, anatomy, physiology, etc., that are adapted to satisfactorily meet the needs of students majoring in physical education.
5. A standardized nomenclature in physical education.
6. Means of coordinating the several departments, schools and colleges which contribute to the professional curriculum. . . .
7. The determination of the minimum essentials for the preparation of teachers. . . .
8. The organization of graduate work in physical education for specialists, administrators, and directors of physical education. (Elliott, 1927, pp. 56–57)

In undertaking a comprehensive history of professional preparation for physical education in the mid-1940s, I subdivided my investigation into a number of persistent problems, or areas of concern, that have confronted those concerned with teacher education in physical education since it began in 1861 in the United States (Zeigler, 1950). Thus, I was concerned with describing the historical development in each of the following topical headings:

Selective Admission, Placement, and Guidance. The first school had no entrance requirements, but by 1948 complicated routines were involved. The trend in the 1950s was toward generalization of entrance requirements, working toward a continuous, long-range program of selection.

Curriculum—Aims and Methods. The aims and methods of the early schools varied greatly, but toward the end of the nineteenth century some leaders were taking an eclectic and fairly scientific approach. In the period from 1920 to 1950, a unique American philosophy of physical education developed, and the physical educator was conceived as a person of more professional stature. Although many still think primarily of "courses taken," the curriculum is now also being conceived of as all the experiences provided for the development of the professional student.

Curriculum—Length of Course and Type of Degree. The first course for training teachers of physical education extended for a ten-week period, and the successful student received a diploma. Now the professional student in physical education may be awarded the doctor of philosophy or doctor of education degree upon successful completion of a program extending over at least seven years.

Curriculum—Specific Courses and Trends. Early curriculums in the field varied greatly, with some including about as much knowledge of the body as a medical doctor of the time would have been expected to know. The program varied depending upon which foreign system of gymnastics was being propounded. In the twentieth century there was a gradually broadening to include a balanced distribution of general academic, basic science, professional education, and professional physical education courses. In the 1920s the most prevalent specialized curriculum was that of athletic coaching, but in the 1930s the emphasis shifted so that a coach, an academic teacher, and a gymnasium instructor were desired in that order.

In-Service Training of Teachers—Summer Schools, Professional Organizations, Professional Periodicals. In the late nineteenth and early twentieth centuries, a number of summer training programs in physical education began (for example, the Harvard Summer School of Physical Education under Dr. Sargent). This movement really expanded in the 1920s, so that by 1931 the total number of summer sessions was 654, or approximately 28.6 percent of the total number of teachers (273,148 enrolled) (National Education Association, Research Division, 1931). In addition, a number of professional associations have been organized by people with special interests in the field (for example, The National College Physical Education Association for Men in 1897). Either as organs of these associations or separately, a number of professional periodicals were started (for example, *Mind and Body* of The North American Gymnastic Union).

Administrative Problems of Teacher Training. Four other administrative problems were delineated: (1) staff evolution; (2) growth in the number of training programs; (3) teacher certification and state laws involving a steady trend toward centralization of certification in state departments of education along with a progressive raising of minimum requirements; and (4) professional status and ethics, an area in which there has been some development within the so-called education profession.

CONTRASTING PHILOSOPHICAL POSITIONS WITHIN PROFESSIONAL PREPARATION

Broadly speaking, it is possible to delineate among progressivism, essentialism, and a philosophy of language approach to educational philosophy in relation to professional preparation for physical education. In any attempt to do this, the teacher of teachers should keep in mind that progressivism is greatly concerned about such elements as pupil freedom, individual differences, student interest, pupil growth, absence of fixed values, and the idea that "education is life now." The essentialist believes that there are certain educational values by which the student must be guided; that effort takes precedence over interest and that this builds moral stamina; that the experience of the past has powerful jurisdiction over the present; and that the cultivation of the intellect is most important in education (Zeigler, 1963, p. 10). Existentialist "flavoring" in educational philosophy may typically be viewed as somewhat progressivist in nature, mainly because it is individualistic and quite often fundamentally atheistic or agnostic. A philosophy of language approach may be regarded as neither progressivist or essentialist. It is basically concerned with language and/or conceptual analysis. The former is based on the belief that much of the confusion and disagreement over philosophy emanates from misuse of language in various ways; the latter inclines a bit more toward a technique that seeks to define what a term or concept is (as opposed to how it is used). Somewhat broader analytic philosophy provides "a rational reconstruction of the language of science" (Kaplan, 1961, p. 83).

An attempt will now be made to enumerate some eleven aspects of teacher education about which there have been sharp divisions of opinion historically. It has been possible to achieve some consensus on these problems from time to time through the medium of national conferences on teacher preparation, which have been held in the United States since the late 1890s. All factions are in agreement, of course, on the statement that qualified teachers are the most important determinant of the status of the profession, yet there are many areas in which consensus is a long way off—or indeed may never be found. Such disagreement will not necessarily be resolved through employment of the ballot box at national conferences, although the influence of the majority on a contentious issue should be helpful.

Course Emphasis—Technique or Content? The first of the eleven problem areas to be discussed briefly is the question of whether the prospective teacher or coach needs more or less time spent on courses emphasizing technique rather than content. Historically, essentialists are suspicious of the value of so-called general professional education courses; they tend to believe that teaching is much more an art than a science. The idealistically oriented essentialist would be inclined to stress the need for the physical educator to have somewhat more of a background in the humanities, whereas the essentialist with a natural realistic orientation has usually wished to place increased emphasis on the foundation science courses (Zeigler, 1964, pp. 263–265).

Competency versus Courses and Credits. The previous discussion leads to a further problem that has plagued teacher education historically and still has not been resolved. This is the possible use of the competency approach as opposed to the courses and credits approach that has been with the field traditionally since the first professional program was introduced in 1861. As matters stand now, the student takes a certain number of courses while attending college for a required number of years. Upon graduation, the "teacher" receives a degree for the successful completion of 132 semester hours, more or less, and a provisional teaching certificate—a notice which informs local school boards that the recipient is presumably a competent, educated person able to teach physical education to the youth of the state. But these are no guarantee that graduating seniors will be able to function well as intelligent citizens and competent professionals; we need a more effective means of assessing their abilities. For example, what specific competencies have they developed through selected experiences, using subject matter as a resource?

Over the years the essentialist has not been disturbed at all about the pattern in which students take a certain number of specified courses for a required number of years; earn the required number of credit hours with approximately a C plus grade point average; and then go out to teach if they can find jobs. The progressivist, conversely, has been more concerned about what is happening to the individual if this process goes on, especially insofar as knowledge, skills, and competencies are concerned, and specifically as these may be related directly and evaluatively to excellent teaching performance.

Relating Language Analysis to the Competency Approach. When a special committee at Illinois related a language analysis approach to teacher education in physical education in 1963, I was charged with preparation of a preliminary statement employing this ordinary language terminology. The members of the committee were not approaching their task in either an essentialist or progressivist manner; they were merely attempting to define the terms that are typically employed and then to place them in proper perspective. Once this process was completed, when a specific term (for example, "competency") was employed, they would know where it fit into the pattern being developed and *how* the term was being used. (For purposes of this presentation, therefore, this philosophy of language approach is clearly understood as possessing no value orientation like that of progressivism or essentialism.)

The results of this deliberation were as follows: Students enrolled in a professional preparation program in physical education and sport are afforded educational experiences in a classroom, laboratory, gymnasium, pool, field, or field work setting. Through various types of educational methodology (lectures, discussions, problem-solving situations in theory and practice), they hear facts, increase the scope of their information (knowledge), and learn to comprehend and interpret this material (understanding). Possessing various amounts of ability or aptitude, the students gradually develop competency and a certain degree of skill. It is to be hoped that certain appreciations about the worth of the profession will be developed, and that they will form certain attitudes about the work that lies ahead in their chosen field. To sum it up, there are certain special duties or performances students preparing for the teaching profession should fulfill (functions). Through the professional curriculum, they are exposed to specific problems they must face successfully. Through planned experiences, with a wide variety of resource areas to serve as repositories of facts, they develop competencies, skills, knowledge, understanding, appreciations, and attitudes that will enable them to be effective educators (Zeigler, 1975, pp. 290–292).

Specialization or Generalization in the Curriculum? A fourth problem in this century has been the question of whether there should be a specialized curriculum or a generalized program that includes health and safety education (including driver education) and recreation education. Those with an essentialist orientation have felt that the trend toward generalization of function must be halted; many professional educators with such an orientation would prefer that attention be devoted toward turning out good physical education teachers or gymnasium instructors—exercise specialists. The essentialist tends to believe that the field has spawned many of these allied fields, but that they have now grown up and should be allowed to try out their own wings. Some with an essentialist orientation believe that physical training can be considered curricular, but there is almost unanimous agreement that all these other areas are really extracurricular. The educational progressivist, conversely, believed—at least until the disciplinary emphasis of the 1960s arrived—that we should include any and all of these areas within a department or school and as a part of the physical education major curriculum.

Election versus Requirement in the Curriculum.   The pendulum has been swinging surely and steadily back and forth in connection with this problem area from generation to generation over the past hundred years. In a professional curriculum of twenty-five years ago, a student was allowed one elective course in the senior year—and even with this "elective" the young man or woman was urged to select a basic geography course. Now there is almost complete freedom of election in the same university, and a student could graduate without taking anatomy and physiology! The "elective promiscuity" of the 1960s is now being changed, however, and a modified or basic core of courses is being established as a requirement in both the humanities and the social sciences as well as in the biosciences.

Influence of Competitive Athletics.   Most women in the field of physical education have been appalled by the strongly materialistic influences that have beset men's athletics since the early years of the twentieth century. In making every effort to set proper standards for women, it is quite possible that women physical educators in the United States tended to throw out the baby with bath water. During the decades when interscholastic and intercollegiate athletics for women were zealously kept under control and at a very low level, Canadian women physical educators maintained competitive sport for women in educational perspective and at a slightly higher level of competition in the colleges and universities. Now the situation has very definitely changed, and the social influence of the women's movement is bringing about a new emphasis on women's competitive sport. Recent Title IX legislation clearly means that women should have exactly the same opportunities as men in competitive sport, and one wonders whether the women's program will inevitably lose almost all educational perspective in the process. The almost plaintive statement of the American physical educator that "we don't have any problems with intercollegiate athletics;

we are completely separate from them" is almost as frightening as the rationalizations of the politicians caught in the Watergate fiasco. Both educational essentialists and educational progressivists decry the materialistic excesses operating within competitive sport in education, but they seem almost powerless to combat these abuses successfully. Essentialists are probably a little less disturbed because they may see this activity as extracurricular, whereas progressivists, who see this experience as potentially curricular in nature, are greatly disturbed.

Discipline versus Professional Preparation. It is now recognized by almost all that the need for a disciplinary orientation to a body of knowledge for physical education which became evident in the early 1960s has somehow challenged or threatened those who felt the field's primary mission to be preparation of teachers and coaches of physical education and sport for the secondary schools. This would not seem to be an either-or decision situation, because certainly any true profession needs enough supporting scholars and researchers to provide the knowledge necessary for successful functioning. For a variety of reasons, the field of physical education has not attracted a sufficient quantity of scholars in the past, although fortunately the situation has improved in the past ten years. This deficiency has resulted in physical education as a field acquiring a rather massive inferiority complex. Is it any wonder, therefore, that the theory and practice of human motor performance (or human movement) has not been considered acceptable for introduction into the educational curriculum at any level?

The Bioscience versus the Humanities–Social Science Conflict. Another problem that has come into sharp focus recently—although it has surfaced on occasion in the past—is the actual conflict that has developed between those in the field who feel that a bioscience approach is sufficient for its fullest development. Thus, their efforts are devoted fully in this direction, and they decry any expenditures for the development of the humanities and social science aspects of the profession. Of course, this is not the first time in education or elsewhere when haves became worried about have-nots wanting to get support for their work, and the present financial cutbacks in university support may make the problem more acute. Incidents such as isolated efforts by social scientists to downgrade the humanities aspects of the field represent the type of internecine conflict that will inevitably be self-defeating for the entire field of physical education and sport.

The Accreditation of Teacher-Preparing Institutions. Efforts to improve the level of teacher education generally, and physical education specifically, have resulted in several approaches to the matter of accreditation. Over the past forty years or so, a number of attempts have been made to standardize professional curriculums with some positive results. Many national conferences in both general professional education and in this specialized field have been held in an attempt to determine desirable practices for teacher education institutions. From this movement have evolved standards to be used by teams of professionals serving under accrediting agency auspices. The first step was the establishment of evaluative criteria for the rating of professional programs, and at this time individual departments were encouraged to undertake self-evaluation of major programs. More recently, however, the National Council on Accreditation of Teacher Education began conducting institutional surveys as rapidly and as carefully as possible. The entire field of teacher education is involved in this effort, and accreditation is being withheld from institutions that do not meet the prescribed standards. There is a considerable amount of consensus between the essentialists and the progressivists about this development, even if their agreement is not always based upon the same reasons for backing this move by NCATE. The progressivist typically supports the concept of self-evaluation and believes that standards should allow room for flexibility, whereas the essentialist would generally vote to eliminate substandard institutions from the field if their standards are not elevated within a fixed period of time.

Involvement of Students in the Evaluation Process. Yet another problem has been the extent to which students are allowed or encouraged to share in the evaluation of the professional program's progress. Typically, the progressivist has seen a great deal of merit in such a process, whereas the essentialist has avoided the employment of such an evaluative technique. The student unrest of the 1960s and public disenchantment with colleges and universities have forced essentialist professors and administrators to accept course evaluations by students as a necessary evil. The publication of course evaluation manuals by student organizations has met with considerable hostility on the part of segments of the faculty. Demands that such evaluations be employed by committees on promotion and tenure have brought strong reactions by professors who hold that the immature cannot possibly evaluate correctly what they do not fully understand.

Patterns of Administrative Control. The final problem to be discussed here relates to the question of whether the approach to the administrative function within education has a vital part to play in the achievement of the objectives of the professional preparation program in physical education. The educational essentialists tend to see administration as an art, whereas the progressivists view it as a developing social science—that is, all evidence should be brought to bear in the administrative process, while the program is being administered artfully. An educational progressivist serving as an administrator would seek to conduct the affairs of the department in a truly democratic manner and would encourage faculty members to share in policy formation. The chairperson would encourage faculty, staff, and students to offer constructive criticism in a variety of ways. Essentialist administrators tend to function on the basis of ascribed authority centralized through a line-staff pattern of control. They have the ultimate responsibility and, although they may ask for opinions from faculty members—and indeed there are aspects of the university situation now where faculty and even students vote on important matters—they would not hesitate to overrule majority opinion if convinced that incorrect decisions had been made. In the final analysis, there is still no firm understanding in an evolving democratic society as to what constitutes the best type of democratic process within a college or university's pattern of administrative control. But it is most important that undergraduate students observe (and take part in?) the best pattern of administrative control consisent wih representative democracy.

CONCLUDING STATEMENT

One last step will be taken in connection with the analysis of professional preparation as a persistent problem in the field of physical education and sport—the recommendation of six criteria whereby a philosophy of professional education might be developed by any sincere, reasonably intelligent individual practicing in the field. The position taken here is that to be effective, a philosophy of professional education should include the following:

1. The expression of a position concerning the nature of the universe (*metaphysics*). To the extent that such a position is possible, it should be founded on knowledge that is systematically verifiable—or at least recognition of nonverifiability should be admitted.
2. A statement about the possibility of the acquisition of knowledge (*epistemology*). Such a statement should be logical and consistent in its several divisions.
3. A determination of educational aims and objectives in relation to societal aims or values (*axiology*). Such aims should be both broad and inclusive in scope.

4. A *design of action* for education. Education should be meaningful and enjoyable, as well as practical and attainable.

5. A design for implementation of *general* professional education. This should be based on the achievement of knowledge, competencies, and skills through planned experiences.

6. A design for implementation of *specialized* professional education. This should also be achieved through the acquisition of knowledge, competencies, and skills as a result of carefully planned experiences.

Section Four

The Healthy Body

Although we discussed attitudes toward the place of health education (in all its aspects) within the educational system briefly in the first chapter, they are of such importance today that they merit special consideration as a separate persistent problem.

The condition of our bodies has undoubtedly always been of concern. Early peoples found that a certain type of fitness was necessary for life. Muscles, including the heart, *had* to be strong; vision *had* to be keen; and one *had* to be able to run fast. Physical efficiency was necessary for survival. Modern people, more successful than their forebears in making an adjustment to their environment, live longer. Success is dependent, however, on complicated procedures. Sound teeth depend upon competent dentistry. Good eyesight very often depends on the services of highly trained opthalmologists, oculists, optometrists, and opticians. Highly qualified medical doctors and surgeons preserve the health of heart, lungs, and other vital organs. Protruding neck, round shoulders, sagging abdomen, and pronated ankles (including flat feet) are indirect results of the machine age. People's hearts pound wildly when they run fifty yards after a departing bus or subway train, or when they climb a flight of stairs fairly rapidly. Often they have difficulty adjusting elemental emotions to the habit pattern of do's and don'ts that we commonly term civilization. When this occurs, and it is occurring with increasing regularity, people crack under the strain and are referred to a hospital, more victims of what have been designated as psychosomatic difficulties.

HISTORICAL BACKGROUND

A study of past and present civilizations indicates that the sociological states of war and peace produce quite different health emphases.

Freedom from disqualifying defects, strength, and endurance are important to those who want to win wars. When a particular war is over, the society is then able to focus its attention again toward the mastery of its own environment. During such periods, the emphasis in health can be placed on the related questions of longevity and environmental health.

There has always been a great deal of ignorance about sound health practices throughout the world. However, attempts at scientific solutions may be dated as long ago as 1000 B.C. The Egyptians tried to curtail the spread of communicable disease through land drainage and also developed some primitive pharmaceutical knowledge. The Hebrews extended somewhat the health knowledge of the Egyptians in the areas of water purification, waste disposal, food protection, communicable disease control, and maternity care, certain elements of which were incorporated into the Mosaic Law.

The Greeks regarded hygiene, the science of preserving health, as a positive goal. The Spartans preserved the lives of healthy, strong infants and exposed the unfit to die on Mount Taygetus. These hardy youth were then subject to a rigorous existence in preparation for military service. The Athenians, with a much broader educational aim, sought to realize sound personal health for Athenian youth through improved nutrition, a variety of types of exercise, and plenty of fresh air. They were fortunate to have Hippocrates, the father of medicine, who made a sound effort to place medicine on a scientific basis. He saw prevention as medicine's true ideal. He classified the causes of disease into those brought on by external conditions such as climate and those caused by internal conditions such as lack of exercise and poor health habits. Unfortunately most of this "knowledge" was based upon false premises that were not corrected until many hundreds of years later with the beginnings of the science of bacteriology. We do have the Greeks to thank, however, for the ideal of the sound body developed through their recommended program of health gymnastics.

The Romans adopted many of the advances the Greeks had made, although they were basically suspicious of them as foreign. The only significant forward step in public health made by the Romans seems to have been in the area of sanitary engineering. The city of Rome had a well-organized sewer system and a tremendous aqueduct (as did many other cities in the empire). Military hospitals were evidently constructed in a sanitary manner as well. Even though Rome's location and the actual environment have been called "healthful" by some, there is evidence of a number of epidemics, especially during the flooding periods and the warmer season of the year. As the Roman economy improved, the dangers of overeating became a problem. There was continuing concern that the people were not leading the same healthy lives they had in the earlier days. Writers of the time stressed the need for healthful exercise and recreational activities, especially for the sedentary, but often to no avail. Galen, a famous physician of the time, wrote a number of essays on the subject of healthful exercise, while deploring athletic contests that promoted excesses and often resulted in the maiming of participants. A type of early medical science began to develop with all sorts of specialization. Some of these physicians had talent, but many were quacks of the worst order. State medicine, encouraged by Caesar, ultimately vanished in the waning days of the empire, mainly due to the pseudoscience of early Christian saints.

During the Middle Ages, Greco-Roman civilization and culture all but disappeared, including public health and medical practice. Leprosy spread all over Europe, but the rigid establishment of isolation camps eventually brought about its eradication. The recognition that the various communicable diseases were spread by contact with infected persons was an important step taken in preventive medicine. A type of quarantine was even established for ships entering ports. It has been estimated that plagues and epidemics killed off approximately one-quarter of the population of the time. It is not surprising that people sought an explanation in God's wrath and other superstitious beliefs.

Many factors brought about the general awakening known as the Renaissance in the fourteenth century. A new spirit of inquiry that had been dormant for centuries arose. A rediscovery of the writings of Aristotle and the establishment of a number of universities helped to kindle a spirit of adventure and a desire to progress despite existing conditions that made the era anything but peaceful. In the field of medicine Paracelsus (1491–1541) helped to liberate scientific thought from the formalized structure of Galen's teachings. Independent research and thought was greatly hampered by the status-quo attitude of both Church and state. Christianity in the Middle Ages must be credited, however, for the establishment of the first institutions that can be called hospitals. Islamic learning, based to a considerable extent on Greek translations, no doubt helped to stimulate the awakening during the fifteenth and sixteenth centuries. Yet we find that surgery was still largely in the hands of barbers who worked in opposition to physicians and formed their own guild. One significant development during the sixteenth century was Ambroise Paré's surgical technique of tying an artery—a technique necessary for successful amputations.

It would not serve our purpose to trace in detail at this point the various advances made in public health through the efforts of many great pioneers during the early modern period. Without their help we would not have the foundation upon which today's public health knowledge is based. Although the rate of progress may seem slow, an examination of the history of public health reveals that such advancement was often made despite adverse attitudes rather than with the help of public opinion. The period of the Industrial Revolution, for example, with the resultant urbanization and overcrowding, was a great challenge to those concerned. Fortunately, the changing political atmosphere encouraged government responsibility and made possible the advancement of humanitarian ideals. During the twentieth century there has been outstanding progress; nevertheless, it is profoundly disturbing that so many people in the world are still not able to profit to the fullest from these advances. In the United States a gigantic effort has been made to enlighten the public in the areas of personal and community health. The federal government has gradually assumed a larger role in the promotion of public health—this in the face of constant criticism that socialized medicine will help destroy our system of free enterprise.

Health education itself advanced rapidly after the stage had been set by the draft statistics of World War I. It was evident that many of these physical defects could have been prevented by proper measures taken during the school years. Fortunately, money was available in the 1920s to do something about the situation.

Since that time many have concerned themselves with the development of school health education. Simultaneously, public health education in the home and community has advanced through the efforts of public and private agencies. During the 1920s, conflicting ideas arose as to the definition of health and the place of health instruction in the curriculum. Some people conceived of health as freedom from disease, while others saw it as an attribute of a strong, vigorous body. Still others have broadened this concept; the late Jesse Feiring Williams, for example, defined health as "that quality of life which enables the individual to live most and to serve best." According to this definition, the ultimate test of health is the use to which it is put.

IMPLICATIONS FROM EDUCATIONAL PHILOSOPHY

Much of the disagreement over the role of school health education in the educational pattern today stems from differing educational philosophies and from various concepts of health. Perhaps the greatest hindrance to full acceptance of health education in the curriculum is the dualistic concept of the person first as a thinking being and only secondarily as a physical being.

For educational progressivists, sound health is one of the primary objectives of education, and the success of the school health education program depends upon the degree of cooperation among home, school, and community agencies. Educated persons today must understand the difference between health and disease, and know how to protect and improve their own health, that of their dependents, and that of the community both large and small. In addition, physical training, health education, and instruction in profitable use of leisure time should be coordinated within the school program.

A school health education program designed to foster truly healthful living should be composed of three distinct, yet closely related, divisions: (1) *healthful school living*—the development of the type of environment that will facilitate the optimal growth and development of students; (2) *health instruction*—a teaching program organized to develop specific knowledge, competencies, and attitudes concerning health; and (3) *health service*—provision for care when sudden illness or injury occurs, annual appraisal of health status, and health counseling including procedures for the prevention and/or control of communicable diseases.

The realist position is not as clearcut in regard to the place of health education. Some realists view it naturalistically; others take theological considerations into account. The naturalistic realist, for example, would state that he or she is concerned with maximum development of physical vigor and health, but the Thomist and rational humanists are inclined to preserve a certain hierarchy of values "inherent" in liberal education as they view it.

Broudy's position on the place of health education in the school structure (1961, pp. 149–171) appears to be fairly representative of the realist. He believes that the school environment should be healthy and that knowledge about the bases of emotional and physical health belongs in the curriculum. But from here on, other agencies should take up the task. The community, for example, has the responsibility of providing clinical facilities for therapy, and the home must instill desirable health habits. He inquires further whether the school could ever hope to treat the matter of sex education adequately. In fact, Broudy even intimates that adolescents are for the most part so healthy that any discussion of health problems may seem unreal to them.

Perhaps the clearest statement of the idealist position toward health and health education comes from the late Herman Harrell Horne. He omits it under a discussion of the "essential studies" in the curriculum except for incidental mention under biology, but then places "health" first in a list of nine basic values of human living. Horne explains this contradiction as follows: health education belongs at the bottom of the hierarchy of educational values, but the quality of health "enhances the richness of each and all of them [the other values]" (1942, p. 186).

Among Christian idealists, Mormons appear to take the strongest position in regard to the care of the body. According to their faith, the spirit and body *are* the soul of the individual. They conceive of the body as a non-evil component of the eternal soul and look forward to literal resurrection after death. Thus, generally speaking, the idealist values a program of health and physical education highly as a service program which enables people to pursue still higher goals in education and ir life.

The existentialist, as has been noted earlier, wants the school to help the person become an authentic, self-determining individual. When the child realizes that he is responsible for his own conduct, education becomes for him a process of discovery. He *alone* can make the decision that he needs to learn about personal and community health.

Women in Physical Education and Sport

Aristotle believed that women had been fitted by nature for subjection to the male of the species because they had no ability for self-direction. He felt that they were weaker, less courageous, and incomplete. Plato held a different view; he believed that women should have education similar to the pattern he prescribed for men, including the highest type of liberal education and preparation for warfare.

Certainly one of the significant social trends of the twentieth century has been the movement for women's liberation. In past societies it had been erroneously concluded that women simply did not possess the intellectual capacity to profit from the higher types of education. Hence girls and women were typically given no intellectual function; their duty was to bear and rear children and manage the home. This concept has certainly changed considerably for most women in the United States and elsewhere. Egalitarianism has been fostered through such influences as the Industrial Revolution, the various wars, and more democratic theories of state. Women's physical education and sport has been hampered not only by the place of physical education in a particular society, but also by the place that women held in any society under consideration—and to a considerable extent by the ideas that men and women had about women's physical limitations.

HISTORICAL BACKGROUND

Early Societies

In primitive and preliterate societies, education took place largely in the home, where the mother nurtured the young boys and girls until a division of labor took place. At this juncture the mother began the education of the girl in household arts, and the father started the boy on preparation for manhood. The boy's training was designed to test his strength, endurance, skill, and courage. That which might be called drudgery today was typically assigned to women in the large majority of societies, although there is evidence that women and young girls took part in minor amusements and played games.

Egypt. In the Egyptian civilization, for example, there is pictorial proof that women took part in simple ball games, swimming, archery, and dancing. Dancing was not considered proper for members of the upper class, although certain priestesses evidently performed religious dances. With the common people, however, dancing was practiced regularly, and there were numerous professional dancers.

China. Aside from simple childhood games and the popularity of dancing, the large majority of people in ancient China got their exercise from various types of physical labor; time for recreation was extremely rare. The emphasis on intellectual training was such that physical training was deprecated. A few girls whose families had means were educated, but physical activity was not a part of such training. There were a few exceptions, but these were rarities indeed. A simplet yet devastating maneuver like binding the feet kept women quite weak and useless for anything save household management and decoration.

India. Although ancient India had a great many health problems, history indicates that there was considerable concern for health prior to foreign rule in the tenth century, and that a number of sports and games were practiced. Accompanying the decline in physical activities and physical culture were the restrictions laid down by Buddha himself against the popular pastimes of the day. There was often a military class that had to keep fit for combat. Dancing was popular, but then fell into disrepute except for members of the lower classes and professional dancing girls. Generally speaking, there was a complete rejection of bodily activity for women, who were kept in an inferior social position.

Iran and Israel. In Iranian civilization there is no mention of physical education for women whatsoever, but in Hebrew civilization women appear to have occupied an important place, especially in early times. Dancing was often involved in religious worship, but subsequently continued only as a form of recreation and for various secular celebrations. There was a certain amount of physical labor for women in connection with the routine chores of the camps, or perhaps with the flocks in the fields, or in vine culture on the hillsides. Certain health habits and recreational pursuits were considered desirable, the latter especially on the Sabbath. As social life increased, women were confined to a greater extent to the home. They were not expected to possess intellectual acumen. Many did involve themselves in simple games, music, and dancing.

Crete. The Cretan civilization preceded that of the Greeks and extended roughly for a period of four or five thousand years on the island of Crete and at other points in the Mediterranean Sea. It was the first society in which women assumed a relatively important role. Even their deity was a mother goddess, and there appears to have been more equal status in marriage between the sexes. Women are known to have taken part in numerous games and sports. They did other things like hunting, driving chariots, and even bull-grappling, a dangerous sport. There is further evidence that they attended various celebrations and religious festivals. Because of the proximity of the sea, they were active in boating and undoubtedly knew how to swim.

Classical Civilization

Greece. In the city-state of Sparta, presumably the most warlike of the various Greek city-states, the educational system was carefully designed to fulfill the avowed goal of military supremacy. Here women received unusual attention, as it was felt that it was absolutely necessary for them to produce rugged children to be future warriors. They took part in many of the activities of the boys and young men and developed a concept of good health and their place in life. They wrestled, ran, played ball, threw the javelin, swam, and rode horseback. Some even won Olympic victories. Typically, they continued public exercises until marriage and were probably on the average the finest physical specimens that the world has seen to date. There is some disagreement as to whether this training fully accomplished its purpose, although it is quite natural that the Athenians would ridicule these women because of the different standard they held. There is evidence, however, that the dancing of the young Spartan maidens was graceful, and that their demeanor was appropriate to that expected of a woman.

Contrasting Cultures. There were sharp contrasts between the Spartan and Athenian cultures, yet the ideal of service on behalf of the state characterized Athenian life as well. The Athenians gradually developed a concept of education that envisioned harmony of development of all the aspects of the person—physical, mental, moral, and esthetic. They fostered, as perhaps never before or after, an ideal of liberal education for freemen that has been admired ever since. And yet we find that women had virtually no part in the achievements of this civilization save for the function of childbearing and care of the home. Subsequently women achieved greater status as teachers of their children. but the boys were taken away from them when ready for the palaestrae. Lower-class women did have the opportunity to become entertainers in such occupations as dancing, juggling, and the playing of various instruments. Properly modest Athenian women played games as children; learned household arts as young ladies; at times learned to read and write; married early; and were rarely heard of thereafter.

Roman Culture. The status of women in Rome was very low initially, but changed considerably during the time of the empire. In early Rome the average woman was definitely considered inferior, and had little to say about her place in life. Her education came to an abrupt end when she married. Despite these limitations, her station is generally considered to have been somewhat higher than that of her counterpart in Greece. She did learn how to read, write, and cipher and was responsible for the early education of her children. Presumably she took part in childhood games and, in some cases, learned how to swim.

In the later days of the empire women achieved a greater amount of independence, including social and moral equality, as well as the opportunity to gain a divorce and to own property. A developing laxity in morals took place, and adultery was much more common. Many women, however, distinguished themselves in a variety of ways and were trained in the various professions. Their pattern of education changed also, although there is doubt whether coeducation ever existed. Dancing, music, and literature were included, and then were banned later under the influence of Christian asceticism.

The Romans never caught the Greek spirit of total education, although they exercised for health and took part in a number of different sports, especially ball-playing. Women went to the public baths, took part in the simple forms of ball-playing, and watched the spectacles, but on the whole were not very active physically. The exercises of the gymnasium were simply not considered proper for women except in rare instances when such activity was tried and summarily rejected.

The Middle Ages

The Middle Ages was a time when physical education sank to its lowest ebb except for the training of knights in the feudal period, and its appearance in some of the humanistic schools of the Renaissance. The Church opposed athletic and recreational excess during this time, and there developed the concept that the body was evil and its demands should be suppressed. The Romans in their final days so debased sports and games that such opposition was quite understandable. There were some exceptions to this belief, but they were rare indeed. There is very little mention of women during the Dark Ages. During the feudal period, girls received training in the courtly graces in schools conducted at the various castles. There were, of course, the usual children's games that have persisted throughout history. During the transitional period now known as the Renaissance, the care and development of the body received greater emphasis. There does not appear to be evidence that the concept of all-round development was generally recognized, however, and this certainly held true in the education of girls and young ladies. It should be pointed out that the humanism of the early Renaissance gave great promise for physical education, but a growing spirit of intellectualism cut short this hopeful development. In the lands where the Protestant Reformation took hold, study of the classics was combined with that of biblical literature, with the result that the educational aim was somewhat more social than individual. These so-called social humanists promoted a much narrower concept of education and copied Greek and Roman writers slavishly. With this approach there was little room in the curriculum for physical education, music, or art.

Early Modern History

During the sixteenth and seventeenth centuries a number of educators rebelled against the formalism present in education at that time. These educators, known as realists, have since been divided into three categories: (1) the verbal realists, who desired a strong body for the help that it could give the mind as it strove for religious piety; (2) the social realists, who conceived of physical education as an important part of education for an integrated personality, and (3) the sense realists, who desired physical fitness for its contribution to sound health and as a basis for intellectual attainment.

Very little attention appears to have been given to education for girls during this era. Fénelon, Archbishop of Cambrai, provided some stimulus for the education of women by presenting his theories on the subject, but his main contribution appears to be in the direction of liberalizing educational method. Juan Luis Vives, a Spanish scholar, omitted such subjects as music, dancing, and drawing in his proposed curriculum, while including training in Latin and the vernacular, religion and moral conduct, and household and child management. John Locke, whose greatest contribution was made in the latter half of the seventeenth century, was greatly concerned with character development as well as health and physical fitness as a necessary base. He stressed the need for recreational activity as well, mainly because of the refreshment from toil that it provided. But his recommendations were made primarily for boys and young men.

Eighteenth-Century Europe

The eighteenth century is generally regarded as a transitional period insofar as political, social, religious, and educational ideals are concerned. It might be designated as a reactionary period in education, especially in the first fifty years. Formal discipline in education developed as a reaction against the realistic theories. The tendency toward universal education was retarded to a considerable degree as rationalism became an important goal in education as well. The greatest influence on education in this century came in the latter half with the thought of Jean Jacques Rousseau. He was the exponent of naturalism in education—an idea that represented a revolt against the corrupting influence of society and the absolute and dogmatic authority of state and church. His doctrine of naturalism gave unusually strong emphasis to the place of health and physical education in the child's education, because he evidently realized the interrelatedness or unity of the mind and body.

Unfortunately for the women of his time, he did not appreciate the possibility that a woman might possess an individuality of her own. He felt that woman was destined to be a supplement to man. Hence she should be strong physically to bear healthy children. She should also receive sound moral instruction, as this would get her children off to the right start in life. Furthermore, her education should include such skills as singing, dancing, and a variety of household abilities, since the possession of these talents would make life more comfortable and enjoyable for her husband.

The Nineteenth Century

The Influence of Nationalism. The influence of nationalism on education in both Europe and the United States in the nineteenth century was very strong, and helped to bring about state-controlled and state-supported public school systems. In any national school system, physical training designed to maintain and improve the fitness of the populace will invariably find an important place, and it will usually include girls and women as well as boys and men. Thus, the various systems of universal, free, and compulsory education that developed throughout the Western world typically included citizenship, physical, and vocational training.

New Ideals in Elementary Education. Concurrent with the development of nationalism in education, another change was gradually taking place in connection with the actual educational process itself.

Many concerned individuals began to realize that education should involve control of the child's development according to certain psychological principles resulting from the interaction of the individual and his environment. The results of these new ideas were felt primarily only in the elementary school during this century, and subsequently extended to some extent to the other levels.

Women's Physical Education in the United States

During the early years of the nineteenth century educational practices for girls and women in America began to change. This change in practice was true in the matter of exercise as well, which had previously been characterized by formalism. The boys and the men of the early 1800s were following a German pattern as prescribed by Beck, Follen, and Lieber, but there was some variation in the exercise patterns prescribed for girls.

Girls were considered to be quite frail, and it was believed by many that calisthenics were much too strenuous. A new type of wand drill known as Indian Scepter exercises were quite popular for a time. Another trend was the introduction of apparatuses to improve posture and develop strength. Women of this period, according to fashion, were expected to have small waists and weak backs. It is significant to note that—for the first time—walking, riding, croquet, swimming, skating, and archery were being recommended as desirable activities for women.

Other Developments. Around the middle of the nineteenth century, the Turners were promoting German gymnastics as the best program for the schools. At this time, also, George Barker Winship was declaiming that strength and health were synonymous. Furthermore, some colleges became concerned with the health habits and practices of their students. Then along came Dio Lewis with his system of light exercises designed for adult women, as well as for the young and the old.

Post-Civil War Period. After the Civil War, the exercises devised by Lewis and those proposed earlier by Catherine Beecher continued to meet stiff opposition from German gymnastics, Swedish gymnastics, and new patterns being devised by Hitchcock, Sargent, and others. Interest in athletic participation in various sports and games arose simultaneously. Greater freedom in activity (and dress) was gradually being accepted, although such "freedom" was actually very limited in scope by today's standards. In dancing there were changes as well away from stylized movements with very little bodily action to a more classic form of dance that involved all parts of the body. In early health education, the emphasis had been on the unsatisfactory environmental conditions in the schools; during this postwar period, concern was increasingly related to the harmful influence of bacteria, along with physiology of the body, including the harmful influences of alcohol and narcotics.

Early Twentieth Century

At the beginning of the twentieth century, there was still a great deal of opposition toward the idea of women taking part in interscholastic athletics, but the recommendations of women's organizations in favor of intramural sports did not discourage the women basketball enthusiasts. The first standardized rules guide was published on behalf of the American Physical Education Association in 1901. It is noteworthy that professional women physical educators made every effort to guard women's athletics from many of the difficulties that the men had encountered.

The "Natural" Movement. Another innovation at this time was the widespread effort to bring dancing into the curriculum. A new conflict developed over the extent to which dancing and athletics should supplant gymnastics in physical education programs. Folk dancing became so popular that many felt it and athletics were receiving undue emphasis. These trends, of course, were part of the growing "natural" movement in physical education that attempted to relate our field to current American educational theories. This movement undoubtedly had a relationship to the growing interest in play and recreation, as well as to the competitive athletic trend.

There is no question, also, of the tremendous influence that Dewey's philosophy of education had on the natural movement. Wood and Cassidy's *The New Physical Education,* published in 1927, was designed to clarify this approach so that all who were interested might understand what the naturalized program was intended to accomplish. It was based upon a system of motor training to be implemented through "learning while doing." The belief was that it was in agreement with "modern educational theory" and helped the student to realize "concrete goals in activity." The major emphasis was to be on exercise that was more natural, spontaneous, and enjoyable. Education *through* the medium of the physical was to supersede education *of* the physical.

1930 to 1940. In 1930 the American Physical Education Association elected Mabel Lee as its first woman president, and in the following year the Women's Division of the National Amateur Athletic Federation affiliated with the APEA. In 1940 this group (the Women's Division) merged with the National Section on Women's Athletics (APEA). This section, now known as the Division of Girl's and Women's Sports, has exerted a strong, wholesome influence on all aspects of women's sport. The decade from 1930 to 1940 was dominated by a devastating financial depression that, incidentally, gave impetus to the concept of education for wholesome use of leisure. Requirements for teachers were upgraded during this period.

World War II. World War II dominated the decade from 1940 to 1950 and brought increased emphasis on physical fitness for both boys and girls. The time allotment for physical education was generally increased. Their acceptance in the various branches of the armed forces provided additional incentive for women to stress physical activity. Increased interest was shown in a large variety of individual, dual, and team sports, but competition for women was still confined almost completely to the intramural program, with some emphasis on interscholastic competition in specific geographic areas. Interest in all aspects of the dance continued to grow, with special emphasis on modern, folk, and square dancing.

The Postwar Period. Women physical educators have continued to emphasize the need for a broad program of health, physical education, and recreation. Where possible, they have encouraged a program of required physical education for all girls as well as a remedial program for those who needed it. They have taken the lead in the elementary field, and many have made an effort to implement the concept of movement education in the field. They have stressed health education, instruction in carryover activities, and voluntary recreational participation. Recommendations for improved physical fitness from the national level in the latter half of the 1950s and the early 1960s are undoubtedly having an influence on girls' programs at present. The extent to which the desire for increasing physical fitness has influenced the gradual upswing in the caliber of girls' and women's sports has yet to be determined.

PHILOSOPHICAL ANALYSIS

We have now arrived at the point where the question must be asked whether the same set of educational values in physical education and sport that applies to men applies to women as well. Immediately we encounter the issue of whether or not the sexes are actually so different and, if so, in what ways? From an anatomical standpoint, the differences are apparent at once. But such differences are only superficial, as is pointed out by anthropologists, and when one gets beyond the factors of strength and endurance, questions can then be raised as to which is the "stronger" sex. Of course, such attributes are especially important in sport, and this fact must be recognized.

This persistent problem is so important for the future, however, that it demands much more serious consideration than it has gotten for perhaps several thousand years. In our opinion there are far too many men physical educators who are all too willing to ignore the efforts of women in the field and to let them go their own way. The assumption seems to be that men really have nothing at stake in this matter. Nothing could be further from the truth! There appears to be another group of male coaches and athletic administrators who seems all too willing to go along with the prevailing situation in girls' and women's physical education and/or sport in the United States because there is very little conflict between the sexes for the use of equipment and facilities.

The study of history, as has been indicated above, has shown that women have traditionally been considered inferior in comparison to men. A steady change in woman's role seems to have taken place, however, despite the fact that a larger view of cultural sociology reminds us that the truly important functions of life must be continued. Despite what appears to be the urgent need for population control in certain geographic areas, it is not possible to escape the fact that women do have a unique function to fulfill—that of continuing and protecting life. And yet our changing way of life, and the increasing tempo of that change, has caused a considerable amount of uncertainty and confusion. Perhaps the question is whether we can shape the thinking of our society so that there can be concentration to a greater extent on *individual* differences rather than on the time-honored sex difference approach. In this way it is conceivable that all individuals in the United States, regardless of sex, may within a reasonably short period of time have the opportunity to develop to the maximum of their potentialities in keeping with the pattern of evolving democracy.

But despite the declaration of such events as International Women's Year, this daydreaming could well be a bit too experimentalist for the United States (or Canada) at present, so we must return to what in popular jargon would be called a more realistic assessment of the present situation in regard to values in physical education and sport. This means that some women physical educators see educational aims and objectives as relative and experimental, whereas others—the realists and the idealists —look upon them as objective and intrinsic in the universe. For the latter group, therefore, the intrinsic values are most important, and it is logical to construct a hierarchy of values that has direct application to the educational system.

The Three Major Philosophies

With this in mind, it seems reasonable to state that the same major philosophies of physical education and sport—experimentalism, realism, and idealism—apply to women, and that these approaches are modified by certain social influences or forces concerning women's role in society and the educational pattern they should follow. Within the past twenty years, a fourth philosophical position or stance has emerged and been accepted by a substantial number of people. The reference here is to existentialism, which has been referred to by many as more of a "permeating influence" than a full-blown philosophical position. At any rate, those with an existential orientation have been quite individualistic and therefore largely progressivist in their approach. The three so-called major philosophical tendencies, along with the more recent "permeating influence," have been delineated at some length earlier in this volume.

Society's Norm for Women

No matter which of the philosophical tendencies or "stances" a woman physical educator aligns herself with, she also finds herself confronted with the image that society has of the role of a woman. Women physical educators are most anxious, and perhaps rightly so, to preserve a professional image for themselves and their students. Obviously, the present situation for women is in a state of flux, and social influences may well cause this image to change. Many have undoubtedly achieved a certain professionalism, but in so doing they have not necessarily lived up to the highest goals of any of the particular philosophical positions for education and for physical education and sport specifically. The norm projected by society for women tends to be retrogressive in many significant ways. The women in the field must certainly appreciate that the norm is not ahead of social change but somewhat behind, and that it is being modified by many societal influences, not all of them good. Women physical educators must ask themselves if they are willing to change—and to actively seek change for themselves and their students.

Society seems to influence women's fitness and appearance negatively in a number of ways. A socially approved appearance, for example, is often achieved through the use of various artificial contrivances, and they are often not physically fit. I can just hear some of my colleagues asking, "just what do you mean by the term 'physically fit'?" Obviously, we can't get into the subject in detail here, and the reader should understand that no invidious comparisons are being made with male physical educators and coaches (who are probably just as unfit and overweight). It is difficult to write about these matters, and especially so for a man writing about women, but women physical educators are not, generally speaking, setting any better standard than men in this regard—and students are great imitators. In this connection, it should (or could) but probably doesn't make much difference from which philosophical base one is operating. The desired amount of physical fitness is simply not there.

Competitive Sport for Women

Another extremely important subproblem that has loomed larger with each passing year is the matter of competitive sport for women. There is no doubt that athletic competition for boys and young men has been and is being carried to unwarranted extremes in many educational institutions. The leading women in our profession reacted violently to many of these excesses and, to their credit, saw to it that similar problems did not arise in the programs for girls and women. In so doing, they were able to set quite a good, and in many cases an excellent, standard in the other phases of the total program. But in their zeal to meet the needs of average girls—as they saw those needs—they negated one of the basic tenets of a democracy, giving every girl, insofar as possible, the opportunity to develop to the maximum of her potential. The accelerated woman student has been slighted and has turned elsewhere for her competitive athletic experience and coaching. In most cases it has not been possible for her to reach her potential. If competitive sport experience in an educational setting has value, and all the philosophical positions grant this to a greater or lesser extent, then it is the duty of women physical educators to make these presumed values available to girls and young women. The excuse that such a development would immediately place the average woman physical educator in the same untenable position as the average male physical educator might be true to a certain extent, but only if women allow it to develop that way. Second best is not good enough, and we should work for the ideal and guarantee that it is approached under educational auspices.

The Question of Individual Freedom

As North Americans move into an uncertain future, they should ponder the term "freedom"—a state that is described as "the condition of being able to choose and carry out purposes" (Muller, 1966, Preface). Of course, who will really argue that most women—or men, for that matter—are truly serious about realizing the implications of Muller's definition of freedom in their own lives—that is, carrying out their *own* purposes in all regards? Kaufmann makes an irrefutable case against all of us for our "decidophobia"—the fear of making autonomous decisions without the aid of readily available crutches such as political ideologies, religions, philosophical positions, microscopic deviational maneuvers, and all the other "bandaids" of life (1973, pp. 1–35).

Women have usually been second or third class citizens in the world. A certain amount of progress has been made in the twentieth century, yet now we find there is a worldwide ideological struggle that revolves around the concept of freedom. Obviously, if a democratic society wishes to keep its ideals from becoming a mockery, women—and men too—should be encouraged to reach their potential in all phases of life. They should become "incandescent" about freedom, if they wish to prevent the erosion of personal liberty in their lives. Absolute freedom for a person to do anything at any time would result in a truly anarchic state of affairs, to be sure, but the conditions of life under fascistic totalitarianism are well understood by hundreds of millions in the world today. The "crunch" becomes evident in an evolving democratic society when the group dictates to an individual "for his or her own good"—and presumably for the group's own good as well.

Both women and men are caught up by the social forces operating in their cultures. We are being forced to ask ourselves whether scientists like B. F. Skinner have the best answer for the future. In both *Walden Two* and his best-selling *Beyond Freedom and Dignity,* Skinner outlines a society in which the problems of men and women are solved by a scientific technology designed for human conduct. Such prevailing values as freedom and dignity are reinterpreted to help bring about a utopian society. Many will immediately say that they wish to preserve what they think is the status quo, but who would not agree that the values and norms of the United States have been preventing women from the achievement of their potential for excellence in sport? Athletics (sport) is a significant cultural force, and women should not be prevented from competing or cooperating in individual, dual, and team sports with any other person—male or female (Skinner, 1948, 1971). As the saying goes, "you've come a long way, baby," but we must hasten to add that there's still a long way to go.

CONCLUDING STATEMENT

The ultimate goal or objective is, of course, an ideal program of physical education and sport at all educational levels and thereafter into later life for women and men. It just so happens that women in the field at this moment in space and time have been confronted with a major problem that is at once staggering and frightening in its dimensions. The development of women's sport must be carried out in accordance with the best educational practice in a society that has allowed men's sport to degenerate so much that in many cases it may exert a greater force for evil than for good. The task facing women—and those who may have the courage to align themselves with them—may be impossible given the prevailing situation, *but the ultimate goal is worthy of a maximum expenditure of energy and time.* Not to make the effort could result in a tragic situation in which competitive sport for women would drain effort, money, facilities, and equipment away from other aspects of the present program with the end result that both women *and* men would be in exactly the same situation. Sport must be administered for both men and women in an open, democratic manner in which the finest type of educational environment—stressing both competition *and* cooperation—is provided for all. There is no other viable alternative.

Dance in Physical Education

The place of dance in physical education (and recreation) has been a persistent problem throughout history. People have danced for personal pleasure, for religious purposes, to express emotion, for exercise, for money, and for the pleasure of others. As both an art form and a social function, dance will probably always be with us and will reflect the age in which it takes place. Consequently, the statement that it is possible to distinguish the pulse of a civilization by an analysis of its dance forms can probably be substantiated. As Woody has indicated,

> There is probably no better example of the survival of primitive practices in modern life than dancing. What causes this survival, long after certain of the previously assigned reasons for it have ceased to exist? The answer lies in human nature. Insofar as any activity satisfies some original or "instinctive" demand of man it has, and will continue to have, adequate reason for its existence, though some of its earlier ideological associations and justifications may have faded from his mind completely. Such an original satisfier rhythm seems to be. Life is a rhythm; dancing is life, as Havelock Ellis maintains. (1949, pp. 22–23)

In recent years on the North American continent, there have been varied opinions as to where a department or division of dance belongs on a campus. The field of physical education and sport has been the usual place for dance instruction, but there has been a move in some quarters to move dance into the arts faculty. Obviously dance is an art, and maybe such a transfer might serve to put some life back into arts units. Nevertheless, many people do define the discipline of physical education as "the art, social science, and bio-science analysis of human movement in sport, dance, play, and exercise." Further, if schools of education serve the function of teaching people how to teach various subjects, it can logically be argued that teaching young men and women to teach dance to others belongs in courses offered by a school of education. The best approach on any given campus would be to allow those interested in the development of dance to move it in what seems to be the right direction in that particular institution, keeping in mind what unit has helped it to develop down through the years. As I have often said to dance personnel in universities, "If you don't find a home within physical education in which you can grow and develop normally given present financial constraints, I will be the first to help you 'relocate' elsewhere."

HISTORICAL BACKGROUND

Early Societies

In primitive societies certain types of rhythmic expression were "instinctive satisfiers." The ancients prayed and pleaded to their various spirits and deities through the medium of different types of ritualistic dances. When they decided to fight their enemies, war dances helped them to achieve the necessary frenzy for the battle. If food was needed, other types of dances were employed to guarantee the success of the hunt. If they were victorious in battle or successful on the hunt, they danced for pleasure and joy. When the vagaries of climate plagued them and their crops were failing, dances were used in the hope that they would bring more rain or more sunshine as the occasion demanded. And when disease and other illness struck, as so often happened, they danced to exorcise the "evil spirits" that brought these misfortunes. To these early people, therefore, dance was most often serious in nature and only incidentally served physical fitness, health, and recreation purposes. We can safely say that the evidence of anthropologists, archeologists, and historians points to the conclusion that dance was an important factor in Paleolithic culture, the first recognizable human civilization, and continued to be so in preliterate societies.

Egypt. In some early societies, there was a tendency to curb the emotions; thus, an element of restraint gave some forms of dance, perhaps for the first time, an esthetic quality. When an element of drama was introduced, dance rose to the status of an art form and was accorded greater esteem by the more cultured people in that society. In Egypt, for example, dance developed both as an art and as a profession. A religious caste was established that consisted of dancers and singers affiliated with particular shrines. Egyptian professional dancing, contrary to popular opinion, was extremely flexible and acrobatic in nature. Professional dancers were men and women who danced for the entertainment of the upper classes at celebrations and other festivities. The lower classes took part in the folk dances of their regions.

The Hebrews. From the Old Testament we learn that dancing was part of the life of the early Hebrews. It was an important feature of many religious ceremonies, along with singing and various types of instrumental music. Dancing of an informal nature, along with the more stylized folk dances, continued to play a role in Hebrew life, but the earlier emphasis on dancing at religious rites evidently waned in later centuries.

China. In ancient Chinese upper-class families, dancing occupied an important place in the education of youth, particularly that of boys. Many different kinds of dances were developed for purposes such as worship, war, and the driving out of evil spirits. These dances seem to have varied somewhat under the different dynasties, but were usually accompanied by music and the recitation of poetry. The development of a written philosophy of dancing was, of course, a distinct advance over the dances of primitive peoples. Kings recognized the power and importance of music, dancing, and formal ceremonies in the lives of the people; it has been said that the worth of rulers was often adjudged by the quality of the dance prevalent during their period of control. Chinese dance is said to have begun more than two thousand years before Christ, but it should be mentioned for our purpose here that women seem to have danced much less than men; that their role in life appeared to revolve around the typical household responsibilities; and that the custom of foot binding in certain social classes limited their physical exercise, including participation in the dance, severely and made women assume a decorative role.

India. Ancient Indian dance was closely associated with religious practices and was evidently held in high favor. This admiration for the expression of "rhythmic energy" continued into the sixth and fifth centuries B.C., and dance and music were included in the education of youth. But for various reasons, including greater class consciousness and the fact that it became professionalized, dance soon became an activity in which only lower-class individuals took part. It was difficult to erase its popular appeal, however, and men and women still enjoyed it on many occasions. There were still many temple dancers, and professional women dancers and musicians were popular for the entertainment of guests at the homes of the wealthy.

Crete. Dancing was very much in evidence in ancient Cretan civilization. Along with music and sport, it played an important role in the religious life of these people. Women achieved a relatively high status in this society and were prominent in religious ceremonies that included dance as a form of worship. There were gay, spontaneous folk dances, religious ceremonial dances of a stately nature, lively dances including outstanding tumbling routines, and war dances.

Sparta. Spartan girls and young women were extremely active physically; it is to be expected that they would be involved in dancing as well. They danced at celebrations, and at times in company with young men. Dressed in what even today would be considered rather scanty attire, they danced on certain occasions while the young men watched. Dancing and music were regarded as basic to the education of youth, as both had a relationship to religion and war. Their national heritage was very important to the Spartans, and many dances related to the culture were conducted with great dignity. There were a number of dances, however, that we today would characterize as gymnastic dancing.

Athens. Athenian girls and women led much different lives from those of their counterparts in Sparta; they were regarded as inferior, and they stayed that way. They did engage in certain types of dance, however, at different stages of their lives. Certainly children of both sexes took part in a variety of informal dances. Dancing and music were also part of the education of young ladies in the more wealthy homes. Many of the slave girls did acquire great facility in the dance, but this type of activity would not have been proper for the Athenian maiden.

It is interesting to note the extent to which both Spartan and Athenian men took part in the dance in its many forms. There was theatrical dancing, gymnastic dancing, and folk dancing, not to mention dance that was more specifically religious and that which was related directly to war and peace. If anything, it could be said that the Athenians were more dance-conscious than the Spartans. This was because their whole conception of education was pointed toward the harmonious development of all aspects of human nature—physical, mental, moral, and esthetic. When the Hellenic civilization declined, the quality of the dance declined along with it.

Rome. Dancing served a purpose in Roman civilization, but its status was below that given it by the Greeks. In the early days it was associated with religion and war. Later, during the reign of Nero, it was held in high esteem. Thereafter, dance experienced a decline; it became a matter of tricks, acrobatics, and feats of juggling often performed by slaves to provide entertainment. When this happened, it was naturally considered an unworthy activity for a true Roman. It is therefore no wonder that no further progress was made in the art of dance. It continued as a popular activity for the lower classes, but then waned in popularity with the advent of Christian asceticism. In general it can be said that the Romans saw some purpose for dance in religious festivals, but did not understand the role that it had played in Greek life.

The Middle Ages

The Early Period. During this period dance had very low status, probably due to the corruption of dancing in the Roman era. The Christian Church accepted dance at first as a means of liturgical expression, but subsequently banned this form of dance because of its pagan origins. Folk dance did continue in the Middle Ages; in fact, it appeared to be one of the few opportunities that people had for freedom of expression. The so-called Dark Ages were characterized by Christian asceticism, and dancing as a *natural* activity was considered "of the body" and therefore evil.

The Renaissance. The people of the Renaissance rediscovered the grace and dignity of the earlier classical civilization. The place of dance in the culture began to rise again as it developed as an art form. Traditional folk dances were refined by dancing masters who devised various forms of the dance that became socially acceptable. In this period we see the beginning of dance theory, albeit at an elementary level. During this time men and women danced together at court activities. There were solo dancing routines, dances for couples, and dances for small groups. So-called European court ballet became fashionable, and then declined toward the end of the sixteenth century. During this time professionals performed what was known as pantomime dance for the enjoyment of the people. At the end of the sixteenth century, a closed couple dance known as the *volta* came into existence. It was to have a great influence on dance in the future.

The Modern Period

The Seventeenth Century. In 1661, the National Academy of Music and Dance opened in France, and dance gradually became a real art. Only men appeared in the ballets; they wore masks when depicting feminine roles (women did not take part until 1881). The minuet started as a peasant dance and achieved great popularity as it was gradually refined into a "dance of courtship" in polite society. During this time the English round and longway dances were popular, although they were really not new developments—the circles and files were merely adaptations of basic forms from earlier societies.

The Eighteenth and Nineteenth Centuries. Changing social conditions appear to have caused a decline in the popularity of the minuet toward the end of the eighteenth century. French leadership in the dance was superseded by the many variations of the German waltz in the so-called Romantic period of European history. The Viennese waltz was the classical dance of the latter half of the eighteenth century and only began to wane about 1830 when numerous variations developed. The polka was really the only popular dance that rivaled the waltz in any way.

With the onset of a radically new, revolutionary attitude toward the rights of individuals, dance could not help but be affected and change accordingly. Changes were taking place in the traditional ballet, which began to become a theater art in its own right. Costume changes became increasingly frequent, and scenes depicting contemporary social developments were often displayed. Further reforms in the ballet were characteristic of the nineteenth century, a time in which the potentialities of the "natural man" were being realized. The Romantic period saw the birth of the romantic ballet, with a new role for women. The ballerina achieved great esteem as a solo performer, and the male dancer found himself in a supporting role for one of the first times in history. By 1850, however, the golden age of ballet seemed to have passed.

The United States. To say that the introduction of dance in its various forms into the physical education curriculum in the United States has been an uphill struggle would be to put it mildly. In pioneer life many forms of recreation were viewed suspiciously. Children's dances and folk dancing brought over from Europe, however, were impossible to suppress and gradually became increasingly popular. As social life developed, the parties became gayer and more sophisticated in the eastern cities, and "polite" dancing was generally accepted. The recreational life of the westward-moving frontier group developed as well, and social dancing, of a folk- and square-dance nature, was increasingly evident despite the opposition of some of the fundamentalist religious sects.

The nineteenth century was actually a transitional period in attitudes toward play and recreation. The first use of anything resembling dance in physical education came around 1850, when some of the recommended calisthenics were really elementary dance forms. In one of the handbooks published for young ladies, John Locke and others are quoted as being in favor of dancing instruction for children because of the "graceful motion" and "confidence" it gave. Girls were not, however, supposed to be "brilliant" in their performance of any of the dance figures. Three names may be mentioned for the part that they played in the development of dancing as an integral part of physical education: (1) Catherine Beecher, who introduced some elementary dance figures into her system of calisthenics; (2) François Delsarte, who actually developed a "couple dance" without calling it that, and whose Eurhythmics became a worldwide movement of esthetic, systematized rhythmic training; and (3) Melvin B. Gilbert, who began the era of the so-called esthetic dance in physical education in the 1890s. His teaching at the famous Harvard Summer School of Physical Education did much to spread its popularity throughout the country.

The Twentieth Century. The twentieth century has witnessed a truly remarkable development in the dance. Many would say that the body has been rediscovered as a means of communication through the medium of dance. The great Isadora Duncan, who had made a study of Greek culture, introduced a spirit of individualism and freedom with emphasis on a natural form of expression. This development symbolized a revolt against three centuries of more or less formalized ballet technique. Working from the premise that emotional states are typically expressed through movement, early natural dance broke away from tradition and attempted to convey the gamut of emotional experiences through bodily movement. The main purpose was not so much to create a spectacle as it was a desire to communicate and to put self-expression into the dancer's movements—movement in which the performer was free to respond to various emotional states without necessarily being limited to a particular musical form.

Miss Duncan's work was ably carried on by such outstanding dance teachers as Gertrude Colby, Margaret H'Doubler, Mary P. O'Donnell, Martha Hill, and Martha Graham, to mention only a few. Gertrude Colby saw natural dance as a dance form indigenous to the American culture—a form in which the body is used correctly and that is also based on established psychological laws. It became an art form that could draw on drama, music, color, design, and pantomime for its full expression. It paved the way for later "modern" dance and served as a means of unifying various, somewhat diverse approaches to the teaching of the dance.

In the early years of this century, Louis Chalif came to New York from Russia and offered a course in dance for teachers. With a background in ballet and a developing interest in esthetic dance, he applied a certain amount of this influence to the teaching of folk dance. He was an outstanding teacher himself and evidently an indefatigable enthusiast, as evidenced by the short courses he conducted in many centers across the country. Although some questioned the educational soundness of his type of dance instruction, there is no question but that he was a great influence in the establishment of dance in America. Elizabeth Burchenal is credited with helping to establish folk dance more soundly within the educational system, along with Mary Wood Hinman.

Another interesting development was the advent of clog dancing and subsequently tap dancing within physical education programs in the United States. Mary Wood Hinman recognized the worth of this dance form, and she continued to promote it despite a good deal of early criticism about its worth as a dance form in education. This trend in dance was not to be denied, however, and for a period tap dancing was tremendously popular and became known in other countries as an American contribution to the art of dancing. Marjories Hillas and Anne Schley Duggan have been prominent in applying this dance form to education.

After 1912 a new era of social dancing that reflected the social attitudes of a vigorous, thriving country began in the United States. America broke away from the traditional, standardized European dance forms that had dominated up until this time. This new wave of interest owed much to the influence of Vernon and Irene Castle, who popularized the movement. The beginnings of jazz and ragtime soon resulted in a variety of popular dance steps that were doomed to extinction almost before they started. The turkey trot, the bunny hug, the Charleston, and innumerable other dance crazes (such as the twist and the frug in the 1960s) have superseded each other in fairly rapid succession since the early years of the century, and each has been enjoyed by teenagers and young adults. They have been counteracted to a degree by the efforts of professional ballroom dancing instructors, who have made an effort to offer more refined dance steps for public entertainment such as the tango, the hesitation, the waltz, the fox trot, the Lambeth walk, and the rhumba.

Modern Dance. Modern dance grew out of natural dance in the late 1920s and made rapid strides in the following decade. For a while in the 1930s the influence of Mary Wigman and her German modern dance, a further development of earlier expression gymnastics, was strong, but this form was fairly soon absorbed by the rapidly growing and expanding American modern dance. A dance section was established in the American Physical Education Association in 1932, and various outstanding summer schools of the dance were inaugurated at Bennington College, New York University, Connecticut College for Women, and other institutions. As early as 1926 the first major program in dance had been begun at the University of Wisconsin under the leadership of Margaret H'Doubler, and many others have started since that time. In 1951, the Juilliard School of Music in New York City organized a dance department, and recognition by this prestigious institution tended to further its establishment as an art form.

Despite the advancement of modern dance and its acceptance in modern education, as evidenced by the development of dance education teacher preparation programs across the country, there is still much room for progress. A significant body of research knowledge is lacking, although the American Alliance for Health, Physical Education, and

Recreation has published bibliographies of dance research in recent years. The Committee on Research in Dance sponsored a Preliminary Conference on Research in Dance at the Greystone Conference Center, Riverdale, New York, from May 26 to 28, 1967. The proceedings were entitled *Research in Dance: Problems and Possibilities.* CORD—the Committee on Research in Dance—is a group established in 1964 on the basis of ideas expressed by some members of the U.S. Office of Education to some dancers who were members of AAHPER, the National Dance Guild, and the Dance Notation Bureau.

A certain amount of curriculum standardization for prospective teachers seems desirable, and an improvement of the interaction between the dance teacher and the professional performer would add further strength to the development. Articulation within the dance curriculum at the various levels of the school system is needed as well. Further analysis must be made of the reasons why modern dance especially, and many of the other dance forms, seems unacceptable to the majority of male physical education teachers of North America. Square dancing and social dancing continue to be popular throughout many parts of the country with the masses, and interest in folk dancing is persistent. Tap dancing is on the wane and interest in ballet is limited except in certain geographic areas and segments of society. There have been a number of interesting cultural center developments in New York City, Washington, D.C., and elsewhere—all indicating a possible rebirth of interest in the arts including dance.

PHILOSOPHICAL ANALYSIS

At this point we must ask ourselves what implications can be drawn from the major educational philosophies regarding the place of dance in education. This is apt to be a controversial subject and is in need of careful investigation by those who are competent and knowledgeable in both philosophy and the dance. A few tentative opinions will be expressed to offer an avenue of approach to those most vitally concerned. These statements are based on the assumption that occasionally an outsider—in this case to the dance—may be able to offer some insight because of a different vantage point.

It appears to be true that—rightly or wrongly—the public and educators in general view dance as physical movement and associate it with physical education, physical recreation, exercise, sport, and the like. Therefore, we find that dance in the schools is generally equated with physical education. This means that dance, like physical education, might be considered curricular, cocurricular, extracurricular, or completely outside the educational sphere. Carrying this analogy further, the progressivist (experimentalist or reconstructionist) might view dance as curricular, or at least cocurricular. The essentialist would tend to see dance as extracurricular or completely outside the sphere of education. It should be pointed out, however, that the naturalistic realist, although basically an essentialist, could conceivably see dance as serving a useful function within education. This can be explained through the desire of the naturalistic realist to allow the student the opportunity for the full expression of so-called natural instincts, and because modern dance especially promotes a type of animal fitness. We may be able to be somewhat more specific in relation to the major philosophical tendencies of experimentalism (pragmatic naturalism), so-called realism (with diverse positions within it), and idealism (which is metaphysically indefensible in the eyes of the philosophical analysis movement).

Experimentalism. The experimentalist, for example, would see the various dance forms being introduced in an articulated curriculum in such a way as to conform to the child's growth and development pattern, and thereby contributing to total fitness for life in our society. As an integral aspect or phase of human movement in physical education, dance activities do bring natural impulses into play. Dance teachers within an experimentalist educational pattern evaluate the needs, interests, and abilities of the student and are concerned with the progress of the individual in relation to his or her adjustment to the social environment. They believe that a reasonable level of dance skill in the various forms according to the individual's interest—and potential—can be a fine esthetic experience. Dance teachers view vigorous dance activities as making a valid contribution to the physical fitness of the student and believe that such activity should be available to boys as well as to girls. And believing that education for leisure is basic to the curriculum, they view participation in dance as a worthwhile creative leisure activity that helps to ensure desirable individual growth. Furthermore, dance as a natural activity can promote sound mental and physical health, thereby aiding the student to acquire knowledge, competency, and skill for a rich, full life. Obviously the methodology to be employed in the teaching of dance will be identical with that of experimentalist teaching in other phases of the total physical education program. The reconstructionist, as a sort of utopian experimentalist, would agree largely with the preceding statements. He or she is basically most anxious to encourage the student's self-realization as a social being, and dance certainly fulfills this objective, as well as contributing uniquely to creative expression.

Realism. Realists would tend to see dance as an activity that promotes education *of* the physical—that is, if it is vigorous enough. This would appear to be much more important than any recreational aspects of dance participation. Dance has value as it is able to contribute to the beauty and utility of life, and as it helps pupils develop muscles and bodily coordination. Since it helps to establish an adequate physical basis for intellectual life, to this extent it should be included as part of physical training. Since it is part of physical education in schools, it must accordingly yield precedence to intellectual education. Many realists would concur in the belief that social and square dancing skills are important for use in later life, but they see them nevertheless as extra-curricular and feel that they should be taught after the regular school day is over. One reason for this belief is that play and work cannot be identified under the same psychological rubric. However, this does not mean that dance cannot serve a useful function in life. It can help the individual to use leisure for recreation and to achieve balance among the various pursuits of daily living. Normal recreation should provide for change in activity, and such play should be as carefree as possible. For this reason dance, and other physical educational and physical recreational activities, should not be overemphasized and too highly organized. Dance can help in the reduction of just about any psychic tensions that life's problems and stresses may create. Last, dance forms should be in keeping with the fundamental laws of the universe itself. Obviously, realistic educational teaching methodology should be employed in teaching dance as well as other physical educational activities.

Idealism. Idealists in dance education tend to be ambivalent creatures who see dance as making a contribution both to education of the physical and to education through the physical. Despite this belief, however, they would regard dance—and other physical education and recreation activities—as occupying a lower rung on the educational ladder. An idealistic dance teacher sees dance education as one part of the total program that aims to assist us to improve the quality of life through the development of the physical, esthetic, and perhaps religious aspects of our nature. Idealistic emphasis typically strives for perfection through the achievement of the enduring values of truth, goodness, and beauty. Therefore, dance's importance would have to be judged on the basis of the contribution it can make toward the realization of these values for each individual.

The idealist stresses the need for building wholeness of mind and body and would wish to see students develop beautiful and skilled bodies. The supreme worth of personality is readily apparent to idealistic dance teachers, who would teach the subject so that good habits of mental and physical health result. They would not wish the student dancer to become too self-centered, and dance should very definitely be a means to an end—never an end in itself. This would be in keeping with the emphasis on a well-balanced program of physical education and sport for *all* students. Furthermore, such teachers see dance as an activity that affords the performer a spiritual lift through the liberation of powers and through the physical well-being it engenders. It should be a creative experience that helps to provide a physical reserve for life's many physical and spiritual burdens. The progressive idealist regards the traditional attitude taken against dance by many major religious groups in modern history as being uninformed, unappreciative, and illogically biased concerning the role that dance can fulfill if taught well within an educational setting.

To the extent that the idealistic teacher of dance can help students realize the eternal values through choice of the right kinds of dance experience without flouting the moral order of the world, he will be progressive enough to disregard a dualistic theory of work and play. Such dance experience, even under religious sponsorship, can actually serve to help a society improve moral and ethical standards. Dance experience can help the individual to offset the psychic disintegration taking place in the world by providing creative experiences that can be spiritual in nature. It can assist individuals to relate themselves to that which is beautiful in life and can be one of many forces in leisure that has unique potential for the good of humanity.

Existentialism. A person with an existentialist orientation or stance is regarded in this approach as being progressivist because of the great concern for individuality. It would be very important, therefore, to stress creative physical activities such as modern dance. Such activity can be chosen by the individual based on knowledge of self. Thus, the authentically eccentric child and young person can and should be made to feel at home, so to speak, through the medium of dance. Further, dance can provide a way for youth to commit themselves to values and to people, an experience perhaps more important than ever before.

The Use of Leisure

Citizens in the industrialized world now have more leisure than ever be-fore, but the promotion of the concept of education for leisure depends a great deal on whether the prevailing educational philosophy will allow sufficient support for the inclusion of such programs in the educational system. When people achieve leisure, what will they do with it? What have they done with it in the past? Shall it be used for play, as typically conceived, or for recreation education? Our objective in this section is to trace the use of leisure throughout history and then to analyze how it *should* be used according to the major philosophical trends in Western educational philosophy.

As we begin this historical outline of the use of leisure, a few brief definitions seem to be in order. "Leisure" will be used to explain the time a person has free from his work and does not need for sleeping or basic survival activities. For our purposes we will accept the definition that "play" is an instinctive form of self-expression through pleasurable ac-tivity that seems to be aimless in nature. The term "recreation" seems to have developed a broader meaning than "play," although they are com-monly used interchangeably. Typically, recreation embodies those ex-periences that people engage in during their leisure for purposes of pleasure, satisfaction, or education. Recreation is a human experience or activity; it is not necessarily instinctive; and it may be considered pur-poseful.

HISTORICAL BACKGROUND

Early Societies

In primitive and preliterate societies, there probably was not so sharp a division between work and play as in civilized societies. Adults had a difficult time with basic survival activities and enjoyed very little leisure. Such leisure as a particular family or tribe was able to earn was probably used for play activity of an aimless nature, conjecturally quite similar to that of animals. Later, embryonic cultures developed certain folkways and ceremonials of a more controlled nature. Inclement weather, even in our own day a mighty influence, may at least have afforded some leisure time.

A division of labor (with resultant leisure for some) occurred in Egypt, Mesopotamia, China, and India, generally considered the first great civilizations of the world. These social developments came about through favorable environments and men's correct responses to certain stimuli. The wealth accumulated through the toil of the masses was soon in the hands of a relatively few individuals; historically, these people were the first to enjoy anything like an extended period of leisure. Some used this free time to speculate and learn more about their environment; others developed various arts and skills, or participated in sports. Still others squandered the time in meaningless pursuits. In Egypt, for example, we find a great accumulation of formal knowledge that became available because religious leaders acquired wealth and leisure.

The Athenians developed a very high standard of living and, during their golden age, used their leisure wisely. Although Athenian democracy is often acclaimed as an ideal, the existence of three social classes (freemen, noncitizens, and slaves) must not be overlooked. Education was confined to native freemen, and Athenian women were regarded as inferior creatures to be kept on a low intellectual plane. Nevertheless, Athenians did have a revolutionary idea: a many-sided education, involving training of the mental, moral, physical, and esthetic aspects of human nature, an ideal the world had not seen before and has not been able to realize since.

It has been said that the Romans never did more than merely perpetuate the Greek ideal of liberal education. Here again we find a stratification of society with the senators and the equites enjoying far greater wealth and social status than the plebeians; toward the end of the republic there were as many as 5 million slaves in Italy. As usual, wealth determined leisure, and leisure determined the extent to which a person would be educated. Leisure was, in fact, synonymous with freedom.

How did the Romans use their leisure? Accumulated wealth led to unnecessary luxuries and selfish individualism. Social standing was determined to a large extent by the amount of one's personal fortune, and crass materialism became the leading philosophy of the time. Crime increased at all levels and often went unpunished. As the way of life changed, the formerly active Roman found himself unemployed and with no source of income. The state fed and entertained these people with great exhibitions, and a passion for the games and the circus grew. Many baths were provided for the physical recreation of the masses as well. Another strong factor in Rome's decline was the misuse of political power by the senatorial class, which resulted in a series of civil wars just before Augustus came to power. What once had been an extremely strong state disintegrated as the rich exploited the poor, civil freedoms gradually vanished, and moral fiber weakened.

The Middle Ages

In the period known as the Middle Ages, the same social system existed, with minor variations. The ruling class had its own pattern of leisure and pretty well decided what the masses, villagers and peasants, would be allowed to do. Whereas the knights did their jousting at tourneys and the gentlemen engaged in hunting and hawking, fencing, dancing, gaming, and other such activities, the common folk had their fairs, drama, celebrations, and festivals. Recreations were often carried to excess, and such activities were typically frowned upon by the third social class, the Church.

The Church glorified asceticism and hard labor. Leisure activities were generally condemned, as they tended to destroy godliness; the spirit was to control the flesh and keep it from vices. Thus, any types of recreation gratifying the bodily senses were to be put aside because of the resulting harm to the individual seeking salvation. A total of eight weeks was typically set aside for a multitude of religious celebrations. These periods were specifically designed for purposes other than leisure pastimes. Such restrictions were difficult to enforce, however, no matter how many rules and regulations the Church laid down. We should not forget that leisure was still not something you *earned;* it was the property of one particular class in society.

The Renaissance was the beginning of a most important time for modern people. There were, of course, many influences that gradually brought about the change in attitude away from the narrow, "other-worldly" atmosphere which existed prior to the Renaissance. Intellectual advancement of a scientific nature had been taking place among non-Christians, and the Christian world finally began to realize this in the late fourteenth and fifteenth centuries. A number of humanists of this time made a strong effort to renew the earlier concept of a sound mind in a sound body—a concept that still remains only an ideal in the twentieth century. Vast economic changes were also occurring, as commerce developed throughout the known world. The rise of free cities, the developing spirit of nationalism, and the growth of industry and banking all contributed to a new way of life.

The real meaning of the Renaissance and the centuries immediately following may well be found in the spirit of inquiry that developed—a type of scientific inquiry which swept aside dogmas. The founding of many universities contributed greatly to this spread of knowledge and learning, as did the development of paper and the printing press. The power of the Church declined somewhat, as attention shifted to the problems of individuals attempting to carve out a good life on earth.

One may well ask why it took so long—that is, so many hundreds of years—before the possibility of earning and using leisure became a reality for the average person. This is not a simple question to answer. For one thing, there have been many wars, and these automatically destroy the surplus economy that is absolutely necessary for a high standard of education and leisure. Second, the traditions and mores of a civilization change slowly and probably only under concerted intellectual, social, political, and economic pressure. It took revolutions to overthrow absolutist regimes before the concept of political democracy had an opportunity to grow. Third, the almost absolute power of the Church over all aspects of life had to be weakened before the concept of separation of church and state could become a reality. Fourth, the beginnings of the natural sciences had to be consolidated into very real gains before advanced technology could lead us into an Industrial Revolution, the final outcome of which we still cannot foresee.

Not the least of these changes was the rebirth of naturalism during the early days of the Renaissance. Actually, unrefined naturalism has been considered by some to be the oldest philosophy in the Western world, dating back to about five hundred years before Christ. Thales, who lived in Miletus in Asia Minor, believed he had found the final stuff of the universe within nature. He and his contemporaries saw an order in nature that was both logical and exemplary for people to follow. Both their intuition and their reason told them that we should allow nature to take its course. Here was a philosophy that bore a close relationship to the individual humanism of the twelfth and thirteenth centuries. The educational aim was the development of the individual personality through a liberal education, with the "humanities" replacing the "divinities." The world of nature should be studied; the real life of the past should be examined; and the joys of living should be extolled. Physical education and sport were considered to be natural activities that should be encouraged. Naturalism emerged in the eighteenth century as a full-blown philosophy of life with obvious educational implications. These implications were expressed magnificently by Jean Jacques Rousseau, who encouraged educators to study the child carefully and then to devise an educational plan based on this examination. The results of this approach became evident in the educational innovations of the next two centuries both in Europe and North America. For the first time, play was recognized as a factor of considerable importance in the development of the child. The aftermath of these new ideas has been of untold value to health, physical education, and recreation.

North America

Before leisure could be used in North America, it had to be earned. Furthermore, certain prevailing ideas about idleness had to be broken down. Neither of these occurrences took place overnight. Recreational patterns have gradually emerged as the United States and Canada have grown and prospered. Initially, people originated their own recreational pursuits in an unorganized fashion. Following this, all types of commercial recreational opportunities were made available, some of dubious value. And, finally, public and voluntary agencies were created to meet the recreational needs and interests of the populace. These patterns of recreation are now proceeding concurrently in the twentieth century, and careful analysis is most difficult.

From an economic standpoint we now find ourselves in a very favorable situation, as the average work week has been cut almost in half. Many people are now choosing leisure instead of more work, because they want to enjoy life. Many others are being forced to accept an increased amount of leisure, although they do not have all the material possessions of life that they might wish to have.

From a historical standpoint, the Puritans equated play with idleness, and hence evil, and tried to suppress it by legislation. At the same time the Virginians were enjoying a variety of recreational pursuits with relatively few twinges of conscience. The eighteenth century saw a marked change in recreational habits as some leisure was earned. Such activities as dancing, hunting, horse racing, barn raisings, and all sorts of community enterprises characterized this period. After 1800 a transitional period set in, as sectionalism caused many different patterns of recreation to flourish. The movement toward urbanization gave commercialized recreation the opportunity to develop unrestrained, yet we might say that recreation as an organized structure of the democratic way of life was only in its infancy in the late nineteenth century.

The twentieth century has been characterized by the greatest surplus economy the world has ever seen. We have witnessed a vast new development that may be called an organized recreation pattern. The outlines of this pattern had been barely discernible toward the end of the nineteenth century, but in the past fifty years the development of public and voluntary agency recreation has been absolutely phenomenal. Further social and economic changes have taken place; professional associations have developed; professional preparation for recreational leadership has mushroomed; and city-supported recreation programs along with community centers in schools form a network across the United States and Canada.

PHILOSOPHICAL ANALYSIS

We face the final quarter of the twentieth century with a good deal of apprehension. Behind us are all sorts of wars, depressions, and examples of inhumanity, as well as much that gives us hope for the future. We are in the middle of a cold war that could spell utter devastation, and yet we look ahead idealistically, realistically, pragmatically, existentially, materialistically. On the home front we seek to control the tides of the business cycle. We try to comprehend the peaceful and the shooting revolutions going on all about us. We hear that automation may bring about a situation where people will be paid not to work. Education for leisure would seem to warrant serious consideration in the face of such a development.

History shows that no civilization has survived for long when the people had too much free time. Can we continue our unprecedented development as a continent where most people will find happiness and satisfaction despite the fact that we are increasingly crowding people together in heavily populated cities and suburbs? To answer these questions in relation to the use of leisure, we should examine our philosophical positions with their implications for education. What we decide as professionals, and what others will accept, will exert a considerable influence on the place of health, physical education, and recreation in our educational systems and, subsequently, in our communities at large for our mature citizens.

Experimentalists, who believe that it is only possible to find out if something is worthwhile through experience, do not like the "fractionation" that is taking place within our field, so they would immediately protest against discussing recreation education separately. For them education for the worthy use of leisure is basic to the curriculum of the school —a curriculum in which pupil growth, as defined by the experimentalist, is all-important. Second, play should foster moral growth, and third, over-organized sport competition is not true recreation, since the welfare of the individual is often relegated to second place. Experimentalists make it quite clear that it is a mistake to confuse the psychological distinction between work and play with the traditional economic distinction. All citizens should have ample opportunity to use their free time in a creative and fruitful manner. They would not condemn a person who watched others perform with a high level of skill in any of our cultural activities, including sport, so long as the individual kept the spectator role in the proper place.

Furthermore, they would view with favor a carefully planned program of interscholastic sports (athletics) that is built on a sound physical education and intramural athletic base.

Reconstructionists believe that reality is evolving and that there is no such thing as a preestablished order in the world. Thus a fixed or universal curriculum in physical, health, and recreation education is unthinkable. Their curriculum would be developed through the employment of shared planning to determine what specific contributions the field might make to the program of general education and to our use of leisure. If the "community school concept" were employed, the student could well be offered about an hour and a half a day for recreation and relaxation alone. "Carryover" games and sports with opportunities for wholesome educational play would undoubtedly contribute to total fitness. The reconstructionist goal is *social self-realization;* hence, creative artistic expression through recreational activities such as rhythms and dance should be emphasized. Intramural sports, compared to interscholastic athletics, rank high. Democratic method should be used to aid the group to fulfill goals—goals which themselves are the result of democratic consensus. Self-expression is important for human development, and sound recreational use of leisure would promote this particular goal.

Realists, those who accept the world at face value and who believe our experiencing it changes it not one whit, sharply differentiate work and play. Play serves a useful purpose at recess or after school, but it should *not* be part of the regular curriculum. They would agree that the use of leisure is significant to the development of our culture, but they would also be quick to point out that winning the cold war is going to take a lot more hard work and somewhat less leisure. They see leisure pursuits or experience as an opportunity to get relief from work, as things that serve a re-creative purpose in life. The surplus energy theory of play and recreation makes sense to them. So does the more recent biosocial theory of play—the idea that play helps the organism to achieve balance. They would tend to deprecate the fact that the "play attitude" seems to be missing almost completely in many organized sports. Play (and recreation) is therefore very important to realists; it should be "liberating," with people developing their potentialities for wholesome hobbies through recreation. As they see it, recreation can serve as a safety valve for the reduction of life's psychic tensions. Even though play should not be considered as a basic part of the curriculum, we should not forget that it provides an indispensable seasoning to the good life. Extracurricular play and recreational activities and a sound general education should suffice to equip the student for leisure activities in our society.

Idealists, having both a firm belief in an intrinsic system of educational values and an extreme concern with individual personality and its development, are ambiguous about the role of recreation in the school and in adult life. It is the duty of idealists, therefore, to reassess the contributions that recreation and play can and do make in education—education as they define it.

Another difficulty that confronts idealists is deciding on the roles of physical education and recreation. Perhaps only *physical* education should be included in the educational hierarchy, and all other recreational needs should be met by the recreation administrator (either within the school system or in the community). On the other hand, an idealist might view favorably a theory of recreation and play that grants educational possibilities to these activities. The self-expression theory of play suggests that the individual's chief need in life is to be able to give expression to his own personality—a theory obviously quite compatible with the conception of the person as an organic unity. Idealists believe that the person is a purposive being who is striving to achieve those values which are embedded in reality itself. To the extent that idealists can realize the eternal values through the choice of the right kinds of play and recreation without flouting the moral order in the world, they will be progressive enough to disregard a dualistic theory of work and play—a theory that has plagued us in North America down to the present day.

There are distinct signs that specific Protestant denominations are becoming increasingly aware of the role that recreation can play in the promulgation of the Christian idealistic way of life. In the United States such recognition has been largely a twentieth-century phenomenon. Recreation has developed to the point where it is now clearly one of the major social institutions in American life. If "the ideal suggests the integrated individual in an integrated society growing in the image of the integrated universe," then all types of recreational experience and activity can seemingly make a contribution to the realization of this "ideal." We are warned that we are faced with a "recreational imperative."

Existentialist thought gives play an important place. Personal liberation is highly desirable, and this is most certainly a function of play. In sporting activities individuals can be free as they select their own values and achieve self-expression. Children can create their own world of play and thereby realize their true identities. Obviously, varsity athletics, as typically conducted, would be almost completely antithetical to existentialists. Existentialists at play want no prescribed formations, no coach calling the plays and destroying the players' "authenticity," and no crowd exhorting them to win at any cost. A perfect example of the use of language analysis to help us better understand the use of leisure in sport and athletics is provided by James Keating (1964, p. 28).

Amateur, Semiprofessional, and Professional Athletics

The relationship of these three areas to one another, to the educational system, and to the entire culture must be more fully understood. This brief treatment should help the physical education and sport teacher to comprehend the issues at stake. Sport (a pleasurable diversion) and athletics (a highly competitive activity) are both parts of the very lifeblood of our field and offer the possibility of great benefits and satisfaction to participant and coach alike. They are significant cultural influences that offer the possibility of good or bad to the society. Thus we should ask ourselves, "In what way may sport and athletics be used for the service of humanity?"

People engage in games and sport today for many reasons. Psychologists have revealed some of the complexities of determining motivation. Do people really know why they do a particular thing, or are they suppressing their reasons? Or have these reasons been "determined" for them by their home and social environments? Keeping these reservations in mind, we ask: Do we take part in games and sport for fun, for re-creation, for self-expression, for health, for exercise, for competition, or perhaps because of the money or other benefits it might bring us? Or do we do it for a variety of reasons, some stronger at times than others? Or perhaps we have never even given it any thought at all!

HISTORICAL BACKGROUND

Early Societies

Primitive and preliterate peoples undoubtedly felt the urge to play; often they took part in games as part of religious observances. And there is no denying that sport served a very practical purpose as well. It gave them the opportunity to practice skills upon which they relied for survival.

The urge to play is probably older than any so-called human culture, since animals play in the same ways that humans do. It has been stated that civilization has contributed no significant aspect to the general concept of play, although we must admit that considerable thought and investigation have been devoted to the matter. It is possible that scientific investigation will eventually give us the answer to the question, or perhaps we may never really know the reason. Did God give us a play instinct, or did nature give us play—play whose very essence defies all analysis; play that appears to be completely irrational; play that is both beautiful and ridiculous at one and the same time. It is free and voluntary and seemingly not concerned with the serious business of life. Yet it can be and often is completely absorbing; it starts and stops at a given moment; and it has rules.

It is the so-called higher forms of play with which we will concern ourselves primarily, and especially those types that eventually became semiprofessional and professional in the Greco-Roman period. But before we come to this phase of the development, we should consider briefly the early relationship of sport to religious observances. Here we find the idea that play is dedicated to the deity. The ritual or performance is played or "represented" in a designated area. It may be a sacrifice, a performance, or a contest. The hope is that the gods will observe the sacred contest and give their approval by causing the event to actually take place. Such a contest might be between the hero of the particular culture involved and some arch foe which is vanquished by superior skill, wile, or good fortune.

A great many of the primitive games obviously served an extremely useful purpose. Contests involving the use of a club, a spear, and a bow and arrow developed proficiency in the use of weapons. Other activities such as wrestling, fighting, running, horse racing, and swimming were also highly useful activities in life and the struggle for survival, and these sports today are "vestigial remains" of earlier civilizations. These games demanded in most instances such attributes as strength, endurance, skill and dexterity of movement, as well as control of the passions. Thus inclusion of this vigorous play activity would seem to be warranted in all educational systems in some form or another.

Similar sports and recreation were part of life to a greater or lesser degree in all the early civilizations. Egyptians took part in all sorts of gymnastic exercises and field sports. This was especially true for the nobility and for those whose profession was arms, but the masses had their games and amusements as well. In Babylonia and Assyria the skills of hunting and fighting were shown preference, and there are many passages in the Bible that refer to the physical activities of the Hebrews.

The early aristocrats in China were active sportsmen. The contests in swordsmanship brought this skill to a high level, and wrestling, jiu-jitsu, and boxing were very popular during particular eras, as were butting and football, the latter a game in which a round ball was kicked within a prescribed area. Even the games of polo and golf may trace their origins to ancient China. In India, boxing, wrestling, and hunting were popular activities for warriors. And in Iran, a nation in which the warrior was very prominent, most of the accepted sports had a close relationship to the arts of war, with the possible exception of polo. This latter activity was extremely popular for a considerable period of time, and the Persians became very skillful at it.

The Cretan and Mycenaean warriors engaged in similar warlike sports around the sixteenth century B.C. Hunting, for example, was a favorite of these people. The art of bull-grappling was an unusual sport of the Minoan age, practiced by both men and women. The activity was evidently connected with religious observance. Other sports included boxing, wrestling, hunting, and fishing, as well as acrobatic dancing by both sexes.

Greece and Rome

Although Spartans went to the extreme in the physical training of both men and women, the Spartan government was actually against extreme specialization in athletics. Spartans did compete very successfully, however, in wrestling, boxing, jumping, running, and throwing of the javelin and discus in the early Olympics. Boxing and the pancratium were activities in which the Spartans were not allowed to enter in the various sacred games, but there is evidence that they were encouraged at home. Hunting was extremely popular in this warlike nation. Ball-playing was also a favorite activity of Spartan youth.

In Athens, young men spent a great deal of time in the palaestra being trained by a man known as a paidotribe. This specialist was responsible for general physical development of youth, while the gymnast was more of an expert in specific athletic contests. The paidotribe trained boys from the age of seven to about fifteen in a variety of activities, and in many instances, parents selected this instructor with great care. Concern was expressed, however, about early overspecialization in preparation for subsequent participation in the Olympic Games. Eventually boys graduated from the palaestra, and the sons of the wealthy went to the gymnasium for further training in sport. Some talented boys were selected for further instruction even though they came from poorer families—possibly the first athletic scholarships! But they did find difficulty in taking sufficient time away from their daily work.

Training in the gymnasium was much more vigorous, and the aim was a much higher degree of perfection. Here we see the appearance of the first "wealthy alumnus" who assumed the role of a sort of graduate manager of athletics. He was known as the gymnasiarch, and it was he who directed the gymnasium and the various festivals. Some of these gymnasiums were really elaborate structures with many rooms and facilities. Again we find a close connection between sport and religion; in each gymnasium there was a shrine where a particular deity was worshipped. The fact that there were public gymnasiums also indicates the responsibility that the city-state felt for the physical training of its youth. A system of "ephebic" training was subsequently instituted to bring to a climax the preparation of the warrior-citizen between the ages of eighteen and twenty.

From time to time, games and sport succeeded in unifying the city-states of Greece, where nothing else, not even religion, could. Of course, it has been said that the real religion of the Greeks was their concern for beauty, strength, and health. The need for the highest type of physical skill and conditioning was quite understandable, as they were involved almost constantly in one type of struggle or another. Sparta achieved early distinction through military triumphs, made possible largely through training in sport. The Athenians recognized this and pursued athletics most vigorously, especially when the city-state's freedom was endangered. The Hellenic ideal was to meet life head-on and to win.

All sorts of games and festivals were conducted at the various levels of society. Private sporting contests led to local games. Then there were contests within the different city-states for representatives from the various communities. These games were expanded still further into regional events such as the quadrennial Panathenaic games established in 566 B.C. The greatest contests, of course, were the Panhellenic games—the most famous of these being the Olympic Games held first at Olympia in 776 B.C. These contests were so important that a sort of international truce was declared for a period before, during, and after the games.

Elimination contests in all events were held throughout the land prior to the games, with only freeborn Greeks allowed to compete. Upon their arrival at Olympia, athletes were carefully examined and took the Olympic oath promising to obey all the rules which were established. Great dishonor and shame was the fate of the athlete who cheated or otherwise broke the strict rules; hence such infractions were rare. Approximately 45,000 spectators filled the stadium and held their places day in and day out over the five-day period despite miserable sanitary conditions. The pentathlon was a most important event that included the broad jump, the discus throw, the spear throw, the stadium sprint, and wrestling. The victor had to score first in three of the five events.

Other events included boxing, the pancratium, various running races, horse races, and chariot races.

The winner of an event received a laurel wreath—a crown of wild olives placed on top of a woolen fillet wound around the head. Soon all sorts of prizes were awarded, including vases and oil from the sacred olives which was dispensed in amphorae (vaselike containers with handles). First prize was usually worth five times as much as second, and the "youth" classification winners received slightly higher awards than those in the "boys" group. For example, the winner of the pentathlon for boys received 30 amphorae of olive oil, while second place was awarded 6. But the winner of the pentathlon for youth earned 40 amphorae, and the second-place contestant received 8. The winner of the chariot race with full-grown horses was awarded 140 amphorae, possibly because this event was more expensive for the participants. Such awards did not exceed contestants' expenses at any rate, so soon there were more semiprofessional boxers and wrestlers than horse and chariot racers.

There did appear to be a relationship between politics and athletics as political decline set in. After the Peloponnesian War, Athens had many economic problems. The Macedonians with their professional soldiers and improved methods of warfare sealed the fate of the amateur citizen-soldier at Chaeronaea in 338 B.C. After that, the former social ideal was never regained, as Athens' sphere of control continued to decline. There developed an intellectualism and a decline in physical fitness as mercenaries took over the defense of the city-state. And as amateur athletics lost influence, professional athletics gained stature. There had been, of course, many indirect rewards for the earlier winners at the Olympic Games, but this was a far cry from the subsequent professionalism.

But even in the earlier days overspecialization in sport occasioned by the desire to win had tended to tarnish the luster of the so-called amateur ideal. The very nature of sport made it difficult to judge, and the goal of excellence in a number of sports as part of overall harmony seemed to be an unattainable objective. If a man wanted to win, he specialized. The more he specialized, the more time he spent in one particular phase of sport, and the less he had for other aspects of his cultural development and for his livelihood. If he were wealthy enough, of course, at least he didn't have to worry about where his next meal was coming from—often a serious concern for our "amateur" athletes today in certain sports!

Extreme specialization in a particular sport often resulted in distorted musculature. Combative sports tended to have a brutalizing effect on the participants, who were disfigured in various ways. Their habits of eating, sleeping, and living in general became specialized. Specialized trainers and coaches arose and the athletes whom they trained achieved preeminence. As athletics became a career for a certain group of men, it was obvious that the amateur athlete would be foolish to engage in any contest with a professional. The ideal of amateurism survived for a time at Olympia, where the rule of amateurism was rigidly enforced, but the maintenance of such a standard became increasingly difficult. Cities began to compete for the services of the better performers, and the worst type of professionalism soon became a reality. Materialistic influence won out over the earlier idealism of a social ideal; such were the characteristics of sport in the age of decline of the great city-state.

Athletics became a business, and athletes themselves were often exploited in the worst sort of way. The result was that soon various athletic guilds and associations were formed to protect the rights of athletes and to secure them greater benefits. By the middle of the third century, successful athletes regularly applied for and were granted pensions for life under Roman law. But despite all these "advances," which were considerable from a materialistic standpoint, social influences eventually brought about the downfall of the professional athlete. Rome became increasingly decadent and was crumbling before the attacks of its enemies. Christianity condemned the morals of the empire, and in a matter of time, the Roman government officially adopted the Christian religion. The 291st Olympiad appears to have marked the last celebration of the Olympic Games, abolished by Theodosius the Great in A.D. 393. This signaled the death knell of what had become professional sport in the Greco-Roman world.

During the seventh and sixth centuries B.C., the Latins invaded Etrurian territory and founded Rome. Etruscans had related sport to religious rituals; their annual games were extremely important to them. But when the Romans began their own conquests, they used sports to help them achieve efficiency at arms. Later, when the military went professional, games and sport were relied on to maintain health and to give personal pleasure and group entertainment. Thus the significance of games changed from a religious function (to gain the gods' favor for various ventures) to a purely hedonistic one.

The Middle Ages

Sport and athletics in the Middle Ages presented a dismal picture according to present standards. Asceticism and scholasticism dominated the society of Europe generally, and the physical pleasures that might arise for the masses from participation in recreational sports were frowned upon in official quarters. For example, some amusements evidently interfered with archery practice by nobles and were banned, as was "weight-putting" by Edward III. These ordinances were very difficult to enforce, especially during the time of fairs, celebrations, and festivals.

After the Norman conquest of England in 1066, the ruling class developed its own pattern of leisure, which included jousting at tourneys. Gentlemen engaged in hunting, hawking, fencing, archery, and other war-related activities. The historians of the time made only occasional references to purely recreational pursuits. A barren intellectual and philosophical life dominated by Christian dogmatism, along with tribe-like political conditions and rude manners and customs, did much to suppress creativity, esthetic expression, and sporting activity of even a fairly high type.

During the Renaissance and the Reformation the attitude toward participation in sport was gradually changing. In England, for example, during the reign of Henry VIII (1509–1547), there is evidence of a resurgence of interest in athletics. He himself liked to throw the hammer. There were those, however, who were against games and sport for scholars. Roger Ascham opposed athletic activity, whereas Sir Thomas Elyot felt that accomplishment in sport was highly desirable in light of extreme study conditions and flogging. James I and subsequent Stuart kings supported the idea of sporting contests for the development of manliness in their offspring. An annual football match was extremely popular in Chester during the fifteenth century, but was supplanted by various running races after 1500. During the Puritan rule and that of Charles II to 1685, interest in athletics dropped off very sharply. We need hardly add that this discussion has been confined to a consideration of the activities of the sons of the upper class. The average man needed leisure before games and sport could truly become an important part of his life.

The United States

We will now transfer our attention almost exclusively to a brief treatment of the history of sport in American life. The focus will be narrowed, and fairly sharply, to a consideration of what may properly be called amateur sport, semiprofessional sport, and professional sport. Our concern for the status of school and college athletics throughout the discussion will be readily apparent.

The distinctly different attitudes of the Puritans and the Virginians toward recreational pursuits has already been mentioned. With the betterment of living conditions during the eighteenth century, a certain amount of leisure was earned. Such activities as dancing, hunting, horse racing, wrestling, and a variety of so-called community enterprises characterized this period. Life began to change considerably in the United

States after the Revolutionary War as a new spirit of nationalism began to make itself felt. The need for physical training as preparation for military fitness was apparent to many at this time, but the significance of play, and the possible inclusion of it along with physical training in the educational curriculum, was not comprehended. The national history of the United States ran parallel with the history of the academies—schools for boys that aimed to prepare youth to meet life and its many problems. With the great job of carving out the West ahead, it was not long before practical education won out and increased consideration was being given to the physical welfare of the student.

By the end of the first quarter of the nineteenth century, great changes were taking place in the lives of the people due to increasing industrialization and urbanization. The new way of life eliminated many of the vigorous activities that characterized life on an expanding frontier. Leisure patterns were changing: There was considerable commercial entertainment and not too much opportunity for active participation because of lack of play space. There were many, of course, who still had to work long hours for their livelihood. The games and sporting tradition were basically those of England with its class society, so it was logical that we should inherit the English concept of amateurism. Some sports quite naturally seemed more appropriate for well-to-do individuals who were able to afford their own social and athletic clubs.

Interest in a variety of sports increased in the first half of the nineteenth century. Bowling and swimming became popular activities, as did rowing and cricket. Cricket was to be eventually supplanted by baseball, which despite its strong relationship to "rounders," was considered an indigenous American sport. The first intercollegiate baseball game is reported to have been played by Williams and Amherst in 1859. Origins of American football date back at least as far as an intramural contest played at Harvard in 1827, although there is earlier evidence of a sort of football game being played on the New Haven green in 1807. Concurrently, German gymnastics achieved brief popularity around Boston in the early part of the century.

It was not until after the Civil War that interest in athletic sports really began to grow. The war showed very definitely that there was a need for physical training of America's young men. The American Gymnastic Union (Turners) promoted the introduction of German gymnastics in public schools vigorously and successfully. Innumerable athletic leagues, both amateur and professional, were formed, and college and university students promoted such activities despite considerable opposition from faculty and administration.

Rowing, baseball, and football were the first intercollegiate sports to be organized to any extent, although track and field should probably be included in this listing as well. The first intercollegiate rowing race was between Yale and Harvard in 1852; the first baseball game, between Amherst and Williams in 1859; the first football game, between Princeton and Rutgers in 1869; and the first intercollegiate track and field meet was an Ivy League affair in 1874 with Harvard, Yale, Princeton, Columbia, and Cornell participating.

After 1870, intercollegiate athletics grew so rapidly, and so many problems developed, that college and university administrators and faculty realized that something had to be done; sport had to be made to conform to certain acceptable standards, or it had to be eliminated. Intercollegiate football was especially troublesome because of a disproportionate number of injuries and flagrant practices. In 1905, representatives of about thirty institutions held a meeting that resulted in the formation of the Intercollegiate Athletic Association of the United States. (The name was later changed to the National Collegiate Athletic Association.) This organization has done all in its power to promote sound intercollegiate athletic programs; from the outset, though, it was urged that individual institutions assume responsibility for high standards of conduct in the administration of interscholastic athletic competition. Obviously, this has been a most difficult goal to achieve.

Another extremely important organization in the history of athletics in the United States, and throughout the world for that matter, has been the Amateur Athletic Union of the United States. This group was formed by interested sportsmen in 1888 to remedy a serious situation in non-school and college athletics, controlled at that time by undesirable individual promoters. The AAU has accepted the traditional British viewpoint that "an amateur athlete is one who engages in sports for the pleasure and physical, mental, or social benefits he derives therefrom and to whom sport is nothing more than an avocation." The promulgation of this ideal has persisted to the present day. In addition, the AAU was instrumental in reviving the Olympic Games in 1896. In the United States, the country was divided into a number of districts with all the athletic clubs within a district forming an association that had representation at the national level. There gradually developed a number of allied governing bodies in certain sports over which the AAU does not have full jurisdiction.

While all this was taking place, certain early twentieth-century educators were stressing the value of play in the total educative process. This had a marked effect on the secondary schools, whose enrollments had been increasing sharply. School playgrounds were being developed, and the popular literature of the time stressed that participation in sport tended to improve young people's attitudes toward desirable group behavior and citizenship. Thus, sports and games gradually began to rival gymnastic instruction in the school program. A survey conducted on a national level in 1905 showed that the majority of superintendents of public school systems approved of including interscholastic athletics in the school program. There were opponents and those who gave half-hearted approval, however, and it was stressed that such athletic competition had to be regulated carefully and should not be overemphasized because it served the needs and interests of only relatively few students.

Thus high school athletics began at the end of the nineteenth century and during the early years of the twentieth century. There was a pattern to follow—that of the colleges and universities. Such a pattern was a help, but it did bring about overemphasis that many claim has never been corrected. As on the college level, leagues that standardized regulations for control of interschool competition were formed. Eventually statewide athletic associations were needed, and the final phase took place in 1920 with the organization of the National Federation of State High School Athletic Associations. Down through the years many difficult problems have been faced and overcome through the dedication of interested educators, but the matter of overemphasis plagues us even today.

Another interesting trend has been the rise of intramural sport competition at the college level, and to a certain extent at other educational levels. Stark social influences such as war and depressions have influenced sport and physical recreational development appreciably. World War I, for example, brought about almost universal physical education legislation in the United States, making possible the introduction of sports skill programs into what had been formerly "physical training" periods. So it was that physical education periods in the schools, with California taking the lead, changed to sessions where sport rather than gymnastics dominated in the years between the end of the war and the early 1930s.

The decade from 1920 to 1930 was an interesting one in many ways, and the growth that took place in sport participation was no exception. Tremendous spectator interest in many high school, college, and professional sports developed. There was a demand for huge athletic stadiums which, once constructed, had to be filled. Athletic coaches and playground leaders were desperately needed, and the number of professional preparation programs increased sharply. During this period the NCAA emphasized the need for faculty control of athletics rather than administration by students and alumni. Conference formation and the elimination of seasonal. coaches had been stressed during the previous decade. Thus, concern in the 1920s was more a matter of the standardization of rules for the various sports and the development of programs for championships at the national level. The seemingly ever-present problem of subsidization and recruitment was so bad that several groups, including the NCAA, requested a survey by the Carnegie Foundation in 1926. The report, entitled *American College Athletics,* was published in 1929 and contained a serious indictment of practices in men's intercollegiate sports. There was no question but that semiprofessionalism had arrived in American college sport.

Also during this period the Olympic Games program was enlarged to include many more sports, a greater number of participants, and competition for women. The classic definition of an amateur accepted by the AAU many years before continued, although times and conditions had changed; it became a matter of principle—a principle which, according to the AAU, was the only means by which the United States could be represented honorably in the quadrennial games. The decision regarding the amateur status of the participants from a particular country rested solely with the country that was certifying its own athletes as amateurs. What others did under the guise of amateurism was not our concern; what we did was our problem, and how we did it will make a most interesting study for future sport historians!

The period since 1930 in the United States has been one in which interest in competitive sport and physical recreation has continued unabated, and has, in fact, grown. The use of leisure has become an urgent concern. High school athletics have attained new heights, as have college athletics and international competition. Competition in sport has helped to promote a concept of internationalism. But who can deny the undercurrents of nationalism present in the cold war athletic contests between the United States and the USSR? Furthermore, behind the scenes, the gnawing, persistent problem of amateurism has plagued us and made a mockery of the high ideals for which we strive. The words of that cynic haunt us: "Amateurs? There ain't none!"

And so in the 1970s the United States still finds itself the scene of a titanic struggle between the Amateur Athletic Union and the National Collegiate Athletic Association for control of what is still called "amateur sport," although an attempt by anyone to offer a blanket definition of that is an absolute impossibility. A dictionary, of course, goes along with the norm, explaining an amateur as one not rated as a professional, and a professional as a person who has competed in sport for a stake or purse, or gate money, or with a professional for a prize, or who has taught or trained in sports or athletics for pay. Which brings us back to that cynic who says, "An amateur is a guy who won't take a check!"

Some one group is going to win this struggle, but not before the United States is terribly embarrassed or before many fine athletes are hurt in one way or another. What appears to be needed is some frank, straightforward thinking that takes into consideration that the United States has entered the second half of the twentieth century, and that history may seem to be repeating itself *but not in the same way.* As often as this theme has been reiterated, we will say it again: Your outlook on this problem will depend a great deal on your philosophy of education.

PHILOSOPHICAL ANALYSIS

The essentialists will generally tend to believe that the classic definition of amateurism has considerable merit. They will be apt to wish to retain the good from the past and to change the status quo very slowly, if at all. If, for example, it can be proved scientifically that a change is needed, certain people holding philosophical positions within educational essentialism would be willing to accept change. Others are skeptical about so-called scientific proof in certain areas of human life; rather, they believe that "right is right, and wrong is wrong."

The progressivists believe that there are no values that are absolutely fixed and that changing times demand new methods. They appreciate the contributions of the past, but do not regard them as sacrosanct. They would be willing to accept a new approach to this perennial problem in sport if it worked; their attitude is that we can only arrive at a solution to this problem by trying out some of the proposed solutions on a trial and error basis.

The experimentalists believe that physical education classes and intramural sports are more important to the large majority of students than interscholastic and intercollegiate sports and deserve priority if conflict arises over budgetary allotment, staff allotment, or use of facilities. They can give full support to team experiences in competitive sports, because these can be vital educational experiences if properly conducted. They believe further that "physical" educational, athletic, or recreational activity at a reasonable level of skill can be an esthetic experience of a fine type. If stress is placed on the continuous development of standards to guide conduct, a significant contribution may be made to moral training through laboratory experiences. Thus, the planned occurrence of educational situations within sports competition is important to the experimentalist.

The reconstructionists would stress intramural sports and voluntary physical recreational activities. In team competition particular stress should be placed on cooperation and the promotion of *friendly* competition. Extramural athletic competition can be introduced when there is a need, inasmuch as striving for excellence is important in individual development, but this aspect of the program must be kept in balance with the total curriculum. Educators must zealously guard against the exploitation evident in many interscholastic and intercollegiate competitive athletic programs. Sport was created *for* us, and we cannot permit materialistic influences in our society to "win out" over sound educational philosophy. Instruction in carryover games and sports (the whole concept of education for leisure) should have an important place in the curriculum.

The realists are typically concerned with the adequate training and development of the body itself. They give "qualified approval" to competitive sport, because they believe that it contributes to the learning of sportsmanship and desirable social conduct. Some realists might agree that every child should be *required* to learn a team game and an individual sport that could be played as an adult before graduation. Competitive athletics, however, are extracurricular and come after the official school day is over. The underlying reasoning, therefore, is that work and play cannot be identified under the same psychological rubric. Play for young adults is "carefree activity performed for its own sake" and for the sake of re-creation. Unfortunately, this "play attitude" is quite often missing from organized sport.

The idealists definitely favor sport and athletics in our culture; after all, witness the status accorded such activity in ancient Greek idealism. They believe in the transfer of training theory, which implies that attitudes of sportsmanship and fair play learned through desirable athletic competition can and do transfer to life situations. The Christian idealists believe that coaches should fulfill the moral and ethical demands of their calling by setting a good example for their charges to emulate; the athlete, therefore, should strive "for that same perfection that we seek on our athletic teams" in his or her individual life. The desired moral and social values that sport can yield must be made realities. The teachers of sports are actually in a unique position, because they can be among the most influential members of the school community in the shaping of these values. But they must be careful not to let students become too self-centered; sport should be a means to an end, not an end in itself. Extreme specialization may warp the personalities of all concerned. As Oberteuffer has emphasized time and again, we cannot be satisfied with scores instead of character.

The existentialists challenge the profession by asking: How is it possible to preserve the individual's authenticity in individual, dual, and team sports where winning is so often overemphasized? In true sport, as opposed to competitive athletics, a young person may personally select the values he or she wishes to derive from activity. We should play, therefore, for actualization of self and *should use sport for our own purposes.* In this way we will find personal liberation and release.

CONCLUDING STATEMENT

This brief summary of the background of sport and competitive athletics in the Western world has indicated that athletic competition is accepted to a greater or lesser degree as an integral or ancillary phase of the educative process. *No one can deny that vigorous competitive sport has become a vital phase of our American way of life!* A great many of us are coaches of one or more sports at the different levels of public education, and there is no question but that we can make our influence felt as to the direction that we believe athletic competition should take in the future. Such influence as we may have in the future determination of policy will achieve results only as we are articulate, logical, and consistent in the arguments we present to our colleagues, who are often not quite convinced of the worth of our enterprise. Hence our task is to make a case for athletics based on a carefully conceived philosophy of education. In the past we have tended instead to rely on the great interest competitive sport generates in the student population and in the community.

What influence we can have at the conference level, at the district and national level in the various sports-governing bodies, and at the international level depends largely upon the degree of "enlightened participation" we are willing to assume whenever and wherever the opportunity presents itself. True professionals, who are dedicated to the promotion of the highest and finest type of sport competition, cannot be satisfied just with doing their own work; they must fight off any tendency to leave the work to others in the professional associations and the sports-governing bodies where policies for the future are being formulated. The average coach feels that he or she, as merely one individual, doesn't have much to say about this problem of the amateur, semiprofessional, and professional in sport. But, united with other like-minded coaches, he or she could strongly influence the future of American sport. It is true that any such progress will necessarily involve cooperative effort with the NCAA, the AAU, the National Association of Intercollegiate Athletics, the National Federation of State High School Athletic Associations, and other similar groups, but has it not been characteristic of our American democratic way of life to work things out amicably for the good of all?

It may well be that we will have to reevaluate some of our treasured assumptions about the amateur code in athletics. What *are* the reasons today for the sharp distinction between the amateur and the professional? History tells us where the ideal originated, but it also tells us that the conditions which brought it about do not exist in America today. It is quite possible that we are trying desperately to perpetuate a concept which has outlived its purpose. Must we persist in the ideology that in sport and athletics it is a question of black or white—the professional being the black one, and the amateur, the white? Can't we recognize and identify the many shades of "gray" that inevitably exist in between?

What is so wrong with a young athlete being classified as a semi-professional? Do we brand the musician, the artist, or the sculptor in our society who develops his or her talent sufficiently to receive some remuneration as being a "dirty pro"? Why must this idea persist in sport —a legitimate aspect of our culture? The answer to these questions may well lie in the fact that we are not willing, almost subconsciously, to accept sport as a legitimate and worthwhile aspect of our culture.

The materialistic image of today's professionals in sport and athletics does not help very much either. Granted they are a different breed than their predecessors, especially in such sports as basketball and football, but even here they are "professional" in the limited sense of the word. They are usually after all the money that physical talent can bring on the open market. They see professional athletics as a means to an end—security and ultimate happiness in life. There is nothing basically wrong with using a talent in this way, but a greater societal good would result if they would attempt to make themselves professional in the broader sense of the word. Everything considered, these people have an unusual talent they have developed to a high degree in a cultural activity that has proved itself important in our society. Furthermore, it is probably true that professionals who have reached their peak are better qualified in this sphere of activity than they will ever be in any other. What would be more natural than to expect them to become true professionals and to devote the rest of their lives to the promotion of sport with the youth and adults of their country? There is absolutely no reason why professional athletes, those who typically love their sport, cannot devote their lives to a social ideal and become really fine professional individuals, whose primary aim in life is to serve others. Such an approach can work; the country is dotted with men and women who have made it work. It is not as idealistic as it may sound. It would do much to help us look at the "amateur controversy" in a new light.

We cannot agree with the cynic who says that there are no more amateurs in sport. This is not true. There are, and will always be, amateurs in the only logical sense of the word today. The amateur is the beginner, the dabbler, the dilettante. This is not saying that he or she "loves" the activity any more or less than the semiprofessional or professional. As a matter of fact, he or she isn't well enough acquainted with it to "love" it. When the businessman goes out to the local golf course early on a Sunday morning and turns in a neat score of 125 for eighteen holes, he is displaying all the traits of an amateur in what should be today's parlance.

Proficiency in the chosen sport, and the amount of time spent practicing it, should certainly be considered when we classify people in sports. The boy who plays the trumpet in the high school band is an amateur. If he qualifies to play in his college dance band on Saturday nights and receives $15 weekly for his efforts, he is a semiprofessional. Who would criticize him for this? Let us assume that this young man is majoring in music and goes on after college to become either a professional musician or a professional teacher. We find this perfectly commendable in our society. But there are a great many people in the United States who can't visualize this in athletics. The first time an athlete takes money for playing a favorite sport, he or she is a professional and *presumably* could be barred from any attempt to participate in the Olympic Games. Obviously, such a stand is ridiculous today.

It is, of course, the excesses and overemphasis that are feared. The United States is committed to a great educational experiment on a grand scale. We are the only country in the world where 40 to 50 percent of the young people go on to some form of higher education in the more than 2000 junior colleges, community colleges, colleges, and universities. Semiprofessionalism to a fairly high degree in college sport can possibly be justified only for physical education majors and those who might wish to become professionals in those sports that bring in fairly high gate receipts. Because winning teams in college sports bring prestige and gate receipts, competition for fine athletes is keen. The NCAA and the NAIA have made athletic scholarships legitimate with certain stipulations. Many people felt that the Western Conference (Big Ten) was only being realistic when it removed the "need factor" from its athletic tender plan; others felt this was a serious mistake. Other important colleges and universities admit students on the basis of their intellectual attainment and many other factors, of which athletic accomplishment is one. Then scholarship aid is given on the basis of the parents' total financial position—their ability to pay for their child's college education. No matter which approach is used, the athlete is still being subsidized to a greater or lesser extent. It is extremely difficult to say which approach is right and best for the individual and for society. One thing is certain: Whatever help the young person receives should be known by all and should be in conformity with established rules and regulations.

The Role of Administration (Management)

As our society continues to grow in complexity, amazing social changes are taking place. The continuing Industrial Revolution, coupled with literally fantastic advances in science and technology, has placed our most modern societies in a most difficult situation. These factors, along with the exploding population and the resultant development of immense urban and suburban areas, have created a situation in which a certain percentage of the manpower has been forced to concern itself increasingly with the management of the efforts of the large majority of the people in our society. The ability of a relatively few individuals to master this task to a reasonable degree has meant that the world as we know it could continue to grow and develop. This is not meant to imply that a great many people have not organized and administered all types of enterprises in the various aspects of life in the past. The point here is that most recently an "organizational" or "administrative" revolution has taken place, and will continue to take place, because of the extreme complexity of our evolving society. Thus, it is administrative theory and/or thought that is relatively new rather than administrative practice. Such practice, closely related to the broad processes of historical evolution, has been affected by the many social forces at work during these centuries.

HISTORICAL BACKGROUND

Social organizations of one type or another are inextricably related to our history as a human and social animal. In early societies there were family units, clans, and tribes. Superior-subordinate relationships evolved according to the very nature of things, as human beings produced goods, fought wars, organized society politically, formed churches, and developed a great variety of formal and informal associations. In certain eras these organizations within the various groups and communities became very large. They grew, changed, developed further, changed their functions along the way, and then in most cases vanished as the particular civilization declined. The central theme seems to have been that of *change*— change that was made to strengthen the organization, change that meant more and perhaps better administration as the organizations grew. If power is required to accomplish a given task in a certain way, then people must be organized and programs must be administered to foster the desired development. Generally speaking, and this statement can be misinterpreted, the more formal the organizational structure is, the more power can be summoned to effect the desired goals. Leaders use money to bring about the necessary combination of human and physical resources (that is, the power) to get the job done. As these resources are combined in various ways, many different and improved techniques are developed that may hasten the end result. Somehow social change takes place as people develop the desire, the physical resources, and the technical knowhow to perform the task in the most expedient manner possible. The desire, of course, originates from the ideals and values of the culture—values that aid the leaders in attitude formation.

In a recent, truly monumental study, Gross traces the historical development of administrative thought (1964). He points out that it was only recently that "administrative thought emerged as a differentiated field of sustained writing, conscious observation, abstract theory, and specialized terminology" (p. 91). He explains how rulers in ancient times were expected to be wise, good, bold, willing to compromise, unscrupulous, and well-advised. Still further, various plans of administrative education were developed as formal organizations grew. Then after the Industrial Revolution really gathered momentum, certain basic changes began to take place in what might be called "administrative technology." It was subsequently accompanied by larger organizations with more subdivisions, directed by more administrators, creating a greater amount of bureaucracy.

The United States

The American people have always had faith in education as the guardian of a democratic government, as probably the best assurance of a forward-looking society, and as an open door to every person for the realization of his or her potential. Education has become a tremendous public business, with the normal community using over half its tax money for schools. It is estimated that over 40 million people have some direct connection with public education, not to mention private education. The business of education will continue to grow; with an ever-expanding population and still unmet challenges, it would be folly to predict otherwise. The school has truly been a remarkable social experiment in the United States, but it must keep abreast of social needs for continued progress.

There is a definite need for efficient administration based on sound theory and scientific evidence in such a large businesslike organization as the modern school. The many problems presented to administrators involve a seemingly unending chain of details, and the tempo of school life is steadily increasing. Well-prepared and ethical school administrators are ultimately responsible for the efficient performance of a myriad of duties. It is very important for them to realize that their position and resultant functions exist as a *means* to an end. American education will always need more and better qualified administrators.

Administration has undergone a process of gradual evolution that parallels the growth of the school system itself. Originally no one even thought of administrators and school board members in our schools. The school was administered democratically by the people at town meetings. As towns grew this became impractical, and town selectmen were delegated the responsibility. In 1827 Massachusetts became the first state to enact a law requiring towns to have separate committees for the schools. Ten years later the first superintendency was created in Providence, Rhode Island. New York had had a state superintendent in 1812. The functions of the early superintendents were only vaguely defined, because the boards of education refused to recognize their professional status. It took a full century for school boards to accord the superintendent his rightful function as a professional expert in the area of school management.

There has been a parallel development at the college and university level. The creation of a board of overseers and a corporation at Harvard College in 1642 and 1650, respectively, pointed the way for democratic administration of higher education in the United States. There have been variations in form, but the principle of centralized administrative authority exists in almost all American colleges and universities today. The administration is responsible to a group outside the school, the composition of which varies according to the source of financial support.

It is often not understood that, by constitutional law, the individual state has the power to make adequate education available to its citizens. Much of this power, along with the necessary details for execution of the school program, has been delegated to the local community. The members of local school boards can never be allowed to forget, however, that they are acting as agents of the state. Basically, the functions of school administration are legislative, executive, and inspectorial; the board's function is to legislate with the aid of professional guidance. Individual board members, therefore, are an elected group who see to it that the schools are operated efficiently. A board should have rules and regulations as to its functions, organization, and responsibilities. A large part of the superintendent's job is to advise the board in such a way that the group functions harmoniously. As individuals, board members have no power to act, and they should never assume executive duties; their power to legislate the conduct of the schools stems from group action only. The board represents the public; it legislates, it employs, and it appraises the status of education in the local community.

In this way our pattern of education has developed. The superintendent of schools acts as a "professional guide" to the board of education. Upon his or her recommendation, the board employs school principals who should display many of the same characteristics an excellent superintendent possesses. Principals are the professional representatives of the superintendent in a particular school. They receive their authority either verbally or in writing, which makes them agents of the board of education. Ideally, there should be rules and regulations that govern the principal's position. Merely stating that "the principal shall be responsible for the efficient operation of the school" allows for too broad an interpretation on the part of this executive. In the professional relationship of principal and teacher, a correct understanding and full appreciation of the role of each is extremely important. Both should understand that they are co-workers in a common enterprise with joint responsibility for the pupil.

When the term "administration" is used in education, it is usually associated with such words as superintendence, direction, management, planning, supervision, organization, regulation, guidance, and control. In common usage we think of it as the process of directing people in an endeavor. This function is carried out in a variety of ways by many people in the field of physical, health, and recreation education. The typical approach to administration is to ascertain those principles and operational policies upon which we can base our own theory and practice. Administration, in its simplest form, could probably be likened to a football coach blowing a whistle to call the players together at the beginning of practice. To carry this parallel further, it is obvious that the coaching of a football team involves different types of activity. The more complex the activity, the more specialization becomes necessary. Thus, the football coach, as an administrator, must devote long hours to planning, organization, coordination, and evaluation, in addition to teaching.

PHILOSOPHICAL
ANALYSIS

The phenomenon of organized physical education, including competitive sport, that has taken place on this continent within the past hundred years has today become a vast enterprise which demands wise and skillful management. The appointment of a director of physical education, an athletic director, or a chairperson with some "combined" title is an ordinary occurrence. These men and women have assumed many of the attributes of a profession. We should keep in mind, however, that a *recognized* profession needs an organized body of knowledge based on research. Thus, the "perpetuation of our species"—the administrator of physical education and athletics—as a profession requires that some organizational structure be developed within educational institutions whereby the body of professional knowledge, whatever its status, may be transmitted to those who follow.

Let us focus our attention on the professional preparation of athletics administrators in years past. Generally speaking, many, if not all, of these men and women worked their way up through the ranks in some sort of an apprenticeship scheme. Admittedly, such a method of preparing administrators is not unique to athletics. A similar pattern was evident earlier in just about any profession that you might wish to examine. This is in contrast, of course, to the way administrators are chosen at the college and university level. Here they are selected on the basis of research endeavor and scholarly eminence—and probably also because they possess certain desirable personality traits.

There have been many charges that the above-mentioned professional schools are offering "trade-school" programs. To combat these attacks and in an effort to achieve some academic respectability, they gradually raised the academic standards of their faculty members and also brought representatives of related, more basic disciplines into their own educational structures. This appears to be exactly what is happening now in the area of sport administration.

In many institutions the administration of athletics is now big business within big education and, unfortunately, there is practically no theory or ongoing research about the administrative task taking place. The professional preparation of athletics administrators is being carried out by physical educators almost universally in a haphazard and poorly articulated fashion. And who is employing the results (or theory) available from a *documented* body of research knowledge about administrative theory and practice? How long, for example, can a profession function successfully with the following types of unwritten theoretical propositions as a base:

1. Under conditions not so carefully controlled, football coaches and athletic directors behave as they damned well please.
2. A discipline and/or profession, most anxious to gain strength and influence, should divide itself according to sex and move in opposite directions.

Philosophical Analysis as a Supplement to Administrative Theory

If and when a truly definitive inventory of administrative theory and research becomes available, such knowledge can then serve as a foundation to be made available to all men and women in sport serving as administrators and managers. Such synthesis and integration of knowledge into concepts would inevitably have considerable practical value in providing the finest type of operational base. The logic of this approach seems incontrovertible, but there appears to be one major flaw with such an assumption. Value-free, scientific investigation may in time tell us how to bring about an effect, but it will *never* tell us whether it is desirable to function in a certain way in our own educational system in this culture. It is at this point that individual and group values come into the picture—a condition from which we cannot and should not wish to escape. (Some philosophical positions are, of course, based on a truth-is-wrought-from-experience, problem-solving approach, and adherents to such beliefs would view this point somewhat differently.) Basically, however, now and in the future administrators have a responsibility to examine themselves and to construct their own personal philosophy so that they may be effective professional persons within their own social system and culture.

At first glance, administrators may not see the need for such a disciplined approach; they may believe they are now serving their profession effectively, and that their common sense—a sort of "theoretical group bias"—is serving them quite satisfactorily. Possibly the best rebuttal is that the commonsense system of decision making and future planning is not suffiiently forward looking in a society where the *rate* of change is increasing geometrically. Sound administrative theory should enable administrators to "put their vehicle into high gear and to follow a reasonably straight course." We need to improve on common sense, and the argument is that a philosophical approach differs in degree from an outlook based on what the "average colleague" would do to plan for the years ahead. Certainly progress has been made in this century, but there are now too many signs that recurring problems are still being handled in the same old way.

Slice it whichever way you will, an evolving democratic system allows the promulgation of many different educational philosophies. Some of these positions or "stances" are much more favorable to the enterprise of sport than others. This means that sport administrators need to understand their own philosophical stances in order to meet persistent problems logically and consistently, but almost equally as important is the development of the ability to assess others with whom they come into contact so that they will understand their attitudes and opinions better. Further, how can an administrator exert any leadership in athletics when he or she is merely reflecting social forces and transmitting ideas that may have worked fairly well in the past?

To achieve the status of amateur philosophers, we recommend that sport administrators examine themselves to the best of their ability and find their place on a somewhat loosely knit educational philosophy spectrum in accordance with some of the ideas expressed under the leading philosophical tendencies. We must keep in mind that educational progressivism is greatly concerned about student freedom, individual differences, student interest, possible gradual change of values, student growth, and emphasis on lifelike problem-solving educational experiences. Conversely, education essentialism's position is that there are certain educational values by which the individual must be guided; that effort takes precedence over interest and builds moral stamina; that the experience of the past has powerful jurisdiction over the present; and that the cultivation of the intellect and reason is most important in education.[1]

Traditionally, departments of physical education and/or athletics, just like other departments in a school, seem to have operated on the basis of a group of unexpressed major and minor principles. Such principles, probably necessary to the proper formulation of operational policies, exist, explicitly or implicitly, beneath every specific act of teaching in a particular field. Still deeper, a consistent and logical philosophy of life and/or religion should be the foundation upon which at least the administrator or the majority of the department rests. Unfortunately, emergencies and practical considerations, as well as individual personalities and possibly conflicting administrative patterns, force a department almost constantly to make exceptions to its "prevailing" philosophy. At times, a program takes on the appearance of a patchwork that bears little resemblance to any common philosophy. For these reasons, it now seems logical to draw some inferences for prospective administrators from the leading philosophical tendencies. There are many who would immedi-

---

[1] To determine the consistency of his or her own administrative (management) philosophy, the reader is referred to the self-evaluation checklist developed by the writer in *Administrative Theory and Practice in Physical Education and Athletics* (with Marcia J. Spaeth), Englewood Cliffs, N.J.: Prentice-Hall, 1975.

ately say that to do so in connection with *any* of the major philosophical positions would be skating on very thin ice indeed. It does seem, however, that every administrator needs such a framework of action and that he or she should get some guidance from these basic beliefs. If this is not possible, philosophy will continue to find its work taken over by newer disciplines.

Experimentalism

The experimentalist approach to administration, as revealed in the persistent problems already discussed, is basically open-minded and un-biased. The administrator makes every effort to conduct the affairs of the department as a democratic undertaking in which all the various indi-viduals concerned have the opportunity to share in policy formation as well as the rest of the operation. Students and staff are not afraid to come to him or her with their problems. When a staff member or student is criticized, it is done in such a way that a minimum of antagonism occurs. The individual concerned is encouraged to present his or her side of the story. The end result should be that the person leaves with a desire to improve his or her performance to live up to the confidence of the ad-ministrator.

Experimentalist administrators encourage both staff and students to offer constructive criticisms in a variety of ways. All departmental policy is decided through democratic procedure. Administrators see themselves as chairpersons at meetings. They may well speak to the various issues and problems at hand, perhaps without the formality of leaving the chair. Their "democracy-in-action" approach is quite apparent throughout the program and is reflected in the attitudes of the staff and the students toward the enterprise. A staff member given responsibility finds that the authority to carry it out is present as well. Such administrators treat staff members as co-workers. They encourage staff study projects and want all staff members to improve themselves professionally. When staff members do something that merits praise, these administrators see that their work is recognized both within and without the department.

Through the best possible personal relationships, experimentalist administrators create an atmosphere in which all can make a full con-tribution to the progress of the department. If such an administrator resigns, it would not be difficult for a qualified staff member to assume the position. A successor does not have to learn the tricks of the trade through bitter experience.

Such administrators realize that among the many relations and de-terminants that influence a person's behavior in any given situation, emotional acceptance rates high. They view administration as a develop-ing social science. They know that they can't expect cooperation on the part of all concerned to develop by chance, so they seek to involve all staff members in policy formation and to keep the lines of communication open. In this way there is a much greater possibility that the goals of democratic, experimental education will be realized.

Realism

A realistic approach to administrative control is entirely predictable. The administrator, possessing ultimate responsibility, makes decisions affecting the rest of the staff and the students. "Authority is therefore centralized in a line-staff pattern of control" (Morland, 1958, p. 295). The administrator tends to function as a business executive who has been hired to make wise, clearcut decisions when the situation so warrants. The administrator may ask staff members for opinions and may have committees investigate certain problems and come up with recommendations. But the eventual decision is up to him or her. As one investigator stated: "As an administrator my decisions are dictated by the impersonal results of objective experimentation. However, I stand ready to modify procedures as more effective methods are established." The school board, which retains ultimate responsibility, typically delegates the administrator a certain amount of responsibility commensurate with the authority granted to get the job done. Teachers have little choice but to carry out the directions of their superior, no matter what their personal feelings may be. The realist feels such administrative theory is compatible with life in an evolving democracy, because there will always be "some chiefs and many Indians." Someone has to call the shots. bear the brunt of the responsibility, and accept the rewards or suffer the consequences. The idea of taking a vote to get majority opinion before any departmental action is taken may sound good in theory, but it does not centralize the responsibility on one pair of shoulders, and may well result in nothing but "pooled ignorance" concerning a controversial issue. Basically, it is simply not a very *realistic* approach! Besides, it is humanly impossible in large organizations to take time to have a vote on everything. School boards, as one unit of control, should hire administrators, set policy, back up decisions made by administrators in line with such policy, reward them if their "batting averages" on decisions are quite high, and fire them if they prove to be incompetent.

Idealism

Idealistic educators face a predicament that must be resolved in order to reach a logical and consistent administrative policy. On the one hand, idealism is a strongly essentialist philosophy of education. Because of an absolute moral law in the universe, and because education's aim is to help the child adjust to the fundamental realities disclosed by history, idealists firmly believe it necessary to conserve and transmit the established value pattern. On the other hand, the idealist philosophy of education places great emphasis on the freedom, growth, and development of the personality. Despite their "will to perfection," idealists are most concerned with instilling the skills and techniques necessary for social responsiveness. If we hope to develop the correct attitudes in children, they must come indirectly "by example, inspiration, and contagion" (Zeigler, 1964, pp. 237–238). This leads us to the view that the personality of the teacher is tremendously important! In the idealistic tradition, great teachers and leaders have respect for the student's personality and intelligence. Ideal teachers do not superimpose their will on others. They do not demand respect; they earn it by their manner and bearing. As a good friend to their pupils, they have a keen desire to show them what democratic living is like, because they realize that the pupils in turn will help to democratize others. Is it too much, therefore, to suggest that there are many implications here for the idealistic administrator—to hope that an improved type of democracy in educational administration will someday become a reality despite the line-staff pattern of control that is apparently a hallmark of essentialist educational philosophy?

CONCLUDING STATEMENT

To draw this discussion to a close, we can broadly state that the essentialist believes in certain inviolable theoretical principles of administration. These principles provide many answers to administrative problems and can greatly help the neophyte. Essentialists would view administration as an art, not a science. They would argue that many fine administrators have never had a course in administration, and that such courses would not help significantly. In general, they approve of the practice, in higher education especially, of selecting administrators from the ranks of scholars and/or research scientists, who will then learn to administer an educational organization on the job.

The progressivists, and many social scientists, tend to believe that no practical rules exist which can be applied in an automatic fashion to the organizational problems that actually arise. They would view administration as a developing social (behavioral) science; that is, an area where scientific evidence about individuals and their interrelationships with others can provide important keys to the decision-making process.

If a person is aware of these new developments and has had an internship experience, it seems to the progressivist that he or she will have a much better chance of becoming a successful administrator—all other things being equal. The argument here is that an administrator's practice should be based on the ever-increasing knowledge available to us through the behavioral sciences particularly. Then it is a question of applying this knowledge skillfully to the task at hand.

Progress as a Concept

Has progress in physical education and sport been made through the agency of the school and other educational agencies? This section will attempt to answer that question with a brief consideration of the concept of progress itself. We shall also discuss educational progress and its relationship to educational philosophy and conclude with a statement about the need for consensus in physical education and sport.

In the first two subsections conclusions of particular scientific and educational authorities will be presented. The writer will rely on his subjective judgment in the third subsection relating to physical education and sport. Any fusion of the past and the present, which this effort undoubtedly is, cannot escape the element of controversy and struggle. Thus the writer recognizes that it is literally impossible for him to have historical perspective or to be completely unbiased.

Furthermore, readers may find that they (1) have already made a number of judgments for themselves; (2) are currently in the process of making these judgments; or (3) will make these judgments for themselves once they understand the problems more fully. One's judgment could well be determined by one's mood or by the prevailing mood of the times. The man or woman who thinks profoundly in the light of the occurrences of the twentieth century cannot be blamed for being pessimistic or skeptical at best. If he or she can be classified as a pessimist, he or she will probably feel that our future prospects on this earth are not good at all. Perhaps you are an optimist, however. At any rate, your considered philosophy—that is, you the reader as a professional person—will have much to do with your future plans and the way you go about executing them. Keep in mind also that thoughts expressed in words are just that and nothing more. Others will judge you and your efforts by your deeds as a professional person—not by what you say you believe. Hopefully, they won't prejudge you. You live your philosophy every day of your life. That is why it is so important to know where you are going and why you want to get there. It is for this reason that this particular persistent problem has been placed at the end of the book.

A DEFINITION OF PROGRESS

Any study of history inevitably forces a person to conjecture about human progress. A world-famous paleontologist, George Gaylord Simpson, after twenty-five years of research, offers us his assessment of the concept of progress in evolution (1949, pp. 240–262). His study has convinced him that it is necessary to reject "the over-simple and metaphysical concept of a pervasive perfection principle." That there has been progression he will not deny, but is this "progress"? The difficulty comes when we assume that change is progress; we must ask ourselves if we can recommend a criterion by which progress may be judged.

We are warned that it may be shortsighted for us to be our own "judge and jury" in this connection. It may well be an acceptable *human* criterion of progress to say that we are coming closer to approximating what we think we ought to be and to achieving what we hold to be good. It is not wise, according to Simpson, however, to automatically assume that this is "the *only* criterion of progress and that it has a *general* validity in evolution. . . ." Thus, throughout the history of life there have been examples of progress and examples of retrogression, and progress is "certainly not a basic property of life common to all its manifestations." If it is a materialistic world, as Simpson would have us believe, a particular species can progress and retrogress. There is "a tendency for life to expand, to fill in all the space in the livable environments," but such expansion has not necessarily been constant (although it is true that human beings are now "the most rapidly progressing organism in the world").

It is true further that we have made progress in adaptability and have developed our "ability to cope with a greater variety of environments." This is also progress considered from the human vantage point. The various evolutionary phenomena among the many species, however, do not show "a vital principle common to all forms of life," and "they are certainly inconsistent with the existence of a supernal perfecting principle. . . ." Thus, Simpson concludes, human progress is actually relative and not general, and "does not warrant choice of the line of man's ancestry as the central line of evolution as a whole." Yet it is safe to say that "man is among the highest products of evolution . . . and that man is, on the whole but not in every single respect, the pinnacle so far of evolutionary progress" *on this earth.*

With these sobering thoughts, with the realization that evolution (of human and other organisms) is going on and will probably continue for millions of years, we can realize how futile it is to attempt to predict any outcome for the ceaseless change so evident in life and its environment. We can say that we must be extremely careful about the possible extinction of our species on earth, because it is highly improbable, though not absolutely impossible, that our development would be repeated. Some other mammal might develop in a similar way, but this will not happen so long as we have control of our environment and do not encourage such development. Our task is to attempt to modify and perhaps to control the direction of our own evolution according to our highest goals. It may be possible through the agency of education to ensure the future of our species; one way to accomplish this would be to place a much greater emphasis on the social sciences and to work for an ethically sound world-state.

PROGRESS IN EDUCATION

Now let us transfer our attention from Simpson's concept of progress in evolution to the more immediate problem of the United States at the end of the twentieth century—to the type of society we may have by the year 2000. Here we find a country in which the people have developed a great faith in material progress. Because technology has advanced so rapidly in the past fifty years, leaders in the various walks of life are devoting a great deal of time and money planning for the years immediately ahead. Specific industries are spending millions of dollars investigating the possibilities of the future, as are branches of the armed forces, several nonprofit foundations, various universities, and professional associations. By 2000 the United States will probably have a population of 330 million. These people will have to be housed, transported, fed, entertained, cared for medically, and educated in large supercities and their environs. The threat of greater stress and strain looms large, unless greater "creature comforts" can be provided and unless life can be made meaningful. It seems imperative to devise better uses of leisure, because there seems to be some likelihood that a great many men and women will have to be paid to be idle—idle, that is, from today's standpoint. And yet those who are brighter and more energetic, and who desire responsibility, recognition, and power, will seemingly gain such rewards only through work. Where does education fit into the picture?

At present there are approximately 60 million young people enrolled at some level of our vast educational system, and the fantastic sum of $50 billion a year is being spent to finance this gigantic enterprise. Unfortunately, however, many people are not happy with this situation. The enormity of the structure is staggering and almost incomprehensible to any one individual or group. Of course, debate about what should comprise a fine education is entirely healthy. Naturally enough, many of the same questions have been asked and debated since so-called educational progress began: How can we determine what is a good education (that is, what criteria shall we employ?)? How should the current situation modify educational practice? What type of environment should be provided to guarantee the best educational outcome? And, specifically, what is the function of the school?

Throughout the course of history until the golden age of Greece, a good education had been based on the transmission of the cultural heritage and the society's particular methods of survival. The Greeks, however, became so prosperous that for the first time it was possible, for a few at least, to depart from previous educational norms. Plato proposed an educational scheme in *The Republic* in which the Greeks might look forward to an ideal society. But the populace was not ready to put this proposal into practice, or to accept Socrates' critical approach to current educational practice. Even the great Aristotle took sides against Plato in this respect. In his *Politics* he called for an educational pattern conforming to the actual political state in existence.

Throughout the Roman Empire and the Middle Ages such practices continued, despite the fact that from time to time certain educational theorists offered proposals of greater or lesser radical quality. Thus, when a society declined, those involved in the educational system had no ideas about societal rejuvenation and were in no position to be of significant assistance. During the Renaissance new ideas and practices developed outside of the traditional educational pattern. Then, later, after humanism had made itself a strong force and had brought about the inauguration of a special school to foster its spirit, the introduction of science into the curriculum faced the same barriers all over again.

As Brubacher points out, this pattern continued in the eighteenth through the twentieth centuries as political and economic revolutions took place (1966, pp. 584–587). The school always played "the secondary rather than the primary role . . . in periods of social transition." This was true in the French Revolution, the American Revolution, the Industrial Revolution in England, the Russian Revolution, and the several upheavals in Germany and Italy—even, to a great degree, in the so-called period of progressive education in the United States in the twentieth century. All of which leads to the conclusion that political leaders have never in world history viewed the school as an agent of social reconstruction.

Yet in modern history there have been a number of educators who believed strongly that the school was not living up to its potential in the preparation of the young for future leadership roles. Such people as the Marquis de Condorcet, Adrien Helvétius, Immanuel Kant, Jean Jacques Rousseau, Johann Heinrich Pestalozzi, Wilhelm August Froebel, Horace Mann, John Dewey, and George S. Counts have seen the need for the schools to serve a more creative function—to provide young people with the knowledge, understanding, and attitudes whereby they could more effectively lead the way. Such an approach would require great understanding on the part of an enlightened citizenry and complete academic freedom. The most controversial of issues would be the order of the day in such a school environment, and infinitely greater respect and confidence would have to be accorded to the teaching profession. This is not to say, of course, that great progress has not been made in regard to the matter of academic freedom; however, such freedom has been gained for the most part at great personal loss to individual teachers.

The question whether our educational institutions have made progress insofar as quantity and quality are concerned must be considered briefly. The almost self-evident answer is yes, even in those countries that have not provided educational opportunities for more than a selected minority. In the United States more than 45 percent are presently going on to some form of higher education. Of course, there are some who contend that it is wrong to have approximately five "levels" of higher education ranging from community colleges to select Ivy League institutions. When this question is raised, the emphasis in the discussion necessarily shifts from quantity to quality—to a degree at least. With societies changing their economies, and often their political regimes, from one type to another, the body of knowledge has grown and the curriculum has expanded immeasurably. Knowledge about the teaching and learning process has also expanded, but not to the same measure. The cost of new facilities and equipment now comprises more than half the community's operational budget.

Even with all this advancement there are many who are not satisfied with the quality of education being offered our young people. Their main reason is that the school's end product is not the most "desirable"; enter the question of educational philosophy! Determining a hierarchy of educational values is most difficult in a pluralistic society such as ours. As encouraged as we might be by the fact that the individual counts for more in the United States today than perhaps ever before in human history, we are still confronted by the ever-present struggle between educational essentialists and educational progressivists. The one thing that we can be really thankful for is that our type of society allows us the freedom for such continuing debate.

THE NEED FOR CONSENSUS

From the standpoint of educational philosophy, therefore, any evaluation of qualitative as opposed to quantitative progress would depend upon the extent to which educational practice approximated a particular philosophical ideal. Therefore, your personal decision about progress that our field may have made in solving the specific persistent problems enumerated in this volume cannot help but be highly subjective. *Your personal evaluation should be based on the philosophical tendency to which you subscribe.* Naturally it will be conditioned by your personal background and experiences—including the scientific evidence available—that have caused you to develop a set of attitudes. Professional maturity depends upon a sound philosophical base.

Philosophical investigation of a normative and analytical nature over the past fifteen years within this and related fields has convinced me of the vital importance of a continuing search for, and the possibility of, consensus among the conflicting philosophies of physical education and sport in the Western world. We have been proceeding amoeba-like for so long with our own biased and eclectic statements of philosophical position that even the current attempt to delineate our own individual positions represents a vast improvement. These words are not meant to be critical of any one individual or group of individuals; such philosophical ineptitude is actually characteristic of the large majority of practitioners in the educational world.

The difficulty of achieving consensus is exactly the problem. It is really questionable, although I am sufficiently reconstructionist in my personal philosophy to believe in such approaches strongly, whether the American Alliance for Health, Physical Education, and Recreation can hope to achieve true consensus by the conferences that are held periodically. With such a careful effort being made to have both sexes, all educational levels, the various educational agencies, and other related groups represented, such meetings usually result in a group in which progressive Christian idealists and pragmatic experimentalists (including a few reconstructionists) predominate, and only a sprinkling of naturalistic realists, rational humanists, and moderate (Catholic) realists is evident. The outcome is consequently predetermined. If a vote on an issue is taken, the realists are hopelessly outnumbered. When the conference report is published, "complete loyalty to God, mother, and country" is proclaimed resoundingly, the progressivist banner is gallantly waved, and there is just enough of an eclectic taint to the entire document that the realist, who might well have conceived of such a conference as pooled ignorance anyhow, acts blithely disinterested or is perhaps sullen but not actively mutinous about the end result.

It is fortunate that there is *more agreement in practice than in theory.* From another standpoint, also, a certain amount of agreement in theory at least is necessary in order to disagree. To make *any* progress there must be agreement on the issues and on an interpretation of the rules for debate.

There are actually a number of methods available by which greater consensus can be achieved. A formidable task, but perhaps not an impossible one, is to attempt to break down communications barriers. The study of semantics, the language analysis movement in philosophy, and the developing social science of administration should tremendously expedite the matter. The development of a truly international language, taught in all countries in conjunction with the mother tongue, would be an enormous aid to communication as well.

It is interesting and important to note that there are some common presuppositions among the different educational philosophies; in fact, among these rival philosophies there are definite points of agreement, as well as large areas in which many points are somewhat similar and often overlapping. In the field of education, for example, some of the areas of practical agreement are that (1) the safety of the child is basic; (2) the school has a responsibility to provide a health service unit; (3) teachers need a certain educational background and experience; (4) boys and girls should be educated for at least a certain period of time; and (5) there are certain cardinal principles of education. *The Central Purpose of American Education,* published by the Educational Policies Commission, after reaffirming earlier statements of 1918 and 1938, states a central purpose—the development of the ability to think, which is not meant to be thought of as exclusive (1961, p. 12).

The extent of class involvement in the discussion of controversial issues is one area where there is a difference of opinon. Many would argue that students should be free to arrive at a solution, but it is recognized that they will have to be careful in many situations about how they express themselves in certain areas of politics, religion, or problems of a particular social nature. It could be stated further that race heritage ought to be the common heritage of all, but the difficulty comes when we get down to the specifics of how much race experience should be included in the curriculum, or what should be emphasized, or how it should be taught. And so it goes as increasingly less consensus is apparent (Brubacher, 1962, pp. 350–354).

What common denominators may be found in the specialized field of physical education and sport, in health and safety education, or in recreation education? The answer to this question might be as follows:

1. The belief of the large majority of physical educators that *regular* physical education periods should be *required* for all schoolchildren through grades ten or eleven.
2. The importance of a child developing certain attitudes toward his or her own health in particular and toward community health in general.
3. Leisure should be put to worthy use. It is understood that in America many people are presumably enjoying a greater amount of leisure than has ever been available before.
4. Physical vigor is extremely important, but there is no general agreement among the men, or between men and women in the profession, about what really constitutes physical fitness. There are national norms, but no national standards (or agreement on whether there should be standards).
5. There should be an experience in competitive athletics. This applies both to boys and girls, but the amount of emphasis and the time when this should be made available are points of contention.
6. Boys and girls who need therapeutic exercise for remediable physical defects should be helped.
7. Character and personality development is important. We believe generally that our specialized field can make a definite contribution toward the achievement of this objective, but we have very little scientific evidence to support this claim.

Having stated these common denominators, it would appear that the time for a consensus *on what it is that we do* is long overdue.[1]

The potentialities for pure and applied research in physical, health, and recreation education (including sport and competitive athletics) are limitless. The unique nature of the field and its role in education relates quite obviously to physiology, anatomy, psychology, sociology, history, philosophy, anthropology, chemistry, medicine, economics, political science, and administrative theory. If we are completely honest we will have to admit that there are still only relatively few *qualified* researchers possessing "physical educators' hearts" (that is, people with professional

[1] *The Contribution of Physical Activity to Human Well-Being* was seemingly as important a project as AAHPER's Research Council, or the association itself, has ever undertaken (*Research Quarterly*, XXXI, 2, Part II, May 1960). This type of endeavor must be updated, "sharpened," and clarified regularly with a format similar to that of the publication, *Human Behavior: An Inventory of Scientific Findings*, by Berelson and Steiner (1964).

preparation in physical education and sport, with *sound* backgrounds in at least one of the fields mentioned above, with a knowledge of research method and appropriate techniques, and who are really interested in *this* field and its future). Many more bright, idealistic young people seek admittance to the field, but the quality of our undergraduate and graduate programs of professional preparation, *including our research efforts,* must be improved immeasurably. Time is running short!

Epilog

It is a rare week that goes by when I do not talk to some young man or woman about his or her future in physical education—whether he or she wants to be a teacher and coach, or to become actively involved in some other facet within the field. When such people ask what the future holds in store for them as physical educators, I suppose I should reply that they hold their own future *and* that of the field in their hands. Life is what *we* make it.

But such a reply smacks of an idealism that we, in more pessimistic moments, view as passé. Today the average physical education student is typically realistic and often quite materialistic as well. The young man contemplating a major in physical education probably makes this decision on the basis of his athletic experience with a high school coach. He has admired his coach very much. He has assessed his own personal athletic ability, his liking of people, and perhaps his scholastic attainment—or lack of it because of poor study habits. Then, often against the presumably better judgment of his parents, he makes up his mind to be a coach and a physical educator in that order. He sees himself coaching a successful high school football or basketball team, and then possibly going on to bigger and better things as a college coach.

As a counselor, my task is to explain to this young man in a few well-chosen words that the field of physical education and sport is much more than simply being an athletic coach, as important a task as that can be. This is very difficult, and I am not always certain just how much to say. I don't want to bore him with my experiences in the various aspects of the field, including coaching. So much depends on his prior experiences. I usually tell him about the advantages and the disadvantages, emphasizing the former more than the latter. I conclude by telling him that, even though he may have heard that the field is overcrowded for men at the present, there is ample room for a well-qualified, conscientious, devoted professional educator. As he is leaving, I tell him to keep in touch and not to hesitate to contact me or my associates if he has a problem, and I wish him good luck.

But after he leaves, I begin to wonder if I have said and done the right things. Of course, perhaps nothing I could have said or done would change his thinking radically. I do hope sincerely that his university experience will be such that he will emerge upon graduation as a fine, competent young teacher of physical education and sport ready to assume professional leadership of the highest type.

What happens to this young man? Many influences affect his development, both good and bad. Eventually he acquires certain knowledge, competencies, and skills. He may be a good student, a fair student, or a poor student. Rarely is he an outstanding student. He develops a set of attitudes. Only very occasionally does he show an inclination after graduation to be really active in at least one professional organization in his chosen field. I wonder where he has failed—where *we* have failed.

The large majority of physical educators haven't had the opportunity, or haven't taken the time, to work out their own personal philosophies. Granted that along the way there has been a great deal of discussion about aims and objectives, but it has usually been carried out in such a helter-skelter fashion that they want no more of it. They are anxious to learn the much more tangible competencies and skills that they can use on the job. And so they leave us as graduates not really knowing why they are doing anything and where they are going, so to speak.

Physical educators need exactly the same sort of progression in history, philosophy, and administration of physical education and sport that they usually follow in anatomy and physiology and the subsequent applied aspects of these subjects. Individuals striving to function intelligently in society need an understanding of the historical foundations of our society and of education in our society. They will then be able to study and fully appreciate the historical backgrounds of their own field and the persistent problems that have been faced through the ages. Second, a professional person needs a philosophy of life and/or religion. Do our professional students ever take an introductory course in philosophy or in the philosophy of religion? Except for those majoring in physical education in Catholic universities, perhaps not one in a thousand has had this opportunity!

Furthermore, teachers of physical education and sport should have a philosophy of education in harmony with their philosophy of life. Strangely enough, however, philosophy of education courses are often available only as an elective and our students "studiously" try to avoid them. The culmination of this recommended curricular sequence (prior to a course in administration) should be an outstanding course in the philosophy of physical education and sport—a course in which prospective teachers begin to develop a personal philosophy relating to their specialized field that does not clash with their basic beliefs about life and education. The achievement of a "stage of philosophical maturity" may well become a life-long task. The reflective thought required to accomplish this task is a mighty cheap price to pay for a well-ordered life.

We have only to look at our present programs with their shifting emphases to realize that we are, to a large degree, vacillating practitioners. This is true both within the school and in public recreation. If we ever hope to convince ourselves, our colleagues in education, and the informed portion of the general public of our worth, we should as individual professionals at least determine whether we are truly progressivist or truly essentialist in our philosophic tendencies, and then work from there. We simply can't continue as dilettantes or casual eclectics ready to jump in any direction when the prevailing wind blows.

No matter which stage of philosophical development you may have achieved presently—the "ostrich stage," the "cafeteria stage," the "fence-sitter stage," the stage of early maturity, or the stage of philosophical maturity—you may find it necessary to retrace your steps before you can truly build your own personal philosophy logically, consistently, and systematically. Obviously, there is no hard and fast progression to which you *must* adhere. Through the use of the self-evaluation checklist (see Chapter II, Section 1), you may discover that you are quite "pure" already. At any rate, find out where you stand and take up the philosophic quest from there. You simply can't go wrong, *if* you go about it honestly, sincerely, and diligently. People of all ages are searching for meaningful values in their lives. If you help them in just one area, that of physical education and sport, you will have attained the highest of professional goals.

Bibliography

AINSWORTH, DOROTHY S. "The History of Physical Education in Colleges for Women." Ph.D. dissertation, Teachers College, Columbia University, 1930.

ALSTON, WILLIAM P., *Philosophy of Language*. Englewood Cliffs, N.J.: Prentice-Hall, Inc., 1964.

AMERICAN ASSOCIATION FOR HEALTH, PHYSICAL EDUCATION, AND RECREATION. *Democratic Human Relations*. Washington, D.C.: AAHPER, 1951.

————, Division of Girls' and Women's Sports. "Statement of Policies and Procedures for Competition in Girls' and Women's Sports." *JOHPER* 28, No. 6 (September, 1957):57–58.

————. *Evaluation Standards and Guide in Health Education, Physical Education, Recreation Education*. Washington, D.C.: AAHPER, 1959.

————. *Professional Preparation in Health Education, Physical Education, Recreation Education*. Washington, D.C. AAHPER, 1962.

————, Division of Girls' and Women's Sports and Division of Men's Athletics. *Values in Sports*. Washington, D.C.: AAHPER, 1963.

————, Division of Girls' and Women's Sports. *Philosophy and Standards for Girls' and Women's Sports*. Washington, D.C.: AAHPER, 1969.

ARCHAMBAULT, REGINALD D. *Philosophical Analysis and Education*. New York: Humanities Press, 1965.

ASHTON, DUDLEY. "Contributions of Dance to Physical Education, Part I." *JOHPER*, 26, No. 9 (December 1955).

————. "Contributions of Dance to Physical Education, Part II." *JOHPER*, 27, No. 4 (April 1956).

ATHLETIC INSTITUTE. *Report of the National Conference on Interpretation of Physical Education*. Chicago, Ill.: The Athletic Institute, Inc., 1962.

AUSTIN, PATRICIA. "A Conceptual Structure of Physical Education." Ph.D. dissertation, Michigan State University, 1965.

AVEDON, ELLIOTT. "A Philosophical Inquiry into the Essence of Recreation." Ed.D. dissertation, Teachers College, Columbia University, 1961.

BAIR, DONN E. "An Identification of Some Philosophical Beliefs Held by Influential Professional Leaders in American Physical Education." Ph.D. dissertation, University of Southern California, 1956.

BAITSCH, HELMUT, et al. *The Scientific View of Sport: Perspectives, Aspects, Issues.* Edited by Ommo Grupe, Dietrich Kurz, and Johannes Marcus Teipel. Published on behalf of the Organizing Committee for the Games of the XXth Olympiad Munich, 1972. Berlin, Heidelberg, New York: Springer-Verlag, 1972.

BALLOU, RALPH B. "An Analysis of the Writings of Selected Church Fathers to A.D. 394 to Reveal Attitudes Regarding Physical Activity." Ph.D. dissertation, University of Oregon, 1965.

BARRETT, WILLIAM. *Irrational Man: A Study in Existential Philosophy.* Garden City, N.Y.: Doubleday, 1958.

BAYLES, ERNEST E. *Pragmatism in Education.* New York: Harper & Row, 1966.

BECK, ROBERT N. *Perspectives in Philosophy.* New York: Holt, Rinehart and Winston, 1961.

BEDFORD, C. M. "The Concept of the Authentic Individual and Its Implications for Building a Framework for an Existential Philosophy of Education." Unpublished doctoral dissertation, University of Southern California, 1961.

BELL, JAMES W. "A Comparative Analysis of the Normative Philosophies of Plato, Rousseau, and Dewey as Applied to Physical Education." Ph.D. dissertation, The Ohio State University, 1971.

BEND, EMIL. "Some Functions of Competitive Team Sports in American Society." Ph.D. dissertation, University of Pittsburgh, 1970.

BENNETT, BRUCE L. "Religion and Physical Education." Paper presented at the Cincinnati Convention of the AAHPER, April 10, 1962.

BENNETT, PATRICIA. "The History and Objectives of the National Section for Girls' and Women's Sports." Ed.D. dissertation, Mills College, 1956.

BOOKWALTER, KARL W., and HAROLD J. VANDERZWAAG. *Foundations and Principles of Physical Education.* Philadelphia: Saunders, 1969.

BOULDING, KENNETH. *The Meaning of the Twentieth Century.* New York: Harper & Row, 1964.

BRAMELD, T. *Philosophies of Education in Cultural Perspective.* New York: Dryden, 1955.

————. *Toward a Reconstructed Philosophy of Education.* New York: Dryden, 1956.

BRAMWELL, AMY B., and H. M. HUGHES. *The Training of Teachers in the United States of America.* New York: Macmillan, 1894.

BRAUNER, CHARLES J., and H. W. BURNS. *Problems in Education and Philosophy.* Englewood Cliffs, N.J.: Prentice-Hall, 1965.

BREED, FREDERICK S. "Education and the Realistic Outlook," in *Forty-First Yearbook of the National Society for the Study of Education* (Part I). Chicago, Ill.: The University of Chicago Press, 1942.

BRIGHTBILL, CHARLES K. *Man and Leisure: A Philosophy of Recreation.* Englewood Cliffs, N.J.: Prentice-Hall, 1961.

BRINTON, CRANE. *The Shaping of Modern Thought.* Englewood Cliffs, N.J.: Prentice-Hall, 1964.

BROEKHOFF, JAN. "Physical Education and the Reification of the Human Body," in *Proceedings of the Second Canadian Symposium on the History of Sport and Physical Education,* ed. P. J. Galasso. Ottawa: Fitness and Amateur Sport Directorate, 1972. (This symposium was held at the University of Windsor, May 1–3, 1972.)

BRONSTEIN, D. J., and H. M. SCHULWEIS. *Approaches to the Philosophy of Religion.* Englewood Cliffs, N.J.: Prentice-Hall, 1954.

BRONZAN, ROBERT T. "Attitudes of University Publics Toward the Contributions of the Intercollegiate Football Program to General Education." Ed. D. dissertation, Stanford University, 1965.

BROUDY, HARRY S. *Building a Philosophy of Education* (2nd ed.). Englewood Cliffs, N.J.: Prentice-Hall, 1961.

BROWN, CAMILLE, and ROSALIND CASSIDY. *Theory in Physical Education.* Philadelphia: Lea & Febiger, 1963.

BROWNELL, CLIFFORD L., and E. P. HAGMAN. *Physical Education—Foundations and Principles.* New York: McGraw-Hill, 1951.

BRUBACHER, JOHN S. *A History of the Problems of Education* (2nd ed.). New York: McGraw-Hill, 1966.

————. *Modern Philosophies of Education* (4th ed.). New York: McGraw-Hill, 1969. (The third edition appeared in 1962.)

BUCHER, CHARLES A. *Foundations of Physical Education.* St. Louis: C. V. Mosby, 1964. (This is the fourth edition of a book first published in 1952.)

BURTT, E. A. *In Search of Philosophic Understanding.* Toronto, Canada: New American Library of Canada, 1967.

BURY, J. B. *The Idea of Progress.* New York: Dover, 1955.

BUTLER, J. DONALD. *Four Philosophies* (rev. ed.). New York: Harper & Row, 1957.

————. *Idealism in Education.* New York: Harper & Row, 1966.

BUTTS, R. F. *A Cultural History of Education.* New York: McGraw-Hill, 1947.

CAHN, L. JOSEPH. "Contributions of Plato to Thought on Physical Education." Ed.D. dissertation, New York University, 1941.

CALDWELL, S. "Conceptions of Physical Education in Twentieth Century America: Rosalind Cassidy." Ph.D. dissertation, University of Washington, 1966.

CARLISLE, ROBERT. "The Concept of Physical Education," in the *Proceedings of the Philosophy of Education Society of Great Britain,* The Annual Conference, 1969, pp. 5–35.

CARVER, JULIA. "A Study of the Influence of the Philosophy of the Church of Jesus Christ of Latter-day Saints on Physical Education in the Church Schools." Ph.D. dissertation, University of Oregon, 1964.

CATON, CHARLES E. *Philosophy and Ordinary Language.* Urbana: University of Illinois Press, 1963.

CAVANAUGH, PATRIC L. "A Delineation of Moderate Realism and Physical Education." Ph.D. dissertation, The University of Michigan, 1967.

CHAMPION, S. G., and D. SHORT. *Readings from World Religions.* Boston: Beacon Press, 1951.

CHAZAN, BARRY I., and JONAS F. SOLTIS. *Moral Education.* New York: Teachers College Press, Columbia University, 1973.

CHISHOLM, RODERICK M. *Theory of Knowledge.* Englewood Cliffs, N.J.: Prentice-Hall, 1966.

THE CHRISTOPHERS. "God's Good Earth—and Ours." (An undated pamphlet published by The Christophers, 12 East 48th Street, New York, N.Y. 10017.)

CLARK, MARGARET C. "A Philosophical Interpretation of a Program of Physical Education in a State Teachers College." Ph.D. dissertation, New York University, 1943.

COBB, LOUISE S. "A Study of the Functions of Physical Education in Higher Education." Ph.D. dissertation, Teachers College, Columbia University, 1943.

————. "Philosophical Research Methods," in *Research Methods Applied to Health, Physical Education, and Recreation.* Washington, D.C.: AAHPER, 1949. (This is the first edition of a useful publication that is now in its third edition.)

COMMAGER, HENRY STEELE. "A Quarter Century—Its Advances," *Look,* 25, No. 10 (June 6, 1961), 80–91.

COWELL, CHARLES C., and WELLMAN L. FRANCE. *Philosophy and Principles of Physical Education.* Englewood Cliffs, N.J.: Prentice-Hall, 1963.

DALY, JOHN A. "An Identification of Some Philosophic Beliefs Held by Australian Physical Educators, with Implications for Administration." M.S. thesis, University of Illinois, Urbana, 1970.

DAUER, VICTOR P. "The Amateur Code in American College Athletics." Ph.D. dissertation, The University of Michigan, 1949.

DAVIS, E. C., ed. *Philosophies Fashion Physical Education.* Dubuque, Iowa: William C. Brown, 1963.

————, and DONNA MAE MILLER. *The Philosophic Process in Physical Education* (2nd ed.). Philadelphia: Lea & Febiger, 1967.

DEMOTT, BENJAMIN. "How Existential Can You Get?" *The New York Times Magazine,* March 23, 1969, pp. 4, 6, 12, 14.

DIVOKY, DIANE, and PETER SCHRAG. "Football and Cheers." *Saturday Review* (December 1972), 61–62.

DOUGLASS, P. F. *et al.,* eds. "Recreation in the Age of Automation," *The Annals of the American Academy of Political and Social Science,* Vol. 312 (September 1957).

DOWNEY, ROBERT J. "An Identification of the Philosophical Beliefs of Educators in the Field of Health Education." Ph.D. dissertation, University of Southern California, 1956.

DUNCAN, ISADORA. *Art of the Dance*. New York: Little and Ives, 1928.

DURANT, WILL. *The Story of Philosophy* (rev. ed.). New York: Garden City, 1938.

————, and ARIEL DURANT. *The Lessons of History*. New York: Dover, 1968.

EDMAN, IRWIN. *The World, the Arts, and the Artist*. New York: W. W. Norton, 1928.

EDUCATIONAL POLICIES COMMISSION. *Moral and Spiritual Values in the Public Schools*. Washington, D.C.: National Education Association, 1951.

————. *The Central Purpose of American Education*. Washington, D.C.: National Education Association, 1961.

EHRLICH, PAUL R., and JOHN P. HOLDREN. "Dodging the Crisis." *Saturday Review* (November 7, 1970), 73.

EKIRCH, A. A. *The Idea of Progress in America*. New York: Columbia University Press, 1944.

ELLIOTT, RUTH. *The Organization of Professional Training in Physical Education in State Universities*. New York: Teachers College, Columbia University, 1927.

ELLIS, HAVELOCK. *The Dance of Life*. New York: Modern Library, 1929.

ESSLINGER, A. A. "Undergraduate versus Graduate Study." *JOHPER*, 37, No. 9 (September 1966), 63–64.

FAGUET, EMILE. *Initiation into Philosophy*. New York: Putnam's, 1914.

FEIBLEMAN, JAMES. *The Revival of Realism*. Chapel Hill: The University of North Carolina Press, 1946.

FEIGL, H. "Logical Empiricism," in H. Feigl and W. Sellars, *Readings in Philosophical Analysis*. New York: Appleton-Century-Crofts, 1949.

"The Fellowship of Christian Athletes." Kansas City, Mo. Pamphlet distributed by The Fellowship of Christian Athletes, January 19, 1962.

FELSHIN, JANET. "Changing Conceptions of Purpose in Physical Education in the United States from 1880–1930." Ed.D. dissertation, University of California. 1958.

————. *Perspectives and Principles for Physical Education*. New York: Wiley, 1967.

FLATH, A. W. *A History of Relations Between the National Collegiate Athletic Association and the Amateur Athletic Union of the United States (1905–1963)*. Champaign, Ill.: Stipes, 1964. (Includes a Foreword by Earle F. Zeigler entitled "Amateurism, Semi-Professionalism, and Professionalism in Sport—A Persistent Educational Problem.")

FLEXNER, A. "Is Social Work a Profession?" in *Proceedings of the National Conference of Charities and Correction*. Chicago, Ill.: Hildmann Printing Co., 1915, pp. 576–590.

FORSYTHE, ELEANOR. "Philosophical Bases for Physical Education Experience Consistent with the Goals of American Education for High School Girls." Ph.D. dissertation, New York University, 1960.

FRALEIGH, SONDRA HORTON. "Dance Creates Man." *Quest,* No. 14 (June 1970), 65–71.

FRALEIGH, WARREN P. "Meanings of the Human Body in Modern Christian Theology." *Research Quarterly,* 39 (May 1968), 265–277.

———. "A Prologue to the Study of Theory Building in Physical Education." *Quest,* No. 12 (May 1969), 26–33.

———. "Theory and Design of Philosophic Research in Physical Education," in *Proceedings of the National College Physical Education Association for Men.* Portland, Oregon, December 28, 1970.

FRANK, PHILIPP. *Philosophy of Science.* Englewood Cliffs, N.J.: Prentice-Hall, 1957.

FRANKENA, WILLIAM K. *Ethics.* Englewood Cliffs, N.J.: Prentice-Hall, 1963.

———. *Philosophy of Education.* New York: Macmillan, 1965.

———. *Three Historical Philosophies of Education.* Chicago: Scott, Foresman, 1965.

FREDERICK, MARY M. "Naturalism: The Philosophy of Jean Jacques Rousseau and Its Implications for American Physical Education." D.P.E. dissertation, Springfield College, 1961.

FRIERMOOD, HAROLD T., ed. *A New Look at YMCA Physical Education.* New York: Association Press, 1959.

FROST, REUBEN B. *Physical Education: Foundations, Practices, Principles.* Reading, Mass.: Addison-Wesley, 1975.

GEIGER, GEORGE R. "An Experimentalist Approach to Education," in *Modern Philosophies and Education,* ed. N. B. Henry. Chicago: The University of Chicago Press, 1955.

GERBER, ELLEN W. "Three Interpretations of the Role of Physical Education, 1930–1960: C. H. McCloy, J. B. Nash and J. F. Williams." Ph.D. dissertation, University of Southern California, 1966.

——— ed. *Sport and the Body: A Philosophical Symposium.* Philadelphia: Lea & Febiger, 1972.

GLADER, EUGENE A. "A Study of Amateurism in Sports." Ph.D. dissertation, University of Iowa, 1970.

GORDY, J. P. *Rise and Growth of the Normal School Idea in the United States.* Washington, D.C.: Government Printing Office, 1903, Chapter XVII.

GREENE, THEODORE M. "A Liberal Christian Idealist Philosophy of Education," in *Fifty-Fourth Yearbook of the National Society for the Study of Education* (Part I). Chicago: The University of Chicago Press, 1955.

GREER, GERMAINE. *The Female Eunuch.* London: Paladin, 1971.

GREGG, JERALD. "A Philosophical Analysis of the Sports Experience and the

Role of Athletics in the Schools." Ed.D. dissertation, University of Southern California, 1971.

GROSS, BERTRAM M. *The Managing of Organizations* (2 vols.). New York: Crowell-Collier, 1964.

HALPIN, ANDREW W. "The Development of Theory in Educational Administration," in *Administrative Theory in Education,* ed. A. W. Halpin. Chicago: Midwest Administration Center, The University of Chicago, 1958.

HARPER, WILLIAM A. "Human Revolt: A Phenomenological Description." Ph.D. dissertation, University of Southern California, 1970.

HAWTON, HECTOR. *Philosophy for Pleasure.* Greenwich, Conn.: Fawcett, 1961.

HAYES, C. J. *Nationalism: A Religion.* New York: The Macmillan Co., 1961.

HEINEMANN, F. H. *Existentialism and the Modern Predicament.* New York: Harper & Row, 1953.

HELLISON, DONALD R. *Humanistic Physical Education.* Englewood Cliffs, N.J.: Prentice-Hall, 1973.

HENRY, FRANKLIN H. "Physical Education: An Academic Discipline." *JOHPER,* 35, No. 7 (September 1964), 32–33, 69.

HESS, FORD A. "American Objectives of Physical Education from 1900–1957 Assessed in the Light of Certain Historical Events." Ed.D. dissertation, New York University, 1959.

HICK, JOHN. *Philosophy of Religion.* Englewood Cliffs, N.J.: Prentice-Hall, 1963.

HILEMAN, BETTY JEAN. "Emerging Patterns of Thought in Physical Education in the United States: 1956–1966." Ph.D. dissertation, University of Southern California, 1967.

HORNE, HERMAN H. "An Idealistic Philosophy of Education," in *Forty-First Yearbook of the National Society for the Study of Education* (Part I). Chicago: The University of Chicago Press, 1942.

HOSPERS, JOHN. *An Introduction to Philosophical Analysis.* Englewood Cliffs, N.J.: Prentice-Hall, 1953.

HUIZINGA, J. *Homo Ludens: A Study of the Play-Element in Culture.* Boston: Beacon, 1950.

HUXLEY, A. "The Politics of Ecology." Santa Barbara, Calif.: Center for the Study of Democratic Institutions, 1963.

HUXLEY, JULIAN. *New Bottles for New Wine.* New York: Harper & Row, 1957.

KAELIN, E. F. "The Well-Played Game: Notes Toward an Aesthetics of Sport." *Quest,* No. 10 (May 1968), 16–28.

KAPLAN, ABRAHAM. *The New World of Philosophy.* New York: Random House, 1961.

KAPLAN, M. *Leisure in America: A Social Inquiry.* New York: Wiley, 1960.

KAUFMANN, WALTER. *Existentialism from Dostoevsky to Sartre.* New York: World, 1956.

———. *Without Guilt or Justice.* New York: Peter H. Wyden, Inc., 1973.

KEATING, JAMES W. "Winning in Sport and Athletics." *Thought,* 38, No. 149 (summer 1963), 201–210.

————. "Sportsmanship as a Moral Category." *Ethics,* LXXV, No. 1 (October 1964), 25–35.

KEENAN, FRANCIS W. "A Delineation of Deweyan Progressivism for Physical Education." Ph.D. dissertation, University of Illinois, Urbana, 1971.

KELLY, DARLENE A. "Phenomena of the Self-experienced Body." Ph.D. dissertation, University of Southern California, 1970.

KLEINMAN, SEYMOUR. "Toward a Non-theory of Sport." *Quest,* No. 10 (May 1968), 29–34.

KNELLER, GEORGE F. *Existentialism and Education.* New York: Philosophical Library, 1958.

KRETCHMAR, ROBERT S. "A Phenomenological Analysis of the Other in Sport." Ph.D. dissertation, University of Southern California, 1970.

KRIKORIAN, YERVANT H., ed. *Naturalism and the Human Spirit.* New York: Columbia University Press, 1944.

KRUG, ORVIS C. "The Philosophic Relationship Between Physical Education and Athletics." Ed.D. dissertation, New York University, 1958.

KUNZ, ROBERT F. "An Environmental Glossary." *Saturday Review* (January 2, 1971), 67.

LANGER, SUSANNE K. *Philosophy in a New Key.* 1948. Reprint. New York: New American Library, 1964.

LARKIN, RICHARD A. "The Influence of John Dewey on Physical Education." M.A. thesis, The Ohio State University, 1936.

LARRABEE, E., and R. MEYERSOHN. *Mass Leisure.* New York: Macmillan, 1958.

LENK, HANS. "Perspectives of the Philosophy of Sport," in *The Scientific View of Sport.* New York: Springer-Verlag, 1972.

LEONARD, GEORGE. *The Ultimate Athlete.* New York: The Viking Press, 1975.

LEONARD, F. E., and G. B. AFFLECK. *The History of Physical Education* (3rd ed.). Philadelphia: Lea & Febiger, 1947.

LEVINSON, HARRY. *The Exceptional Executive: A Psychological Conception.* New York: New American Library, 1971.

LEWIS, DIO. "New Gymnastics." Barnard's *American Journal of Education,* 12: 665.

LIMBERT, PAUL. "Physical Education, Sport, and Recreation." *World Communiqué* (January–February 1961), 3.

LOCKHART, A. S., and H. S. SLUSHER. *Anthology of Contemporary Readings in Physical Education* (3rd ed.) Dubuque, Iowa: Wm. C. Brown Co., 1975.

LOWIE, ROBERT H. *Primitive Religion.* New York: Boni and Liveright, 1924.

LOY, JOHN W. "The Nature of Sport: A Definitional Effort." *Quest,* No. 10 (May 1968), 1–15.

LOZES, JEWELL H. "The Philosophy of Certain Religious Denominations Relative to Physical Education, and the Effect of This Philosophy on Physical Education in Certain Church-related Institutions." M.S. thesis, Pennsylvania State University, 1955.

LUCKEY, G. W. A. *The Professional Training of Secondary Teachers in the United States.* New York: The Macmillan Co., 1903.

LYNN, MINNIE L. "Major Emphasis of Physical Education in the United States." Ph.D. dissertation, University of Pittsburgh, 1944.

MacINTYRE, A. "Existentialism," in *The Encyclopedia of Philosophy.* New York: The Macmillan Company, 1967, Vol. 3, 147–154.

MARROU, H. I. *A History of Education in Antiquity,* trans. George Lamb. New York: New American Library, 1964.

MARTIN, JOHN. *The Dance.* New York: Tudor, 1946.

McCLOY, CHARLES H. *Philosophical Bases for Physical Education.* New York: Appleton-Century-Crofts, 1940.

McGLYNN, GEORGE H., ed.. *Issues in Physical Education and Sports.* Palo Alto, Calif.: National Press Books, 1974.

McGUCKEN, WILLIAM J. "The Philosophy of Catholic Education," in *Forty-First Yearbook of the National Society for the Study of Education* (Part I). Chicago: The University of Chicago Press, 1942.

McINTOSH, P. C., et al. *History of Physical Education.* London: Routledge & Kegan Paul, 1957.

MEANS, R. K. *A History of Health Education in the United States.* Philadelphia: Lea & Febiger, 1962.

MEIER, KLAUS V. "An Existential Analysis of Play." M.A. thesis, The University of Western Ontario, 1971.

MEIER, MILA H. "Play as a Way to Know." Ed.D. dissertation, Boston University, 1968.

MERGEN, FRANÇOIS. "Man and His Environment." *Yale Alumni Magazine,* XXXIII, No. 8 (May 1970), 36–37.

METHENY, ELEANOR. "Philosophical Methods," in *Research Methods in Health, Physical Education, and Recreation* (2nd ed.). Washington, D.C.: AAHPER, 1959.

——. *Connotations of Movement in Sport and Dance.* Dubuque, Iowa: William C. Brown, 1965.

MILLER, DAVIS L. *Gods and Games: Toward a Theology of Play.* New York: World, 1970.

MOOLENIJZER, NICOLAAS J. "The Concept of 'Natural' in Physical Education: Johann Guts Muths and Margarete Streicher." Ph.D. dissertation, University of Southern California, 1965.

MORGAN, WILLIAM. "An Existential Phenomenological Analysis of Sport as a Religious Experience," in *The Philosophy of Sport,* ed. R. G. Osterhoudt. Springfield, Ill.: Charles C Thomas, 1973.

MORLAND, R. B. "A Philosophical Interpretation of the Educational Views Held by Leaders in American Physical Education." Ph.D. dissertation, New York University, 1958.

———. "The Philosophic Method of Research," in *Research Methods in Health, Physical Education, and Recreation,* ed. A. W. Hubbard. Washington, D.C.: AAHPER, 1973.

MORRIS, DESMOND. *The Naked Ape.* New York: McGraw-Hill, 1967.

MORRIS, VAN CLEVE. *Philosophy and the American School.* Boston: Houghton Mifflin, 1961.

———. *Existentialism in Education.* New York: Harper & Row, 1966.

———. *Modern Movements in Educational Philosophy.* Boston: Houghton Mifflin, 1969.

MULLER, HERBERT J. *The Uses of the Past.* New York: New American Library, 1954.

———. *Religion and Freedom in the Modern World.* Chicago: The University of Chicago Press, 1963.

———. *Freedom in the Modern World.* New York: Harper & Row, 1966.

MURRAY, BERTRAM G., JR. "What the Ecologists Can Teach the Economists," *The New York Times Magazine* (December 10, 1972), 38–39, 64–65, 70, 72.

NASH, J. B. *Philosophy of Recreation and Leisure.* Dubuque, Iowa: William C. Brown, 1960.

National Conference on Undergraduate Professional Preparation in Physical Education, Health Education, and Recreation. Weston, W. Va.: Jackson's Mill, May 16–27, 1948.

NATIONAL EDUCATION ASSOCIATION AND AMERICAN ASSOCIATION OF SCHOOL ADMINISTRATORS, EDUCATIONAL POLICIES COMMISSION. *School Athletics, Problems and Policies.* Washington, D.C.: The Commission, 1954.

THE NATIONAL GEOGRAPHIC SOCIETY. "How Man Pollutes His World." Washington, D.C.: The Society, 1970. (This is a detailed map of the earth and its atmosphere with explanatory discussion.)

NEAL, PATSY. *Sport and Identity.* Philadelphia: Dorrance & Co., 1972.

NELSON, EMOGENE A. "Value Patterns of Physical Educators in Colleges and Universities of the United States." Ph.D. dissertation, University of Minnesota, 1970.

NEUMEYER, M. H., and E. S. NEUMEYER. *Leisure and Recreation* (rev. ed.). New York: Ronald Press, 1958.

NEVINS, ALLAN. *The Gateway to History.* Garden City, N.Y.: Doubleday, 1962.

The New York Times. "Nations Demand Agricultural Aid," August 3, 1975.

———. "Foul Air Poses Health Threat to East," May 1, 1970.

———. "Christianity Linked to Pollution," May 1, 1970.

OBERTEUFFER, DELBERT, and CELESTE ULRICH. *Physical Education* (4th ed.). New York: Harper & Row, 1970.

OSTERHOUDT, ROBERT G. "A Descriptive Analysis of Research Concerning the

Philosophy of Physical Education and Sport." Ph.D. dissertation, University of Illinois, Urbana, 1971.

————, ed. *The Philosophy of Sport*. Springfield, Ill.: Charles C Thomas, 1973.

OZMON, HOWARD. *Dialogue in the Philosophy of Education*. Columbus, Ohio: Charles E. Merrill, 1972.

PADDICK, ROBERT J. "The Nature and Place of a Field of Knowledge in Physical Education." M.A. thesis, University of Alberta, 1967.

PAGE, BARBARA. "The Philosophy of the Dance." *Research Quarterly*, IV, No. 2 (May 1933), 5–49.

PATRICK, GEORGE. "Verifiability of Physical Education Objectives." Ph.D. dissertation, University of Illinois, Urbana, 1971.

PEARSON, KATHLEEN. "A Structural and Functional Analysis of the Multi-concept of Integration-Segregation (Male and/or Female) in Physical Education Classes." Ph.D. dissertation, University of Illinois, Urbana, 1971.

PELTON, BARRY C. "A Critical Analysis of Current Concepts Underlying General Physical Education." Ph.D. dissertation, University of Southern California, 1966.

POWELL, SUZANNE M. "Meaning in a Dance Form." Ph.D. dissertation, University of Southern California, 1969.

Professional Preparation in Health Education, Physical Education, Recreation Education. Washington, D.C.: AAHPER, 1962.

Professional Training in Physical Education. Washington, D.C.: U.S. Bureau of Education, Physical Education Series No. 9, 1928. (This is a report of a conference arranged by the Bureau on March 20, 1927.)

PIUS XII. "Physical Culture and Youth." *Catholic Newsletter*, No. 288 (May 26, 1945).

————. "Sports and Gymnastics." *Catholic Mind*, No. 51 (September 1953), 569–576.

————. "Christian Conduct Towards Athletics." *Catholic Mind*, No. 54 (July 1956), 409–417.

RADIR, RUTH A. *Modern Dance for the Youth of America*. New York: A. S. Barnes, 1944.

RAFFE, W. G. *Dictionary of the Dance*. New York: A. S. Barnes, 1965.

Random House Dictionary of the English Language. New York: Random House, 1967.

REICH, CHARLES A. *The Greening of America*. New York: Random House, 1970.

REDEFER, FREDERICK L. "A Call to the Educators of America." *Saturday Review-World*, July 27, 1974, 49–50.

REISNER, E. H. *Nationalism and Education since 1789*. New York: Macmillan, 1925.

REMLEY, MARY L. "Twentieth Century Concepts of Sports Competition for Women." Ph.D. dissertation, University of Southern California, 1969.

RICKARD, R. S. "An Explication of the Role of Aesthetic Value in American

Physical Education: A Conceptual Analysis of Physical Education Literature." Ed.D. dissertation, Stanford University, 1970.

ROBERTS, TERRY. "The Fiction of Morally Indifferent Acts in Sport," in *Proceedings of the First Canadian Symposium on the Philosophy of Sport and Physical Activity*, ed. P. J. Galasso. Ottawa: Sport Canada Directorate, 1972. (This symposium was held at the University of Windsor, May 3, 1972.)

ROLSTON, HOLMES, III. "Is There an Ecological Ethic?" *Ethics*, 85, No. 2 (January 1975), 93–109.

ROSTEN, LEO, ed. *Religions in America*. New York: Simon and Schuster, 1963.

RUDNER, RICHARD S. *Philosophy of Social Science*. Englewood Cliffs, N.J.: Prentice-Hall, 1966.

RUSSELL, BERTRAND. *Education and the Good Life*. New York: Avon Books, 1926.

SACHS, CURT. *World History of the Dance*. New York: W. W. Norton, 1937.

SALMON, WESLEY C. *Logic*. Englewood Cliffs, N.J.: Prentice-Hall, 1963.

SANBORN, MARION A., and BETTY G. HARTMAN. *Issues in Physical Education* (rev. ed.). Philadelphia: Lea & Febiger, 1970.

SAPORA, A. V., and E. D. MITCHELL. *The Theory of Play and Recreation* (3rd ed.). New York: Ronald Press, 1961.

SAVAGE, H. J., et al. *American College Athletics*. New York: The Carnegie Foundation for the Advancement of Teaching, 1929.

SCOTT, H. A. *Competitive Sports in Schools and Colleges*. New York: Harper & Row, 1951.

SEARS, PAUL. "The Steady State: Physical Law and Moral Choice," in *The Subversive Science*, ed. P. Shepard and D. McKinley. Boston: Houghton Mifflin, 1969.

SELDEN, ELIZABETH. *The Dancer's Quest*. Berkeley: University of California Press, 1935.

SHADDUCK, IONE G. "A Philosophical Base for a Physical Education Program Design." Ph.D. dissertation, Michigan State University, 1968.

SHEEHAN, THOMAS J. "Sport: The Focal Point of Physical Education." *Quest*, No. 10 (May 1968), 59–67.

SHEPARD, NATALIE M. "Democracy in Physical Education: A Study of the Implications for Educating for Democracy Through Physical Education." Ed.D. dissertation, New York University, 1952.

————. *Foundations and Principles of Physical Education*. New York: Ronald Press, 1960.

SHIVERS, JAY S. "An Analysis of Theories of Recreation." Ph.D. dissertation, University of Wisconsin, 1958.

SIGERIST, HENRY E. *Landmarks in the History of Hygiene*. London: Oxford University Press, 1956.

SIMPSON, GEORGE G. *The Meaning of Evolution*. New Haven and London: Yale University Press, 1949.

SKINNER, B. F. *Walden Two*. Toronto: Macmillan, 1948.

———. *Beyond Freedom and Dignity*. New York: Knopf, 1971.

SLATTON, YVONNE L. "The Philosophical Beliefs of Undergraduates and Graduate Physical Education Major Students and the Physical Education Faculty at the University of North Carolina at Greensboro." M.S. thesis, University of North Carolina at Greensboro, 1964.

SLUSHER, HOWARD S. *Man, Sport, and Existence: A Critical Analysis*. Philadelphia: Lea & Febiger, 1967.

SMITH, GRAHAME J. C. "The Ecologist at Bay." *Saturday Review* (January 2, 1971), 68–69.

SNYDER, R. A., and W. A. SCOTT. *Professional Preparation in Health, Physical Education, and Recreation*. New York: McGraw-Hill, 1954.

SPEARS, BETTY M. "Philosophical Bases for Physical Education Experiences Consistent with the Goals of General Education for College Women." Ph.D. dissertation, New York University, 1956.

SPENCE, D. W. "Analysis of Selected Values in Physical Education." Ed.D. dissertation, Louisiana State University, 1966.

SPENCER, HERBERT. *Education: Intellectual, Moral, and Physical*. London: Watts, 1949.

SPENCER-KRAUS, PETER. "The Application of 'Linguistic Phenomenology' to the Philosophy of Physical Education and Sport." M.A. thesis, University of Illinois, Urbana, 1969.

SPICKER, STUART F., ed. *The Philosophy of the Body*. New York: Quadrangle, 1970.

STALEY, SEWARD C. "The Four Year Curriculum in Physical (Sports) Education," *Research Quarterly*, II, No. 1 (March 1931), 76–90.

———. *Sports Education*. New York: A. S. Barnes, 1939.

STEINHAUS, ARTHUR H. *Toward an Understanding of Health and Physical Education*. Dubuque, Iowa: William C. Brown, 1963.

STONE, ROSELYN. "Meanings Found in the Acts of Surfing and Skiing." Ph.D. dissertation, University of Southern California, 1969.

STROLL, AVRUM, and RICHARD POPKIN. *Introduction to Philosophy*. New York: Holt, Rinehart & Winston, 1961.

SUITS, BERNARD. "The Grasshopper: A Thesis Concerning the Moral Ideal of Man," in *The Philosophy of Sport*, ed. R. G. Osterhoudt. Springfield, Ill.: Charles C Thomas, 1973.

SUNDLY, JERRY A. "The Desire to Win: A Phenomenological Description." Ph.D. dissertation, University of Southern California, 1971.

TAGGART, GLADYS M. "A Study of the Relationship Between the Goals of Physical Education and Higher Education." Ph.D. dissertation, New York University, 1959.

TAYLOR, RICHARD. *Metaphysics*. Englewood Cliffs, N.J.: Prentice-Hall, 1963.

TESCONI, CHARLES A. JR., and VAN CLEVE MORRIS, *The Anti-Man Culture.* Urbana: University of Illinois Press, 1972.

THOMSON, P. L. "Ontological Truth in Sports: A Phenomenological Analysis." Ph.D. dissertation, University of Southern California, 1967.

TOFFLER, ALVIN. *Future Shock.* New York: Random House, 1970.

————. *The Eco-Spasm Report.* New York: Bantam Books, 1975.

TWOMEY, J. J. *Christian Philosophy and Physical Education.* Liverpool, England: Kilburns (Printers) Ltd., 1958.

UPDYKE, WYNN F., and PERRY B. JOHNSON. *Principles of Modern Physical Education, Health, and Recreation.* New York: Holt, Rinehart and Winston, 1970.

VANDERZWAAG, HAROLD J. "Delineation of an Essentialistic Philosophy of Physical Education." Ph.D. dissertation, The University of Michigan, 1962.

————. "Nationalism in American Physical Education," in *Proceedings of the National College Physical Education Association for Men.* Washington, D.C., December 27–29, 1965.

————. "Sport: Existential or Essential." *Quest,* No. 12 (May 1969), 47–56.

————. *Toward a Philosophy of Sport.* Reading, Mass.: Addison-Wesley, 1972.

VAN LOON, H. W. *The Arts.* New York: Simon and Schuster, 1937.

VAN VLIET, M. L., ed. *Physical Education in Canada.* Scarborough, Ont. Prentice-Hall of Canada, 1965.

WALSH, JOHN H. "A Fundamental Ontology of Play and Leisure." Ph.D. dissertation, Georgetown University, 1968.

WARREN, WILLIAM E. "An Application of Existentialism to Physical Education." Ed.D. dissertation, University of Georgia, 1970.

WATTS, DORIS P. "Changing Conceptions of Competitive Sports for Girls and Women in the United States from 1880 to 1960." Ph.D. dissertation, University of California at Los Angeles, 1960.

WEBSTER, RANDOLPH. *Philosophy of Physical Education.* Dubuque, Iowa: William C. Brown, 1965.

WEISS, PAUL. *The Making of Men.* Carbondale: Southern Illinois University Press, 1967.

————. *Sport: A Philosophic Inquiry.* Carbondale: Southern Illinois University Press, 1969.

WHITE, MORTON. *The Age of Analysis.* Boston: Houghton Mifflin, 1962.

————. *Pragmatism and the American Mind.* New York: Oxford University Press, 1973.

WHITEHEAD, ALFRED N. *The Aims of Education.* New York: Macmillan, 1929.

WILD, JOHN. "Education and Human Society: A Realistic View," in the *Fifty-Fourth Yearbook of the National Society for the Study of Education* (Part I). Chicago: The University of Chicago Press, 1955.

WILLIAMS, JESSE F. *The Principles of Physical Education* (8th ed.). Philadelphia: W. B. Saunders, 1964.

WILLIAMS, J. PAUL. *What Americans Believe and How They Worship.* New York: Harper & Row, 1952.

WILTON, W. M. "A Comparative Analysis of Theories Related to Moral and Spiritual Values in Physical Education." Ed.D. dissertation, University of California at Los Angeles, 1956.

WOODY, THOMAS. *Life and Education in Early Societies.* New York: Macmillan, 1949.

ZEIGLER, E. F. "A History of Professional Preparation for Physical Education in the United States, 1861–1948." Ph.D. dissertation, Yale University, 1950. (Published by Microform Publications, University of Oregon, Eugene.)

———. "A History of Professional Preparation for Physical Education (1861–1961)," in *Professional Preparation in Health Education, Physical Education, and Recreation Education.* Washington, D.C.: The American Association for Health, Physical Education, and Recreation, 1962, pp. 116–133.

———. "Values in Physical, Health, and Recreation Education," *Journal of the Canadian Association for Health, Physical Education, and Recreation,* 29, No. 3 (February–March, 1963), 10–12.

———. *Philosophical Foundations for Physical, Health, and Recreation Education.* Englewood Cliffs, N.J.: Prentice-Hall, 1964.

———. *A Brief Introduction to the Philosophy of Religion.* Champaign, Ill.: Stipes, 1965.

———. "The Educational Philosophy of Existentialism." *Illinois News, Health, Physical Education, and Recreation,* 14, No. 1 (1966). 9–10. (A very concise treatment of the subject.)

———. *Problems in the History and Philosophy of Physical Education and Sport.* Englewood Cliffs, N.J.: Prentice-Hall, 1968.

———. "An Historical Analysis of the Professional Master's Degree in Physical Education in the United States." *Canadian Journal of the History of Sport and Physical Education,* 3, No. 2 (1972), 44–68.

———. "Historical Perspective on Contrasting Philosophies of Professional Preparation in Physical Education in the United States." *Canadian Journal of the History of Sport and Physical Education,* 6, No. 1 (1975), 23–42.

———. *Personalizing Physical Education and Sport Philosophy.* Champaign, Ill.: Stipes, 1975.

———, M. L. HOWELL, and M. TREKELL. *Research Methods in the History, Philosophy, and International Aspects of Physical Education and Sport.* Champaign, Ill.: Stipes, 1971.

———, and M. J. SPAETH, eds. *Administrative Theory and Practice in Physical Education and Athletics.* Englewood Cliffs, N.J.: Prentice-Hall, 1975.

———, and H. J. VANDERZWAAG. *Physical Education: Progressivism or Essentialism?* (2nd ed.). Champaign, Ill.: Stipes, 1968.

Index